The Shikoku Pilgrimage
How to visit the 88 temples

by
Oliver Dunskus

The Shikoku Pilgrimage
How to visit the 88 temples
ISBN-Nr. 9783759766557
Printed and Published by BoD – Books on
Demand, Norderstedt
Copyright© 2024 Oliver Dunskus
Cover Picture by the author

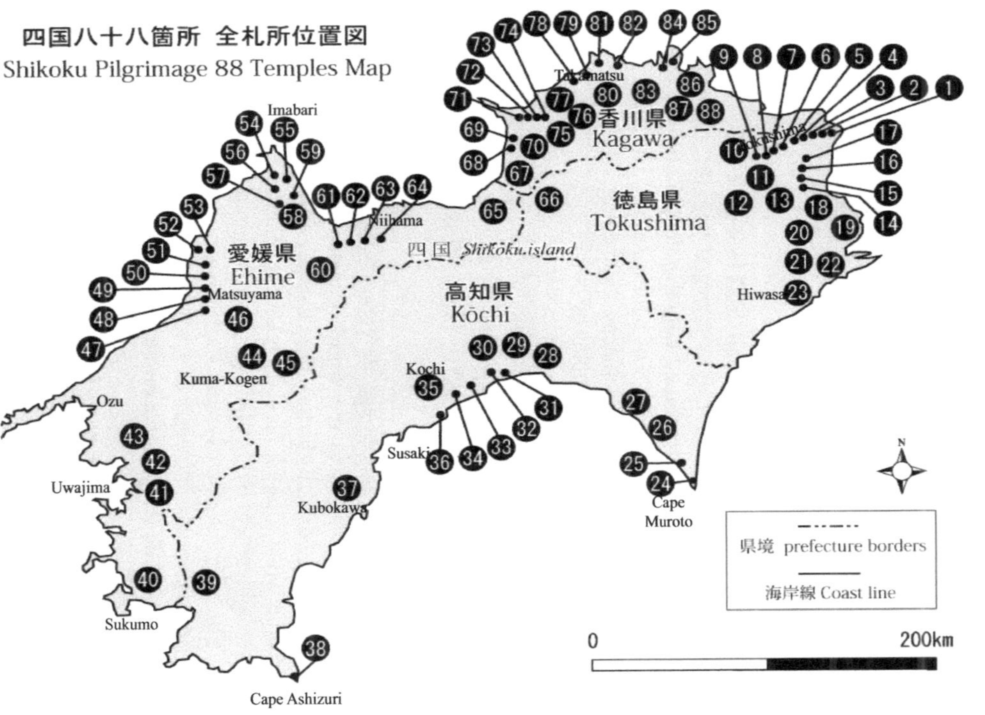

四国八十八箇所 全札所位置図
Shikoku Pilgrimage 88 Temples Map
香川県 Kagawa
徳島県 Tokushima
高知県 Kōchi
愛媛県 Ehime
四国 Shikoku island
Takamatsu
Tokushima
Imabari
Niihama
Matsuyama
Kuma-Kogen
Ozu
Uwajima
Sukumo
Kubokawa
Kochi
Susaki
Hiwasa
Cape Muroto
Cape Ashizuri
N
県境 prefecture borders
海岸線 Coast line
0 200km

Foreword

My first English guidebook about the Shikoku pilgrimage was published in 2021. Many things have changed since then. Corona brought a massive change in the mindset about the pilgrimage, mainly that it has become uncommon to camp outside. Many of the old free of charge "Tsuyado" (free of charge seeping huts) have closed, just like many family run guesthouses did not survive the crisis. Often run by elderly people before Corona, they did not continue their business for various reasons.

The reopening of Japan in Fall 2022 brought a mass of pilgrims back to Shikoku, suddenly confronted with difficulties to find accommodations, combined with the closure of many huts and the new lack of acceptance of wild camping. The good news is that also a number of new places are opening. Also, today, most local pilgrims visit the temples by car.

Another major change, relevant for your planning is that the opening times of the temples is changing to be from 8 am to 4 pm only, some temples even close earlier. It is not the same anymore for all temples.

The Shikoku pilgrimage is often called one of the oldest pilgrimage paths in the world. Located on the fourth largest island of Japan, its history goes back by over 1,200 years to the time when a monk named Kukai travelled to Shikoku to seek enlightenment by meditating in some remote parts of the island. The pilgrimage movement itself, however, started much later, approximately 300 years ago, when it became popular to walk a series of 88 temples in a circle around the island in his honor.

The Shikoku pilgrimage is often compared to the Camino de Santiago (which is a much too general term, as there are a number of pilgrimages that lead to Santiago from different directions, what most people refer to, talking of the "Camino" is the Camino Frances which begins in Saint-Jean-Pied-de-Port). However, the Shikoku pilgrimage is different in many ways: It is a loop, so there is no beginning and no end. It may be completed as a whole or in several stages, and there are no official pilgrimage hostels as such. Instead, the overnight stays need to be organized individually. Also, different to the Caminos, there are not rules with regards to the mode of transportation, and in Shikoku the pilgrims are recognizable due to their white attire.

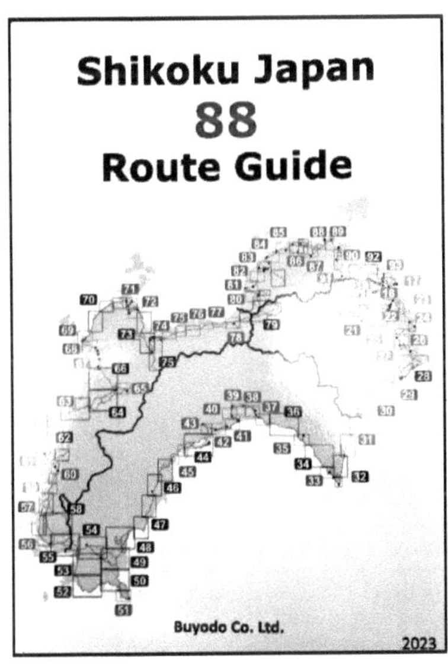

The purpose of this guide is to provide practical help for planning your pilgrimage, and information on the cultural background of the temples. As this is not a map-book, I often refer to the English map book *The Shikoku 88 Route Guide* in addition to this travel guide, which offers a complete map of the 1,200 km path to the 88 main temples and 20 other *Bekkaku* temples. This book is less about deeper spiritual or religious aspects and some popular myths related to the pilgrimage are not covered.

One of the great pleasures of the Shikoku pilgrimage is the interaction with locals, who are friendly and supportive people, usually ready to help wherever they can. As Shikoku is suffering from a declining and aging population, I strongly encourage pilgrims to support the local economy by making use of local places to stay. Consequently, I will also not focus on how the pilgrimage could be done at lowest possible cost, sleeping outdoors or in free shelter huts. In case your budget is limited, I recommend doing as much as you can and returning some other time.

The places where formerly one could stay free of charge in temples or on the roadside are declining and initially were meant for people in need, stranded in the gray zone between being a pilgrim and being homeless. I believe that most of the readers of this guidebook are not in this situation, so these options are not covered in depth.

Most people who come to Shikoku are impressed by the positive aura of the island and its people. I hope you, too, will enjoy this experience.

Symbols

⛩	Shinto Shrines (selected)
🚉	Train Stations (selected)
🚌	Bus stops (selected)
🚡	Ropeway
🍽	Restaurant, Coffee Shop or Snack Bar (outside cities)
🚻	Toilets (All of temples and many shrines have toilets)
🛏	Accommodations (selected)
⛺	Camping Site
🛒	Convenience store or supermarket (outside cities)
T1	Official Temple (On of the 88 Main Temples) with Number
B1	Bekkaku Temple (The 20 Separate Temples) with Number
O1	Inner sanctuary or sacred placed related to a numbered temple
KM	Full Km counting according to the Shikoku 88 Japan Route Guide, 2023 Edition (White numbers in blue square)
△	Peak, pass, highest point of ca limb
↗	Moderate climb, up to 10% or 100 m per km
↗↗	Challenging Climb, above 10% or 100 m gain per km
↘	Moderate Gradient, below 10% or 100 m per km
↘↘	Steep Gradient, above 10% or 100 m per km

The Shikoku Pilgrimage

History

It is not quite clear whether the Shikoku pilgrimage was founded by a Buddhist monk named Kukai, also Later referred to as Kobo Daishi (we will call him Kukai in this book). In old times, people always wandered to visit sacred and spiritual places, even before Buddhism came to Japan in the 6th century AD. There is, however, evidence of Kukai's stays at three of the temples. But actually, the oldest documentation of a pilgrimage trail in Shikoku only dates back to the 17th century in Edo era, when a monk named Shinnen described a walk to 88 temples in Shikoku. Today Kukai is the omnipresent figure in the temples and along the way.

As Buddhism was something "imported" from India via Korea or China, preaching outside temples and monasteries was forbidden, but in the 7th century, a mystic named En-no-Gyoja (634-701) travelled across the country and preached a mix of nature religion and early Buddhism with elements of Taoism called Shugendo. Slightly later, it was Gyoki (649-749) an ascetic monk, who became the first person to teach Buddhism in Japan, supported by Emperor Shomu. Gyoki was well-educated in civil engineering. He passed away 25 years before Kukai was born, and his achievements are possibly underrated.

But who was this Kukai, who is like a permanent companion, whom we see in every temple and on many spots along the way, with his backpack, his sleeping mat, his walking stick and his hat? He was born in 774 near Zentsu-ji (Temple 75) as a descendant of the noble Saeki family and given the name Mao. The family was impoverished, after having fallen into disgrace after some earlier political turbulences, but the youngster was able to study religion and philosophy in Kyoto, which would soon become Japan's new capital. Mao was more fascinated by Buddhist teachings and its ascetic practices than by the widespread Confucian doctrine. Young Mao Saeki spent much time meditating in remote parts of Shikoku, first on a mountain peak near Temple 21, and later in a cave near Temple 24 close to cape Muroto, where he found enlightenment. From then, he called himself Kukai, after the two elements he first saw stepping out of his cave – the sky and the sea. By then he was in his mid-twenties.

Aged 30, Kukai travelled to China with a group of other monks. After a troublesome trip during which some of his companions were lost in a storm, being able to speak Chinese, he was allowed to continue to the capital of Xi'an where he studied esoteric Buddhism for two years. He returned to Kyoto, and after some time at Jingo-Ji, in 810 he was given the position of the head priest at Todai-ji, the largest temple of Nara. Finally, in 816 emperor Saga accepted his request to build a retreat on mount Koya which was only completed in 835, due to major delays in fundraising. In 823, when Kyoto had become the new capital, Kukai became the head priest of To-ji in Kyoto, one of the city's major temples. He passed away the same year, his remains are kept in his Mausoleum at Mt. Koya. Kukai founded Shingon Buddhism, today the largest Buddhist sect in Japan today. One of the key elements of Shingon is the belief that human beings can be enlightened already in their current life through esoteric practice.

Kukai passed away in 835, he was later given the grandmaster title Kobo Daishi, meaning "The grandmaster who propagated the dharma". At that time, the Shikoku pilgrimage with 88 temples did not exist yet, although this is sometimes claimed.

It roughly took another 900 years until in 1687 Shinnen described a pilgrimage path across 88 temples in Shikoku in his book Shikoku Henro Michishirube, at that time still without any particular order. Shinnen put up the earliest sign posts, rest huts and measured the distance between temples, creating a minimal infrastructure for the pilgrims. Some of his sign posts are still existing. This started a pilgrimage movement also among common people, for whom pilgrimage was often the only trip they ever made. Often, a village would collect money and send one person on the pilgrimage with the mission to pray for those who stayed at home or those who had passed away.

Why did it take so long? Quite simply because until the Edo period (1600 – 1868), travelling between the different regions of Japan was generally not permitted and not easily possible as many regions were in confrontation with each other. Only in the Edo period, when the Tokugawa shogunate finally ruled all of Japan, the regions came to peace, the country was ruled more centralized and new laws were introduced, allowing more interaction between the prefectures and allowing travelers to pass borders more easily.

Looking at the history of the temples, we can notice that many of them suffered the similar fates. Apart from occasional fires (from lightning, forest fires or by accident) many temples were affected by two major waves of destruction: First by the armies of Motochika Chosokabe, a Daimyo from Nagaoka in the center of Shikoku, who conquered all of Shikoku between 1573 and 1583, destroying many temples on the way. Sometimes these destructions are also more generally called the "unrests of the Tensho era". The second wave was during the Meiji reformation, when Shintoism, now strengthened by a new emperor back in political power, became powerful again and in all of Japan 40,000 to 50,000 temples were destroyed, and Buddhism was close to extinction. The wave of destruction suddenly stopped and the temples were rebuilt, often in other areas they had been allocated, as the now powerful Shinto shrines reclaimed their former grounds.

Until the 20th century, undertaking the pilgrimage was a hard and dangerous thing to do. Pilgrimage was done in straw sandals in an area with minimal infrastructure (think of walking in straw sandals on mud roads and across rivers). Malaria and leprosy were common and the fact that pilgrims carried along plenty of cash made them an easy target for criminals. Also, pilgrims were not welcome especially on the remote and poorly developed south side of the island. One of the reasons for having a defined pilgrimage path was also that pilgrims were forced by the authorities in some places to pass the areas without delay and on a fixed route, as they were considered being homeless, contagious and were not welcome to settle. Between 1844 and 1866, pilgrims were generally banned from passing the cities of Tosa (Kochi) and Uwajima.

The Pilgrimage Today

Shi-koku means "Four Countries", which refers to the four prefectures of the island: Tokushima, Kochi, Ehime and Kagawa. Today, the route leads along the 88 main temples across the four prefectures. Shikoku has four major cities, one in each prefecture: Tokushima in the east, Kochi in the south, Matsuyama in the northwest and Takamatsu in the northeast. Each of these cities is interesting to visit and offers excellent choices for shopping in case you might need some gear. It is not mandatory to begin with Temple No. 1, nor is it mandatory to visit all of them in one trip. Anything is possible and left to the individual to organize according to his or her own means. Pilgrimage in organized bus tours or by car is not the common way to do it for most Japanese. Apart from some etiquette and general guidelines for behavior there are no rules on how the pilgrimage must be done. Each of the prefectures has its own character which also reflects in spiritual stages, that pilgrims might experience as they walk.

Tokushima Prefecture, formerly Awa (T1-T23, 189 km)
Probably because it is nearest to Kyoto and Koyasan, Tokushima is the first prefecture and this is where the temple count begins. The prefecture stands for "spiritual awakening", and the pilgrim has an easy start: After a 20-minute train ride from Tokushima Station, T1 is just a 15-minute walk from Bando Station. The route begins flat, temples coming every few kilometers as the challenge gradually increases with longer distances and more climbs. After 153 km, the prefecture's last temple (T23) is reached and the route finally reaches the seaside.

Kochi Prefecture, formerly Tosa (T24-T39, 390 km)
The route across Kochi Prefecture mostly goes along the southern coast of the island from Cape Muroto to Cape Ashizuri. The pilgrim is challenged by the sun and by long stretches with minimal infrastructure; the 16 temples being spread over a distance of 455 km. Consequently, this prefecture stands for ascetic training.

Ehime Prefecture, formerly Iyo (T40-65, 365 km)
The route becomes more colorful and the landscape more diverse in Ehime, the prefecture of enlightenment. In

Matsuyama, after passing the Kuma-Kogen mountain range, pilgrims can enjoy the hot springs of Dogo Onsen and look forward to a couple of easier days walking along the beautiful rock coast on the west side of the island.

Kagawa Prefecture, formerly Sanuki (T66-T88, 150 km)
After 945 kilometers, the pilgrims enter Kagawa Prefecture, which represents Nirvana. They will visit 22 beautiful temples over a distance of only 150 km, enjoy local Udon noodles, the bustling city of Takamatsu and receive their certificate of completion before visiting T88 and closing their loop by returning to T1.

There is no "official route" to the pilgrimage as the target is to visit the temples, without following a given route. Over time, the route has often changed when more convenient roads or new bridges had been completed, or even temples had changed their location. However, there is a common understanding of a sort of main route, shown in the Shikoku 88 Japan Route Guide.

In the 20th century, it became common practice to visit Koyasan, after finishing the pilgrimage, the center of Shingon Buddhism, a city of temples which is not located in Shikoku, but two hours by south of Osaka in Wakayama prefecture.

There are over 1800 sacred places in Shikoku. Apart from the 88 *Fudasho* main temples (named T1 to T88 in this book), we find other categories of temples:
- There are 20 *Bekkaku* Temples named B1 to B20, the term *Bekkaku* meaning "counted separately", and they are also c considered a pilgrimage of their own. Many of these temples are just as splendid as the main 88. The numbering of the Bekkaku-temples was only introduced in 1966. The 88 main temples and 20 Bekkaku temples add up to 108 temples, 108 being a holy number in Buddhist numerology.
- Most of the main temples have remote temples or inner sanctuaries allocated to them, these locations are called *Okunoin*. They could be the original holy places which started the temple, places of particular spirituality, or remote locations for ascetic training. When they are connected to any of the main temples, this guidebook uses

the letter O- followed by the temple number. For simplification, I have called all associated sacred spots *Okunoin* although strictly speaking, it may not be correct.

- Another group of temples is called *Bangai*, which means "unnumbered" meaning they are not related to any of the main temples, but they, too, are worshipping Kukai and may be impressive in size or appearance, just as some of the 88 main temples may be rather small and modest. There are several hundred in Shikoku.
- Apart from the different types of Buddhist temples, Shikoku also has over 1,000 Shinto-shrines named *Jinja*, often on the same property as the Buddhist temples. They can be large and majestic, or very tiny, often sharing grounds with Buddhist temples.

Temples and shrines can easily be distinguished by their gates: While Buddhist temple gates are often built like small buildings with walls and roofs, Shinto shrines have the typical Torii gates made of two vertical and two horizontal pillars, the upper one

bent.
A typical Buddhist temple gate (Temple 77 Doryu-ji)

A typical Shinto Torii gate (Kotohira-Gu)

In many cases, temples and shrines can be found on the same area, sharing common history. Historically, Shintoism, before it was the original nature religion of Japan, the Emperor being the head priest. Buddhism was considered something foreign, imported, un-Japanese to some. The emperor was without political power for most of the times (the period between the Meiji era from 1868 and the end of WWII 1945 being one of the few exceptions) as the country was ruled by Samurai clans. Throughout the Edo era (1603-1868), Temples often shared their grounds with Shinto shrines, while the Meiji reformation 1868, in which the emperor took power, brought a phase of strong confrontation between the two religions, during which many Buddhist temples were destroyed and the grounds later divided. The phase of destruction ended suddenly in 1872 and temples were rebuilt.

Traditionally pilgrims follow ten commandments:
1. Do not harm life
2. Do not steal
3. Do not commit adultery
4. Do not lie
5. Do not exaggerate
6. Do not speak abusively
7. Do not cause discord
8. Do not be greedy
9. Do not be hateful
10. Do not lose sight of the truth

Preparations

When to Go

If you do not live in Japan, it is a good idea to start the project with the flight booking. This will set the time for your trip and avoid further postponement. 3-6 months before the trip is a good time for preparation. The best, and most popular seasons for the walking pilgrimage are March and April before April 23rd (which marks the beginning of the Golden Week, a major holiday in Japan where traffic is heavy and many places are booked out). The summer months are not recommended – too much rain, too humid, typhoons, but October is another good month, and later, the winter months in Japan are usually bright and dry. Avoid the period of New Year's Eve and the first week of January. This is a time when the entire country comes to a standstill and accommodation might be difficult.

The walking pilgrim will need 8 to 10 weeks depending on detours and rest days. In any case, a part of the trip will fall into a difficult month. The temperatures are the same across the island between the north and the south, but the south has more rain.

Let us look at the weather you might expect every month:

January	Between 0 and 10°C, month with little rain, dry air and bright days. First week is new year's holiday period, many places are closed. Mountain areas might be cold and snowy.
February	Between 5 and 15°C, good month to go but not warm Mountain areas might be cold and snowy, occasionally rainy.
March	5-20°C, good month to go, be prepared for occasional cold and hot moments, occasional rain.
April	Good month to go. Between 10 and 20°C, Golden Week starts April 23, so be sure to be done or at least to have a confirmed stay early enough in that period. Expect some days of rain. Very popular, might be crowded.

May	More occasional rain, weather becomes warmer with 15-25°C and higher humidity
June	Rainy season, rain approx. every second day, very humid, temps up to 30°C, not recommended for walking. August is hottest month. September is typhoon season
July	
August	
September	
October	Good month to go. Less rainy, sunny but with lower humidity. Very popular, might be crowded.
November	Good month to go but might occasionally be cold, jacket needed.
December	Clear skies and dry weather, good month to go but jacket and gloves needed.

Costs

The costs of the trip can be calculated by adding one-time costs for the trip to Shikoku plus an estimation of costs per day depending on your requested level of comfort and length of stay.

Estimated one-time costs

One-Time Costs	Yen	€ (= 150 Yen)
Flight to Kansai		€1,000.00
🚌 to Tokushima and back	9,000	€60,00
Hotel 1st night	5,000	€35,00
Dinner 1st night	2,000	€13,00
Shikoku 88 Route Guide	1,800	€12,00
Walking staff	1,500	€10,00
Vest	3,000	€20,00
Hat	2,400	€16,00
Stamp book	3,000	€20.00
Total one-time costs		**Appr. €1,200.00**

To the one-time costs, you need to add estimated costs per day

Costs per day	Yen	€ (= 150 Yen)
Hostel per night	4,000	
Food & beverages	4,000	
Average 3 temple stamps	900	
Spending money	1,000	
Total costs per day	**¥9,900**	**€ 66.00**

These estimations are based on a reasonable level of comfort. That would include a nightly hostel or guesthouse stay in shared rooms, eating meals in basic restaurants, and collecting stamps at the temples.

A 2-week pilgrimage to Shikoku will allow you to visit the temples of one of the four prefectures on foot:

One-time costs	€1,200.00
13 x €66.00	€858.00
Total costs for the trip	**€2,058.00**

It takes 8-10 weeks to walk the entire route. An 8-week pilgrimage visiting the 88 temples on foot will cost about

One-time costs	€1,200.00
56 x €66.00	€3,696.00
Total costs for the trip	**€4,896.00**

Hostels are usually paid in cash. Supermarkets accept credit cards, but I recommend carrying money for the trip in case card payment does not work. Japan is a very safe country and the risk of the money being stolen is close to zero. Cash can be withdrawn at ATMs in post offices and many convenience stores. However, some of the ATMs do not accept foreign credit cards, even if they carry the Visa- or Mastercard logo. The ones at 7-Eleven and Family Mart usually work.

What to Take Along

You do not need much. Every hostel or guesthouse offers laundry. I have been on the Shikoku pilgrimage many times and managed to reduce the weight of my backpack down to 6-7 kg, including the backpack itself and a jacket. Everyone is different, but you might take this adventure to find out how light you can really travel.

To start with, here is a list of what you DO NOT really need. Remember, no one cares if you look stylish:
- Too many toiletries. Soap, shower gel and shampoo are always provided free of charge.
- A third pair of shoes

- Hair spray or gel
- Shaving kit
- A large towel (a tiny one will do)
- Cologne or perfume
- Detergent (It is usually provided when you do the laundry)

Here is what I recommend to take along:
- Trekking poles (a good alternative to the wooden staff)
- A soft hat that can easily be squeezed into your luggage. I prefer this solution over the traditional hat.
- Walking shoes (Sneakers or trail runners are good enough, 85% is on pavement, the rest is on trails)
- A lighter second pair of shoes to wear after the hikes.
- 3-4 pairs of socks
- A sweater (think of cold airplane cabins)
- A small towel
- A nail trimmer (your nails, at times, will suffer)
- 2-3 of your oldest T-shirts to maybe throw away during the trip
- Hiking pants (not shorts)
- 2-3 zipper pouches to keep your mobile phone and passport dry during heavy rainfall.
- A waterproof jacket
- Sports tape to protect your feet from blisters, blister-kit
- Sunscreen lotion if you go between April and October
- A mini flashlight (it gets very dark very early)
- A red clip light to be visible in the dark or in tunnels
- The "Shikoku 88 Route Guide" map-book
- Charge cable and adapter
- Battery pack for your mobile phone
- Some tiny souvenirs from home (Key chain, postcards, candy) to give to people who do you favors
- Earplugs to sleep better in case anyone snores.
- Copies of your passport
- A very light bag to take along in case you go on a day trip without your backpack

Should you intend to walk the entire pilgrimage, you should make sure to keep your backpack as light as possible. Check the weight of every item you intend to take along, make a list, including the weight of the backpack itself, check the total weight of your luggage and set yourself a maximum weight limit. It should be possible to get below 8kg.

How to Get to Shikoku

You can begin the pilgrimage anywhere you want, but most people start in Tokushima which is close to Temple 1.

By plane: The closest international airport is KIX Kansai. From Kansai airport there are direct busses to Tokushima, The 3-hour journey costing 5.000 yen one-way.

If you arrive at Kansai Airport in the morning, try to catch an afternoon bus from OCAT to Tokushima and stay there for the night. If you arrive at Kansai Airport in the afternoon, it is better to stay in a hotel in Osaka near Namba Station/OCAT and take a morning bus, in that case the most convenient station to get out is called Naruto Nishi, a highway stop just 2 km from Temple No. 1, on the bus line to Takamatsu.

A more laid-back approach is to take the train from the airport to Wakayama and from there take the ferry to Tokushima.

There are long-distance busses from Osaka Namba OCAT or Osaka Umeda to Tokushima or to Matsuyama. If you get off at Naruto-nishi, you will be less than 2 km from T1. The long-distance busses are very comfortable with generous seat pitch and Wi-Fi. You can also fly via Tokyo and take a connecting domestic flight (from HND Tokyo Haneda Airport) to any of the four larger cities in Shikoku – Tokushima, Kochi, Matsuyama or Takamatsu.

By train: Japan has the world's most dense and reliable railway system. Take the Shinkansen bullet train to Okayama, from there, a limited express (JR Seto Ohashi Line) will take you over the bridge onto the Island to Utazu (near T78), once you are here, there are trains that can take you to T1 with a transfer in Takamatsu if that is where you wish to start. Tokushima is a convenient hub to start from. Allow yourself some time to stroll around and visit the Awa-odori souvenir shop to buy your first pilgrimage gear on the first night. After that, a short visit to a hot spring will help you sleep well after the long trip.

How to Do the Pilgrimage

The basic idea is to go from temple to temple but there are no rules, and everyone may choose the mode of transportation, length of trip starting point and direction they wish, according to their abilities. Many locals go in organized tours or by car, many overseas visitors walk or do a mix of walking and public transportation for some of the longer or more difficult stretches. Your daily distance should be in line with your endurance, but remember you are in an interesting place and there will be many reasons to take a break, so do not plan your distances with too much ambition.

Some people manage to walk 40 km a day and do the entire pilgrimage in one month, but I recommend planning 20 km per day which is approximately 5 hours of pure walking with time to rest and to enjoy the most beautiful moments or discover unusual places. Remember this is not a race, on the contrary, one intention might be to let go of the daily pressures of your life and to find your personal flow. Even if at some stage it might become clear that you will not be able to finish (due to lack of time or injury). Take that as a good reason to come back. Some pilgrims also do it by bicycle. I once did it myself, on a women's shopping bike, which I had purchased locally, but some of the climbs are really tough and some parts cannot be done on the main route. It was a great experience which allowed me to take along more luggage, but my average speed was only 12-14 km/h and many roads were so steep that I had to push.

The stages between the Temples can be anything between a few 100 meters and 84 km. At the temple you take a rest, follow the ritual as you wish, receive a stamp and calligraphy for a donation of 300 Yen, enjoy the marvelous architecture and gardening (more about the temple rituals later), maybe chat with other pilgrims. Slowly, you will make your way around the island, finally making it to T88, the last temple. From there, you may close the loop by returning to T1 and later continue to Koyasan if you want. Stay in one of the many temples and include 2 extra days for this.

There are separate supplements available to use with this guidebook which suggest daily schedules for walkers, cyclists or pilgrims who prefer to use public transportation.

Pilgrimage by Public Transportation

Not everyone is strong enough to do the pilgrimage on foot. And even on foot, you might find yourself in a situation where you might prefer getting a ride, due to pain, frustration, schedule or bad weather. Nothing wrong with that, there are no rules. Trains and busses will take you to most parts of Shikoku, but you should be aware of the schedules, as many connections are not even covered on an hourly basis.

To make travelling convenient for foreigners, the JR stations are numbered so that station names need not be remembered.

With a few exceptions, most of the 88 Temples can be accessed by public transportation and some walking (many of the temples are located on hills).

JR Shikoku offers a Shikoku ticket allowing you to use all railway lines

When taking the train, on major lines you proceed as follows:
1. Find your destination station on the maps near the ticket machines
2. Check the price listed at your destination name
3. Press "English" on the ticket machine if necessary
4. Insert enough money into the machine (They also take bills and give change)
5. Press the button with the ticket price that you found on the map above or next to the ticket machines.
6. Collect the ticket and your change
7. Go to the platform, show your ticket to the station employee
8. Keep your ticket
9. Upon arrival your ticket will be checked and collected
10. In case you did not pay enough fare, you will be kindly asked to correct your payment, there will be no penalties.

Smaller train lines and busses operate by the "one man" principle:

1. Enter through the back door
2. Take a ticket from the little machine at the back door, it will show the station number where you entered. On the first station of the connection, no ticket will be given
3. During the ride, the price of your ride will be shown on a display in front, increasing as the ride gets longer
4. When leaving, leave your ticket, and the right amount of change into the little plastic box at the driver.
5. If you do not have correct change, there is a change machine next to the driver, but make sure you have at least something as small as a 1000 yen bill. Changing your bill into coins and paying your ride are two separate processes.

In case you are not sure about where to get off to visit your temple, tell the bus driver the name of the temple adding "Onegai shimasu" which means "please do me the favor". Bus drivers are familiar with foreign pilgrims in this situation and will tell you where to get off.

There is some etiquette in public transportation:
- Do not speak loudly
- Do not use your mobile phone to make calls
- Do not eat or drink, not even on the platform, unless you are on a long-distance train
- Stay in the back of the bus if you can until your station is coming up
- Queue in the marked spots on the platforms
- Take off your backpack

Pilgrimage Gear

Traditionally, there was no particular attire the pilgrims were wearing. People were on the pilgrimage in their regular traditional clothes, as you can see in old pictures. Their head was protected by a sedge or bamboo hat, because that was the way hats were made, and pilgrims were walking with a staff because that is helpful when walking or in case protection is needed.

White attire was worn occasionally, but it became more popular in the 20th century with the industrialization of the textile industry as clothes became more affordable and temples recognized there was money to be made selling pilgrimage wear. Again, there are no rules but you might enjoy wearing this "uniform" to trigger your mindset.

Today, some temples and shops offer a wide range of pilgrimage clothing gear. The <u>sedge hat</u> is a protection against sun and rain. It may also be worn at an angle so as to avoid eye contact which might improve internal focus during walking meditation. It comes in an inexpensive version (starting from appr. 3000 yen) which needs an additional plastic cover against rain, but also in beautiful hand-made lacquered versions (from 25.000 yen). You will also need a small towel and a sort of crate inside to wear on your head for it to sit tightly and comfortably. (Personally, I prefer wearing a soft hat instead, which I can squeeze into my backpack and a "bandana" which I can dip into cold water, and use to cool my head when the sun burns too hot.)

The traditional sedge hat has four phrases written on it:
- We are suffering because of our worldly needs
- With enlightenment, 10.000 heavens will open
- In the beginning, there was no east and west
- How can there be north and south?
It is worn with the Sanskrit character towards the front.

The <u>staff</u> (walking stick) also symbolizes the presence of Kukai walking along with you. It is made of wood and has a brocade top for the hands and to make it recognizable. Carry it with respect, and clean its bottom end first thing when you arrive at your destination, before taking care of yourself. In traditional places, your staff will be treated with a lot of respect. Also, do not tap it on the ground as you walk over a bridge. As your pilgrimage comes to an end, the staff can be left at Temple 88 and burned in a ritual fire, but if you decide to take it home, you can check it in on your flight. Many pilgrims reported the airline staff taking good care of it and not charging any extra fee. Many pilgrims attach a small bell to it. Its ringing makes the pilgrims heard as they approach, the noise could chase away animals in the forest and the ringing in the rhythm of the steps creates a particular mindset when walking. Personally, I prefer a pair of trekking poles, two of them, they will make steep climbs and descents a lot easier and safer to walk, but I do have bells attached to them.

Formerly, pilgrims used to leave handwritten copies of the heart sutra at the temples, that was before the introduction of printing machines, when copies were not easy to get. This is why the name of the stamp office in the temples is called Nokyo-sho, which means the "Place of Sutra-Presenting". Stamps were given to confirm the reception of the sutra copy. Today, the tradition of sutra copying is still occasionally practiced, but temples hand out their stamps against a small fee.

The <u>stamp book</u> (Nokyo-sho) is a book with white pages or dedicated pages for each temple visit. After every temple visit, you visit the temple office (Nokyo-cho) and collect a calligraphy and 3 large stamps as a documentation of your visit. As you continue your pilgrimage, the book is gradually filled with more and more stamps and calligraphies, documenting your journey, until it is completed and contains stamps of all 88 temples. This should not be missed. To many pilgrims the stamp book is one of the most cherished things they own. Keep it in a separate plastic bag and protect it from moisture (e.g., when hiking in heavy rain). These books come in various sizes and versions, make sure you get one large enough to fit more stamps in case you return to Shikoku some other time, and with enough pages to fit stamps for all 88 temples and some additional white pages for Bekkaku temples. Some stamp books only have white pages, some have 1 or 2 pages dedicated to every temple. If you choose a neutral stamp book not exclusively designed for the 88 temples, you may also use it in other temples.

The <u>white Vest (Hakui)</u> is worn by many pilgrims. There are many good reasons to wear it. It can change your mindset once you put it on, you can be recognized by others as being a pilgrim, it makes you more visible in situations where you might be walking in the dark. In the past it was also considered to be the pilgrim's death shroud, showing that the pilgrim was prepared to pass away. The Hakui has sleeves and usually a convenient zipper pocket on the front. There is also a version without sleeves called *Oizuru* which can be worn on top of regular clothes. In my opinion the sleeve version has the benefit that it is convenient to wear on very sunny stages as it covers your arms, and you may wear nothing or very little underneath, and still be properly dressed, as it is very airy and provides a bit of ventilation. Some people have stamps put on the vests. In that case, it should be considered that the vests can no longer be washed as the stamp ink is not waterproof. The ink will also dilute in rain or by sweat, so in that case it should not be worn anymore and only be stamped, which means you need another one to wear. This type of apparel is usually made of light cotton fabric, the sort used for men's shirts. There are also versions made of breathable technical fabric.

Pilgrims usually carry <u>name-slips</u> called osamefuda. The slips are left at the temples when visiting and they serve as a sort of business card and they are appreciated by people who have done you a favor (Osettai), or by other pilgrims you meet. You might see them inside free accommodation places as well.

Again, there is no rule, but a common format. They are sold in blank at the pilgrimage shops in blocks of 100 and you will have to complete them one by one by pen, adding your name, address and age. People who go on the pilgrimage regularly have them printed before. They come in different colors, indicating how often the pilgrim has already completed the tour: From the 5th time, they are green, from the 8th time they are red, from the 25th time silver and gold from the 50th time the pilgrimage is done. Sometimes you see colorful brocade ones, these are used by pilgrims who have completed the pilgrimage over 100 times and sometimes handed to others to bring good luck. It is hard to imagine anyone doing the pilgrimage so often, but these pilgrims are usually going by car. At the museum of the pilgrim salon between T87 and T88, there are some osamefuda on display including the stamp books from henro who have spent their life walking the pilgrimage 200-300 times before there was public transportation

I recommend keeping your Osamefuda in a suitable pouch or box to keep the dry and avoid wrinkles.

How to fill in the „Osame-Fuda" slips:

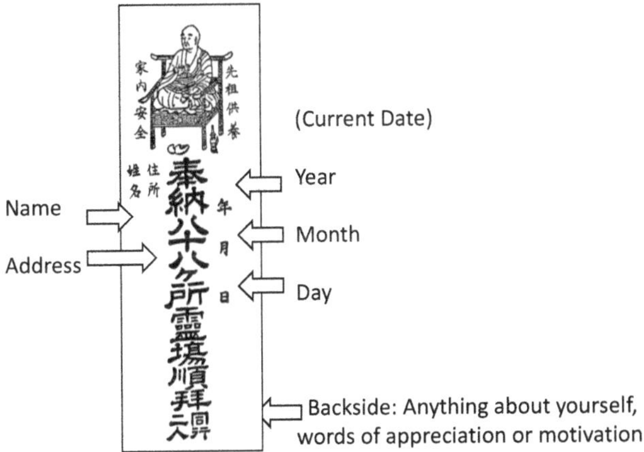

The blank ones are sold at the temple shops. Prepare them to have them ready, 2 for each temple and also as an appreciation to anyone who helps you e. g. with a food gift, a place to sleep, a lift by car

It is practical to carry along an additional smaller bag to keep the pilgrimage gear which you use at the temples – the candles, incense, stamp book, lighter and name slips. It will make your life easier to have these things separately when arriving at the temple. There are special bags available for this.

If you want, you may complete your pilgrimage items with a bell to ring after reciting the sutra, a stole (Wagesa) and a Mala (Juzu) to keep in your hands when praying.

Many temples sell some of these items in larger or smaller choices. If you start in Tokushima, you can acquire some of the items before you start, in the souvenir shop in the ground floor of the Awa Odori Hall, next to the ropeway station at Mount

Bizan. The first temples also have shops for pilgrimage items. A particularly nice shop named Sumotoriya is just before Temple 10, located below the highway bridge. The owner speaks English very well and offers a large choice of quality items. You will probably pass this shop on your second day, so all you might need until then is a stamp book.

At the Temples

These are the Kanji characters for the most important places:

Main Hall	Daishi Hall	Stamp Office	Toilet
Hondo	Daishido	Nokyosho	Toile
本堂	大師堂	納経所	手洗い

Every temple is different, some are over 1000 years old, or recently built, small or large, plain or beautiful, stuck between houses or on mountain peaks, and built with minimalistic architecture or impress with an abundance of decorations. And all 88 temples have their own particular aura. They all have several names: Their official name, the number, an additional name of a mountain and sometimes a sort of nickname. Each of them is devoted to a deity or Buddha and many of them are committed to a particular topic for which people come to pray.

Also, they all share a number of key elements: The gate, the handwashing basin, the bell, the main temple building, a statue of Kukai, the Daishi-do temple building devoted to Kukai, the temple office, public toilets and a spot where pilgrims can sit and rest. Arriving at a temple (they open at 8 a.m. and most close at 5 p.m.) is always an exciting moment, especially after a long walk. You may stop your walking meditation as you approach the first gate, in which two wooden guards (Un-Gyo and A-Gyo) keep a sharp eye on the ones entering. As mentioned, there are no strict rules, but you will make no mistake following the most common temple rituals:

1. As you pass the first gate, stop, take a breath and slowly bow towards the temple
2. Leave your staff/poles in the designated crate
3. Approach the central area (in some cases you might still have to walk for a while.) Drop your backpack at

the rest area, not on the designated benches, but on the floor to leave space for others to sit.

4. Go to the handwash basin, take one of the cups, pour some water over your left hand, then on your right hand, pour some water into your left hand and drink it. Dip the cup into the water again, let the water flow over the handle to clean it and put it back.

5. Ring the bell if you want. In some cases, the bell will be closed to avoid disturbing the neighbors. Listen to the sound.

6. Visit the main hall, the Hondo it is dedicated to the temple's deity, is easy to find by its size and usually the central building of the temple, opposite the entrance.

7. Light a candle and some incense sticks, drop (don't throw) a coin into the big wooden box and leave a name slip in the metal box

8. Step aside so that other people can approach after you. Close your eyes and relax, meditate, pray or say the Heart Sutra, whatever you want. It is also enjoyable to stand next to a group and to recite the heart Sutra together. If you don't know how to pray, just put your hands together and cherish all the good things in your life you can think of in that moment, or think of someone who desperately needs some good vibes.

9. Find the Daishido, the hall dedicated to Kobo-Daishi. Repeat the ritual.

10. Find the temple office, the Japanese name is Nokyo-Sho, hand your Stamp Book (Nokyo-Cho, don't mix that up) with both hands to the kind person behind the counter and just say "Onegai-shimasu" which means "please do me a favor" to receive your stamp and calligraphy. The price is 500 Yen the first time, or 300 Yen when revisiting and more stamps are added.

11. Take a rest at the temple, use the washrooms and enjoy the atmosphere and the entire compound. Take some rest. Have a look at the entire temple area, there might be more things to discover: A particular building, a museum, a hidden cave, you will find out.

12. Pick up your staff. As you leave, after passing the first gate, turn back and bow towards the temple.

Between the Temples

Obviously, the daily routine is to get up, follow the route, visit the temples of the day and arrive at your next accommodation place. It is wise to have reserved your accommodations several days ahead or, even better, as early as possible. Whatever you plan for your day, many temples or a long walking stage, you should build your schedule keeping in mind that the temple offices close latest at 5 p.m., and that it gets dark between 6 and 7 p.m. In order to avoid rushing to reach the last temple before 5 p.m. plan on beginning the day early (between 6 and 7 a.m.) and to plan your distances reasonably. This will allow you to finish your afternoon relaxed and to best arrive at your next accommodation in the late afternoon, with time to shop or eat dinner, take a bath, maybe do some laundry, plan your next day or write your diary before getting to bed early. Many guesthouses like to turn off the lights in the living rooms at 10 p.m. Breakfast is commonly available at 7 a.m. or earlier on request.

If you intend to walk, the best choice is to try following the official pilgrimage route which is shown in the Shikoku 88 Route Guide. Along the route, there are usually arrows and little red stickers on lamp posts and fences along the roads, confirming you are on the right path and often even indicating the remaining distance to the next temple. There will be arrows at important turns, but you should keep the route guide in your bag to regularly make sure you are walking in the right direction and, when in doubt, to be able to identify the temple names in Japanese.

Should you intend to travel by public transportation, make sure to know your next day's schedule and the location of the first station or bus stop the night before.

There are several apps to plan your pilgrimage on your mobile device. I found the Japan Official Travel App very convenient as it also includes low-frequency bus schedules, which you will not find in Google maps.

Where to Sleep

Traditionally it used to be common to sleep in the temples or in free shelters along the way. This tradition has disappeared for several reasons: Depopulation resulting in less people offering traveler services outside of the temples, better infrastructure, higher budgets. Some temples still offer this possibility, right now, in 2023, only 8 temples still run accommodations. In general I encourage the stay in paid locations to support the locals financially.

Wild camping is not allowed, but the Shikoku 88 Route Guide has marked official camping spots in many areas. I do not recommend to plan your pilgrimage sleeping in non-designated areas, so don't improvise. This is not the wilderness, you are always on somebody's property.

There are several types of accommodations, and most of them are shown in the Route Guide:
- Business Hotels: Western-style hotels with small rooms and not many additional amenities, covering basic needs, but lacking a personal touch. You will have your own room and bathroom; the costs will be 6,000 to 7,000 Yen per night without breakfast.
- Ryokan: Traditional hotels, tatami-rooms, futon beds, usually with a common bath, sometimes with a hot spring, price may include traditional set dinner and breakfast. Sometimes with very high standards and usually excellent food. Fixed times for dinner and bathing. A stay including dinner and breakfast may cost over 12,000 yen per person depending on meal choices.
- Minshuku: Similar to ryokan, but cheaper and with lower standard than a ryokan, prices around 7,000 to 8,000 yen per night.
- Henro Houses: Bilingual network with website organized by a private organization providing budget stays without dinner in guesthouses around the island, prices around 3,000-4,500 yen per night, usually shared room but small number of guests.
- Zenkonyado: Free of charge shelters, kept by people living nearby. Some might be convenient; some might be in poor condition. In case you stay in such a place, contact the

owners or neighbors to ask for permission and leave a donation of 2000 Yen with your Osamefuda if you used a futon, be sure you are not staying in a rest hut intended just for day use.

- Tsuyado: Free of charge place to sleep provided by some temples, usually intended for people in need or emergencies. Not recommended for regular planning.
- Shukubo: Pilgrimage hostels run by some temples (mentioned in the Route Guide), comparable to a ryokan or minshuku, traditional sleeping, with option to participate in morning service. 6,000 to 8,000 Yen per night including dinner and breakfast.
- Private guesthouses are marked in the route guide with their phone numbers, prices depend on food option, usually not expensive (around 4,000 – 5,000 Yen per night without dinner.) If dinner is included, it is usually hand cooked and fresh, go for it!

Organizing accommodations is one of the challenges for foreign pilgrims. Many reservations can be done via common hotel websites, or via the Henro House website (check the internet links at the back of the book). Regarding guesthouses, you can ask your current host to make the phone calls for reservations for the next days. Hotels can also be reserved by email or on platforms like Hotels.com, Booking.com or Tripadvisor.com

You might like to improvise your accommodations, but guesthouses do not like to be surprised by unexpected guests, which may force them to improvise. Be respectful. Plan ahead. **Make your reservations early** and try to confirm them one or two days before you arrive. Communication by e-mail in simple English usually works (thanks to translation websites). Also, be sure to cancel your reservation if you do not need it so that your hosts do not shop and cook dinner for a no-show guest.

The Culture of Osettai

One of the great pleasures of the pilgrimage is the positive attitude and the support from the local population. It is common practise to help the pilgrims, especially the walking pilgrims. This tradition is called Osettai.

Osettai can come in many different ways: During my own pilgrimages I have encountered people giving me drinks, bags with fruits or sweets, small souvenirs, paying my food in the restaurant (without telling me) or giving me a lift in the car. But also, temples refusing to accept my stamp fee or offering me tea and cookies, cash money, a car stopping by and offering me a precious golden Osamefuda for good luck, or a Yakuza member paying my dinner bill and inviting me to drink sake with him. I was deeply touched every time. If this happens to you, show your gratitude with a bow, a smile and one of your Osamefuda slips which, of course, you should present with both hands.

Osettai should <u>always</u> be accepted. Even if your intention is to walk the entire pilgrimage, declining a car ride to the next temple as Osettai would be considered rude and egoistic, as you might put your own priorities above the attempt of someone else who wants to do you a favor.

Whatever it is, do not decline but take it as a part of the Henro experience, and remember that also you as a pilgrim may give Osettai to other pilgrims. In addition to your Osamefuda slips, you can also add a little something which you might have brought along, a little, easy to carry souvenir from your hometown, for instance a key chain, a postcard or some sweets from your home country.

Eating and Drinking

Eating and drinking is one of the great pleasures of traveling in Japan. Shikoku is famous for a number of local specialties and its rich choice of fruits. Kochi has a Sunday market which is a paradise for street food lovers. Shikoku, especially Kagawa (formerly Sanuki), is famous for its thick Udon noodles which also make an ideal pilgrim's food. Udon is often hand-made, served in a bowl with concentrated broth or soup and plenty of vegetables and meat added, offering heat, carbs and minerals, just what we need to reheat ourselves after walking in the cold, or in the heat. Udon also comes in a cold version called *Zaru-Udon*, a wonderful cooling summer dish.

Traditional dinner will usually be composed of vegetables, soup, rice and some fish. Along the route, especially on the outskirts of the cities, you will find a large choice of affordable restaurants also serving western food. Often, tea is included free of charge.

Convenience stores are important places for resting. 7-Eleven, Family Mart, Lawson's and the smaller chains provide a large and delicious choice of hot and cold food and drinks, they also have clean public toilets, ATMs and good Wi-Fi. They are open 24 hours a day. Fresh food shelves offering Onigiri rice sandwiches with a wide choice of fillings which are easy to carry along as they are well packed and do not need constant refrigeration. The stores also provide hot water for those who would like to enjoy their instant noodle dishes straight away and health care products or basic electronic products like charge cables or batteries and basic stationery.

One of the specialties of Kochi area is Katsuo Tataki, which is bonito filet barbecued briefly on a hay fire but kept raw inside, garnished with yuzu juice, spring onions and sesame. And needless to say, seafood and fish is excellent all along the coast. Another nice experience is Izakaya, Pubs where Sake, Beer or local liquor is consumed while barbecued food is prepared in front of your eyes by the staff engaging their guests in discussions as they work.

In temples, food will usually be vegetarian but with such a diversity and prepared with such skill that meat will not be missed. Along most parts of the route except remote parts, you will find vending machines offering a wide choice of hot and cold coffees and teas as well as water, isotonic sports drinks and many types of juices and lemonades. Outside stores, beer is only sold at vending machines operated by liquor shops.

While it is easy to find vegetarian food in Japan, there are only very few vegan restaurants, as Japanese cooking usually involves fish broth. Some of the guesthouses and hostels have kitchenettes where you may prepare your own food. In case you have particular food preferences, for environmental or ethical reasons, remember that on a pilgrimage you should take what you get. It is one of the basic ideas.

Shikoku is also a place where Sake is produced, there are around 50 sake breweries across the island, some of them next to the pilgrimage route. When you stay in Kochi, the owner of the Kochi Youth Hostel, a former brew master, can give you an introduction during one of his tastings. While there are other places with a higher reputation for sake, Shikoku's sake still offers a good value for your money and the Kochi Station souvenir shop boasts a large selection.

The Route

Tokushima 徳島

We can begin the pilgrimage anywhere we want, but most pilgrims start at Tokushima. Tokushima is located where Shikoku is closest to Kobe and Osaka. Before the Asahi-Kaikyo Bridge connecting Tokushima with Kobe via Awaji Island was completed in 1998, Tokushima was important as the eastern port city of Shikoku.

As most pilgrims came to Shikoku from Osaka/Kobe, the Tokushima temples were the first temples visited on the pilgrimage which explains why the temple numbers begin near Tokushima.

T1 is located in the north on the outskirts of Tokushima city, in Bando, about 13 km walking distance from the city center. This part is not yet part of the official pilgrimage route, it is usually done by train.

Depending on your ambition and assuming you are starting at T1, there are several options for the first day:

- Walking T1 to T5: Mostly flat walk with 5 temples, 11 km in total, staying at Henro House Morimotoya near T5. This takes 4-5 hours
- Walking T1 to T6: Flat walk with 6 temples, 16 km in total, staying at the guesthouse of T6, this takes about 6 hours
- Walking T1 to T5 including B1: 21 km with 6 temples and a climb, 7-8 hours
- Walking T1 to T6 including B1 is challenging, but possible if you are in good shape and leave early. About 26 km with a climb of 450 m – 8-9 hours. Make sure to leave from T1 before 8 a.m.

Getting to Temple 1 – Ryozenji

Fascination	-
Walking Distance	750 m from Bando Train Station
Elevation gain	-
Difficulty	-
By public transportation	Train from Tokushima to Bando 25-30 minutes, 230 yen
Point of interest	-
Availability of food/drink/public toilets	Plenty in Tokushima Station
Where to stay	🛏 PAQ Tokushima 🛏 Sakura-So Tokushima 🛏 Henro House Ichiban Monzen Dori

To reach T1, take the JR Kotoku Line from T00 Tokushima Station to T05 Bando. The route to T1 is marked by a blue line on the street, starting from the station building. It is a short walk, only 750 m across the village until you will see the temple gate.

T1 can also easily be reached by long distance bus coming from Osaka-Namba or from Kyoto. Book a ride on a bus going to Takamatsu but get off at Naruto-Nishi, a highway bus stop located just 1.7 km from T1.

It is recommendable to have a stamp book from the first temple onwards, however the entire gear/attire can be bought at many places along the pilgrimage, the Sumotoriya-shop just before T10 is one of the best places. There is a gear shop near the entrance to T1 and many articles are also sold at the temple office where you will get your first stamp and where you can register as you begin your pilgrimage.

Henro House Ichiban Monzen Dori is a good place for beginners as the host, a former nun, will accompany you to T1 and give instructions.

Temple No. 1 – Ryozen-ji (Reizan-ji) 霊山寺

Fascination	**
Translation	Vulture Peak Temple
Main deity	Shaka Nyorai
Founded in	Tempyo era 724-749
Location	KM 0
Distance to next temple	1.2 km
Difficulty	Easy
Points of interest	Buddha foot-stone Hondo can be entered Lanterns in Hondo Koi Pond Double Pagoda Statues of 13 Buddhas Stamp office with shop
Okunoin	Toorin-In (Tanemaki-Daishi) 3 km east ⛩ Ooasahiko-Jinja, 1 km north

The pilgrimage begins with a particularly attractive temple. After passing the wooden walkway along the koi pond, we actually enter the Hondo rather than standing outside looking in, as we will in most temples. The many lanterns on the ceiling create a very warm, soothing light and are a tribute to the Okunoin at Koya-san. After worshipping, take a look at the ceiling to see a marvelous gold and silver silk painting of a dragon.

Visitors pray at the white Kannon-statue with the water basin is done to improve relationships. .

Founded by Gyoki by order of Emperor Shomu, Ryozen-ji was once one of the three largest temples of Shikoku, possibly because Ooasahiko-jinja and Ryozenji might have shared the same area. Kukai visited this temple in 815.

This is one of the many temples destroyed in the 19th century, but not in the unrests of 1868-1870, like many others, but it burned down in 1891. The current Main Hall was only built in 1964. The *Tahoto* tower (2-story pagoda) was built in the Oei era (1394-1421)

The stamp office is located outside the temple area, near the parking lot. There, you can sign up in a big book to track your departure and your return from the pilgrimage.

The temple is named after Vulture Peak, a sacred Buddhist mountain in India, a site frequented by Buddha and his disciples.

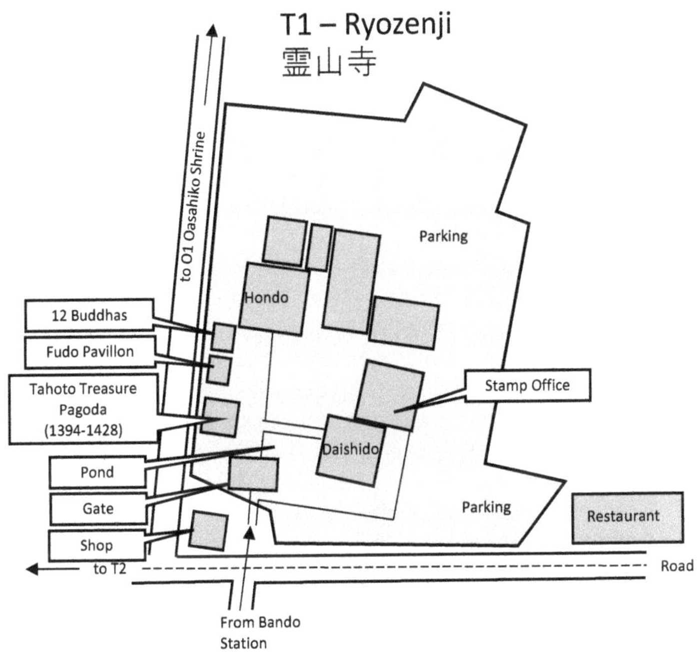

From T1 to T2 – KM 0 to KM 2.

Fascination	*
Distance	1.2 km
Difficulty	Easy and short walk along Road 12
By public transportation	Not necessary, it just takes 15 minutes
Point of interest	🛒 after 1 km Detour to ⛩ O1 Ooasahiko-Shrine Naruto German House, POW Museum German Park
Where to stay	🛏 Henro House Ichiban Monzen Dori 🛏 Morimotoya near T5

According to Laozi "A journey of a thousand miles begins with the first step". The start is easy. It is a short and easy walk directly to T2, but going directly we would miss the beautiful *Ooasahiko Jinja* (Shinto Shrine) and its park which only requires a 3 km detour.

In the first world war, over 1400 German prisoners of war stayed in this area. They built the stone bridges in the park. The German House has a little museum telling the story and showing how they lived, being treated relatively well by the Japanese government which allowed them to be autonomous. They put together an orchestra and the first time that Beethoven's 9th symphony was played in Japan was right here. The actual spot where the prisoner camp was located is 200 m north of the 7-Eleven. Turn right onto the second road after crossing the bridge.

One of the POWs was Herrmann Bohner. who remained in Japan for the rest of his life and convinced his brother, Alfred Bohner, to come to Shikoku and work as a language teacher in Matsuyama. Alfred Bohner's Shikoku Pilgrimage in 1927 made him one of the first foreign pilgrims. His interesting book on the pilgrimage was published in 1931 and later translated into English by David Moreton as "Two on a Pilgrimage".

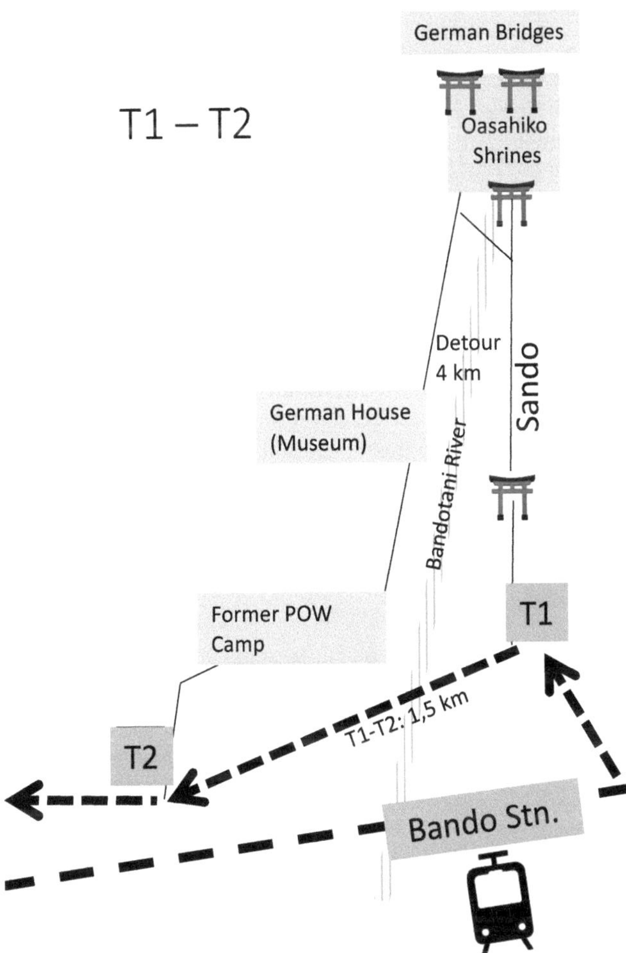
T1 – T2
German Bridges
Oasahiko Shrines
Detour 4 km
Sando
Bandotani River
German House (Museum)
Former POW Camp
T1
T2
T1-T2: 1,5 km
Bando Stn.

Temple No. 2 – Gokuraku-ji 極楽寺

Fascination	**
Translation	Nirvana- or Paradise Temple (Temple of the Pure Land)
Main deity	Amida Nyorai
Founded in	Nara-Period 710-793
Location	KM 2
Distance from last temple	1.2 km, 10 - 15 minutes
Distance to next temple	3 km
Difficulty	Easy
Points of interest	Garden 1200-year-old cedar tree O-Jizo Temple

After passing the newly renovated gate, the path turns right across the temple garden creating an impression of Nirvana. This garden is one of the most beautiful temple gardens in Shikoku. This temple was also founded by Gyoki.

We reach the Hondo (re-built in 1659) after another left turn, and it takes another 50 steps up the stairs to our right to reach the Daishido.

The most impressive spot on the grounds of this temple is a 1200-year-old cedar tree named Chomei-Sugi. According to legend, it was planted by Kukai. People come here to pray for a long life or an easy childbirth. By now, it has reached a height of 31 m.

Temple No. 3 – Konzen-ji (Kensenji) 金泉寺

Fascination	**
Translation	Golden Well Temple
Main deity	Shaka Nyorai
Founded in	Tempyo era 729-749
Location	KM 5
Distance from last temple	2.9 km
Distance to next temple	5.1 km
Difficulty	Easy
Points of interest	Golden Well Grave of Emperor Chokei Benkei (Heavy Stone)
Okunoin	Aizen-In on the way to T4 (KM 8)

The walk to T3 is another easy one, though slightly longer. The old pilgrimage Route runs parallel to Route 12, and after 30 to 40 minutes, we will reach T3 Konsen-ji.

Like T1 and T2, this temple too was built by Gyoki, on behalf of Emperor Shomu, an Emperor who lived during the Nara-Period and strongly supported Buddhism.

The temple is named after the well which is in a little concrete house next to the Hondo. According to legend, the well was built by Kukai who lived in the temple for a while. Its water ensures a long life.

Behind the main hall is the location of the grave of Emperor Chokei (1343-1394) who only reigned for 15 years. (His regency was under dispute, and he was only accepted as the official 94th Tenno in the year of 1926.) The temple was destroyed and later rebuilt by Chosokabe Motochika in 1582.

The garden also includes a large rock, which, according to legend, Benkei, a servant of samurai Yoshitsune Minamoto (1159-1189) was able to lift. Minamoto stayed at this temple to pray before defeating the Taira clan at the battle of Yashima, which marked the beginning of the Kamakura era in 1185. (see T84-85)

From T3 to T4 – KM 5 to KM 10

Fascination	*
Distance	5 km, 1:30 h
Elevation gain	73 m
Difficulty	Easy walk with a short climb before T4
By public transportation	🚌 from Itano Station to Rakan, then walk 2 km uphill.
Points of interest	KM 5 ⛩ Okagami-jinja, Huge Camphor Tree KM 7 ⛩Suwa Jinja shrine 🛒 KM 8 O3-Aizen-In KM 9 ⛩ Yamagami-Jinja 🚻
Where to stay	🛏 Morimotoya near T5 at KM 11

It takes about 90 minutes to reach T4, and we finally leave the villages on the outskirts of Tokushima.

Following the original pilgrimage route that runs just one block parallel to Road 12 for 3 km, after 1 km, we are passing Okagami-jinja, a shrine with an impressive camphor tree on our right. The tree is estimated to by 700 years old and is over 32 m high. It once had to be defended against an order for it to be used in shipbuilding. Take a leaf and rub it between your fingers to enjoy the smell.

After 3 km, we pass underneath the expressway and follow a path through a small bamboo forest leading us to Aizen-In 愛染院, an Okunoin of T3, where they sometimes put up drinks as Osettai to pilgrims. We follow the pathway along the creek.

After another 1 km, the path passes underneath the expressway once again and reaches the street that goes north up the hill at a little shrine called Yama-jinja. From Yama-jinja there is a footpath leading to Temple B1 (appr. 5 km uphill with an average climb of 8%). Instead, we will turn right, follow the street uphill and it is only another 600 m uphill to T4-Dainichiji.

Temple No. 4 – Dainichi-ji 大日寺

Fascination	**
Translation	Temple devoted to Dainichi Nyorai
Main deity	Dainichi Nyorai
Founded in	1394
Location	KM 9.5
Distance from last temple	5.1 km
Distance to next temple	2.0 km
Difficulty	Easy
Points of interest	Main gate with belltower 33 Kannon statues

The temple is situated at about 70 m altitude on the outskirts of the Kuroya river valley. The temple's local name used to be Kurodani-ji. Kuroya and Kurodani are written 黒谷 which means "black valley", referring to the lack of sunlight in this location which is surrounded by steep mountains on three sides.

The main gate has an upper floor with the bell, which you can ring as you pass. The gate and some other parts of the temple were renovated in 2017, after the old gate had become too unstable to carry the bell. It is made of Zelkova wood.

As we continue straight, we get to the Hondo, it was restored in 1799. The path on the right, which connects the main hall and the Daishi-hall (built 1863), contains 33 Kannon-statues, donated by citizens of Osaka in the 18th century. In its long history, this temple has been destroyed and rebuilt several times. T4 is an okunoin of To-ji temple in Kyoto, a temple strongly associated to Kukai. The symbol of the Kyoto temple is displayed at the gate.

This is a well-managed, charming little temple which has been renovated in the last couple of years, managed by a friendly priest who speaks English. This temple has Wi-Fi and maintains its own Facebook page.

Temple No.5 – Jizo-ji 地蔵寺

Fascination	**
Translation	Jizo Temple (temple devoted to Jizo Bosatsu)
Main deity	Shogun Jizo Bosatsu
Founded in	Konin 12 (821)
Location	12
Distance from last temple	2 km
Distance to next temple	5.3 km
Difficulty	Easy
Points of interest	800-year-old Gingko tree Gohyaku Rakan
Okunoin	Gohyaku Rakan

To get to T5, we just have to walk down the hill along the road. It is only a 30-minute-walk.

Just before reaching the temple, we will reach its okunoin, Gohyaku Rakan. It is located to our right, slightly higher than the main temple. Built in 1775, it contains a little museum displaying several hundred statues of followers of buddha. (Gohyaku means 500, and Rakan is the name of the group of followers.) The statues can be visited after paying the entrance fee of 200 yen. The ambience is special and intense, and worth the visit which takes 15-30 minutes. The number of statues today is around 200, the majority of the initial 500 statues were destroyed in an accidental fire in 1921, caused by a worshipper. The okunoin's lawn is also a nice place to take a rest.

Jizoji is a simple temple located around a square, a huge Gingko tree in its center which is over 800 years old. There is a legend that the sacred Jizo statue, carved by Kukai when the temple was founded, is located inside the tree and that also the temple history was carved into it. At this temple, people pray for a long life. Its area is said to have once measured about 40.000 m^2, which probably includes the area of the okunoin, and to have 300 Okunoin all around the island. The temple was founded by Kukai by order of Emperor Saga and was supported by Saga and the two emperors that followed him.

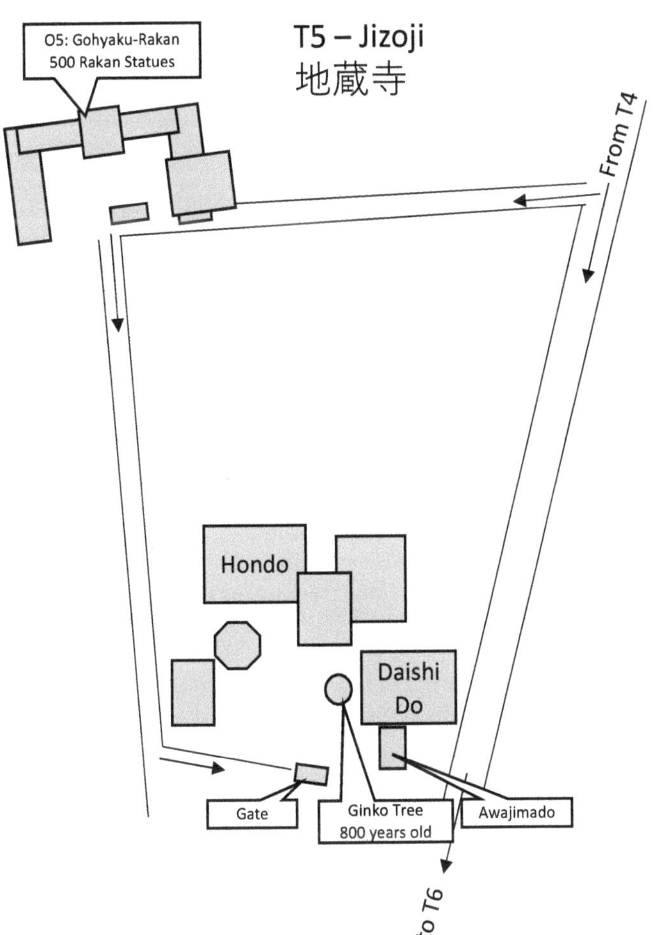

O5: Gohyaku-Rakan
500 Rakan Statues
From T4
Hondo
Daishi Do
Gate
Ginko Tree
800 years old
Awajimado
to T6

From T5 to T6 – KM 11 to KM 16

Fascination	*
Distance	5.3 km
Elevation gain	-
Difficulty	Easy
By public transportation	🚌 from Rakan to Higashibara
Points of interest	KM 12 🛒 🚌 KM 13 🛒 KM 13 Beginning of detour to B1 KM 14 🍴 Udon KM 16 🚌 Higashibara
Where to stay	🛏 KM 16 T6 Anrakuji Guesthouse

The next stage takes us more or less along Road 12, across the flatlands and along the country roads of the Yoshinogawa valley, T6-Anrakuji can be spotted from far, as it is surrounded by large trees.

Unless we made the detour to Bekkaku-1 (Taisanji) we have now walked 17 km as we end this stage, a good distance for our first day.

Turn right for B1 Taisanji

Temple No. B1 – Taisan-ji 大山寺

Fascination	**
Translation	Temple of the Big Mountain
Main deity	Senju Kannon Bosatsu
Founded in	6th century
Detour	10 km starting at KM 13
Difficulty	450 m elevation gain over 7 km of paved road = 6.4% followed by 250 steps
Points of interest	One of the oldest temples
Okunoin	Kuroiwa Daigongen

Taisanji is the first of the 20 Bekkaku Temples. It was founded around 568, which makes it one of the oldest temples of Shikoku and the oldest temple in Tokushima prefecture.

This temple is worth the three to four-hour detour, although its elevation of 450 m may be quite a challenge on the first day of the pilgrimage.

The route is easy to find. At KM 13, there is a "Taisanji right" sign (see picture) next to a rest place, suggesting to take a break before it gets hard. The small road leads uphill with occasional shortcuts for pedestrians. But when we finally reach the lower main gate, out of breath, we still need to climb another 215 steps until we make it to the beautiful plateau with its 800-year-old Ginkgo tree. And another 35 steps until we reach the Hondo.

For those intending to take the challenge and visit the okunoin Kuroiwa Daigongen (the mountain peak was the original sacred spot of this temple), it is another 1.4 km with an elevation gain of 250 m, a 18% climb.

Temple No. 6 – Anraku-ji 安楽寺

Fascination	**
Translation	Temple of Eternal Joy
Main deity	Senju Kannon Bosatsu
Founded in	6th century
Location	KM 16
Distance from last temple	5.3 km
Distance to next temple	1.4 km
Difficulty	easy
Points of interest	Upside-down pine tree

For over 400 years, Anrakuji has hosted pilgrims overnight, maybe because it is the perfect spot to spend the first night, after going from Tokushima to Bando and 17 km of walking to the temples. In the Middle Ages the temple was destroyed by the troops of Chosokabe, and upon rebuilding, this temple was combined with another temple named Suiunji, which no longer exists, but stood closer to the pilgrimage route and often served as a guesthouse.

Like T4, the entrance gate functions as a belltower. Some sites are slightly unusual: The decoration of the buildings is sumptuous and in a somewhat Chinese style (The Hondo was only built in 1965, the one before having burned down in 1955).

There is a 2-story Tahoto pagoda, inspired by the Kompon Daito pagoda at Koyasan (something you will find in several temples) and, for a change, Kukai is shown resting, with his hat off. The upside-down pine-tree, named Yakuyoke no Sakamatsu, is located next to the koi pond, and there is a small statue next to it. At this temple, the Hondo can be entered. Behind the Hondo there is another hall with more sanctuaries and water coming from a well, but it is not open to the public.

The guesthouse can accommodate up to 350 pilgrims, and it has its own hot spring. The mountain name of this temple is Onsenzan, "hot-spring-mountain". Anrakuji and the family who runs it since several generations are strongly engaged in the temple association, and many pilgrimage conferences are hosted in its large guesthouse.

T6 – Anrakuji
安楽寺

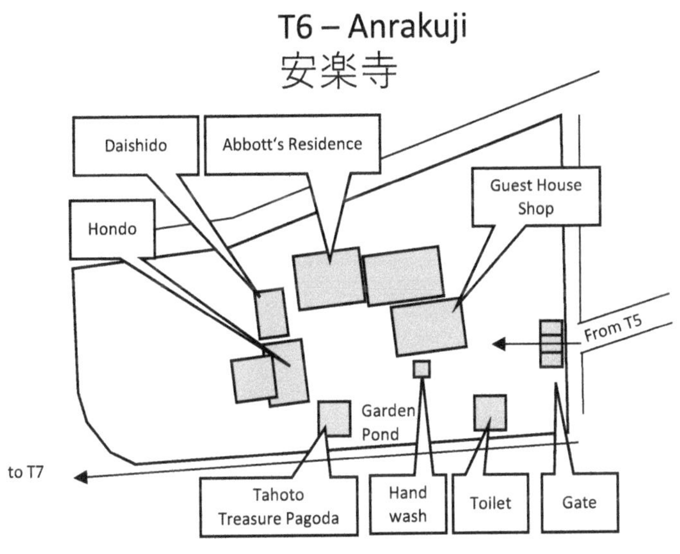

T7 – Jurakuji
十楽寺

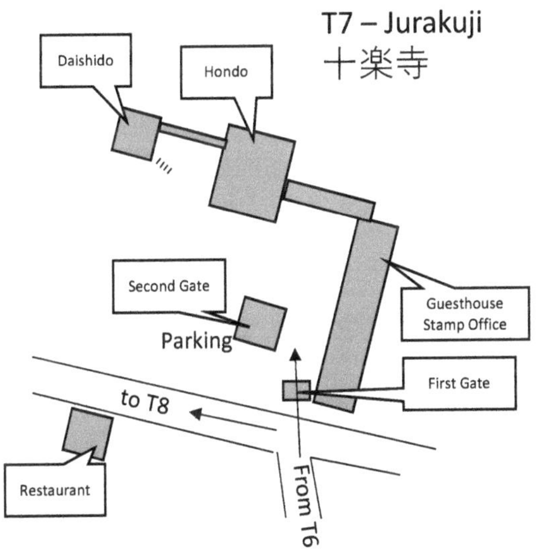

Temple No. 7 – Juraku-ji 十楽寺

Fascination	*
Translation	Temple of the Ten Joys
Main deity	Amida Nyorai
Founded in	806 - 810
Location	KM 18
Distance from last temple	1.4 km
Distance to next temple	4.2 km
Difficulty	Easy
Points of interest	Jizo

After the short walk from T6, we arrive at this smaller roadside-temple. Formerly in a separate location 3 km north, the temple was re-built at this location in 1635, which explains its rather modest location. The main hall was built in 1994. People come to this temple to pray for relief from eye diseases. This temple also offers accommodation in its guesthouse.

From T7 to T8 – KM 18 to KM 22

Fascination	*
Walking Distance	4.2 km, 1 hour
Elevation gain	111 m
Difficulty	Easy
By public transportation	Not available
Points of interest	KM 21 (500 m north, passing the expressway) *Gosho no Sato* - Hot spring and Restaurant
Where to stay	KM 20 Okudaya

The walk to T8 is basically a straight one-hour walk without much infrastructure on the way. We will pass the huge main gate outside the temple area, it is 9 m wide and 12.3 m high, one of the largest in Shikoku. We will see it from afar, and we might wonder where the temple is as we pass it. It is further uphill and we need to cross the road first. The majestic main gate stands alone, and due to traffic rerouting, we need to cross a few streets until we reach the actual temple area.

There is a major hot spring and restaurant (*Gosho no Sato*) near the expressway exit, just 500 m north of the pilgrimage route. The entrance fee to the hot spring and spa is 600 yen.

Temple No. 8 – Kumadani-ji 熊谷寺

Fascination	**
Translation	Temple of the Bear Valley
Main deity	Senju Kannon Bosatsu
Founded in	Konin 6 (815)
Location	KM 22
Distance from last temple	4.2 km
Distance to next temple	2.4 km
Difficulty	Easy
Points of interest	The huge Nyomon

As we continue our walk uphill, we can see a little artificial lake with a tiny island called Bentenjima and a little Shinto shrine on our right, as we enter the temple grounds on our left. The temple grounds stretch up the hill. The distance from the Nyomon (the first gate) to the Daishido at the northern end is about 350 m. After entering from the parking lot, we have to walk another 200 m up the hill until, after passing the middle gate (Chumon) we reach the Hondo and Daishido.

The Hondo and the Daishido were destroyed several times, most recently in 1927, when the temple burned to the ground and its sacred objects could not be saved, and the rebuilding efforts from 1940 were interrupted by WWII, the Hondo was only finished in 1952, and the renovation was completed in 1972.

The Tahoto treasure tower (2-story pagoda, built in 1774) is another building inspired by Koya-san's okunoin.

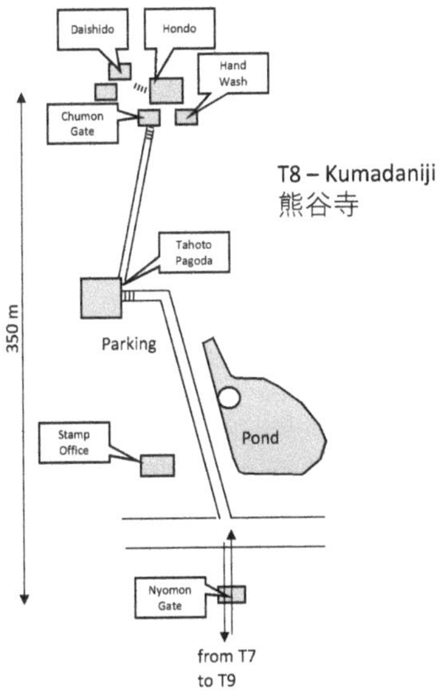

From T8 to T9 – KM 22 to KM 25

Fascination	*
Distance	2.4 km, 40 minutes
Elevation gain	-100 m (downhill)
Difficulty	Very easy
Public transportation	Not available
Points of interest	KM 25 Udon next to T9
Where to stay	KM 25 Tabi-no Yado

This is nother easy stage, as we are heading downhill back into the valley, mostly walking between rice and vegetable fields.

Right next to the temple, there is a little Udon restaurant and a vegetable shop.

Temple No. 9 – Horin-ji 法輪寺

Fascination	*
Translation	Temple of the Dharma Wheel
Main deity	Shaka Nyorai
Founded in	Konin 6 (815)
Location	KM 25
Distance from last temple	2.4 km
Distance to next temple	3.9 km
Difficulty	Very easy

At this temple, it is common to pray for the healing of walking disabilities, hence the many straw sandals shown.

The origin of this temple is said to be 4 km north of the current location on the Hochigakei Mountain but it was burned down by Chosokabe's men in 1582. (There is a spot today named Kyorenji that might fit that location). The temple was relocated and rebuilt in the current location during the Shoho Period 1644-48. But it burned down again in 1859 and was rebuilt and inaugurated by Emperor Meiji in 1882.

From T9 to T10 – KM 25 to KM 29

Fascination	*
Distance	3.9 km, 1 hour
Elevation gain	157 m (60m in the last 400m = 15%)
Difficulty	Easy but very steep at the end
Public transportation	Not available
Points of interest	KM 26 Enkoji KM 26 Azukiarai Daishi (Bangai) KM 27 Shonenji KM 29 Pilgrimage gear shop
Where to stay	KM 30 Yawata-Inn

This is the last stage of the group of temples along the north side of Yoshino-Valley. On the way, we pass a Bangai temple and, on the last kilometer, the village of Ichibacho.

Ichibacho used to be an important location during the pilgrimage as it was usually the second night for the pilgrims. T6, the first night, may not seem that far back but one should remember that in the old days, the roads were not paved and pilgrims usually walked in straw sandals, which they had to replace very often so the distances per day were shorter. Today, there are still several guesthouses and shops on the street leading to the temple.

Sumotoriya, the last shop before passing the expressway, is an excellent shop for pilgrimage and has been in the same family for several generations. The owner, Asano-san, speaks English very well. You can also find high-quality pilgrimage apparel here. This is a great place to get your gear and souvenirs.

Though the walk is an easy one, the last kilometer is very steep and takes us up to the (so far) highest elevation on our route, and as we arrive at the gate - out of breath - we are instructed to climb another 333 steps. So, in case you run out of time and try to reach this temple at 5 p.m. before the stamp office closes, remember that you will need another 10-15 minutes at the end.

Temple No.10 – Kirihata-ji 切幡寺 (Kirita-ji)

Fascination	**
Translation	Temple of the Cut Cloth
Main deity	Senju Kanon Bosatsu
Founded in	Konin era (810-824)
Location	KM 29
Distance from last temple	3.9 km
Distance to next temple	9.7 km
Difficulty	Easy, but last km is very steep
Points of interest	Panorama Pagoda
Okunoin	Hasso Daishi

The unusual name of this temple goes back to the legend of Kukai asking a lady to provide him with some cloth to make some garments, it turned out that she had been the mistress of a samurai who had fallen into disgrace and fled into the temple. She was enlightened when Kukai ordinated her.

Kirihataji too was destroyed by the army of Chosokabe Motochika in the 16th century. It was then rebuilt, and destroyed again in 1900 by a fire.

The 2-story pagoda was brought from Sumiyoshi Taisha Shrine in Sakai, Osaka, in 1868 and took 10 years to erect. Treasure pagodas (Tahoto) usually have round upper floors, but this one has a square upper floor, a rare exception.

The origin of the temple is probably its okunoin, Hasso Daishi, located about 100 m further north and 50 m higher on top of the mountain.

From the temple, there is a magnificent panorama over Yoshino valley and the opposite mountain range, which we will tackle the next day.

From T10 to T11 – KM 29 to KM 38

Fascination	**
Distance	9.7 km, 2.5 hours
Elevation gain	50 m
Difficulty	Easy
Public transportation	Not available
Points of interest	KM 30 Rest hut KM 31 Hachimangu shrine KM 32 Onojima Bridge KM 34 Bridge over Yoshinogawa KM 34 Rest hut KM 35 Detour 700 m to a
Where to stay	KM 30 Yawata-Inn KM 34 Awarakuya Guesthouse KM 37 Henro no Sato Channel-Kan Guesthouse in Yoshinogawa Town

This is a special stage as we are leaving the northern side of the valley, crossing the river and heading over to the south side which is on a different tectonic plate. Simply speaking, we are moving over to a different earth-shell. The quiet flow of Yoshinogawa is the border between the tectonic plates, and we will do that leap in the middle of Kawashima bridge, the second bridge, without being aware of it.

Our walk begins across Ichibacho-village, passing the shops and guesthouses, some of which have been closed over the years. In the past. This village used to be an important location where pilgrims remained until they could pass the river, before the bridge had been built, maybe with no ferry available, waiting for the right moment to cross, with less current and lower water level, making it possible to cross it barefoot, keeping their luggage on top of their heads.

After 1.5 km, just before crossing Highway 12, there is a shelter hut with a public toilet. Nearby, on the highway, Ryokan Yawata offers a more comfortable place to sleep and you can dine in its Udon restaurant.

After another 2 km, we pass a little river and walk across the fields on the fertile soil of Zennyuji-jima island, finally reaching the wider part of the river and crossing it.

There are two bridges over Yoshinogawa: A lower one, Kawajima-bridge, which at times of higher water levels may be flooded and which follows the official pilgrimage route (shown as route A on Route Guide Map 19). The other, higher one, Awa-Chuo bridge, is 2 km east, further downstream, and requires a return to T9 before heading south along Highway 318. This one will take us to Yoshinogawa-City where there we find more infrastructure – a train station, hostels, guesthouses and some restaurants as shown as route B on the Route Guide Map 19.

Yoshinogawa is a good place to stay for the second night, just a few kilometers away from T11 and the hard stage to KM 12 that will be our program for the next day.

T11 is located just 3 km south of Yoshinogawa, an easy walk across the fields. Coming from the town, (Route B) there are some places to grab food along Highway 92 which we cross on the outskirts. This is very important because **we will not have access to food from supermarkets or restaurants for the next 35 km** until we reach the convenience store near T13 one or two days later.

Kawajima Bridge

Temple No. 11 – Fujii-dera 藤井寺

Fascination	**
Translation	Temple of the Wisteria Well
Main deity	Yakushi Nyorai
Founded in	Konin 6 (815)
Location	KM 38
Distance from last temple	9.7 km
Distance to next temple	11.6 km
Difficulty	Easy
Points of interest	Wisteria, dragon painting on the Hondo-ceiling
Okunoin	Daiichi-Nyorai, next to the temple

Fujidera is one of the three Zen-temples along the route. The statue of its main deity is said to have been carved in 1148 and it is considered a national treasure. It has withstood several destructions and temple fires. People come to this temple to pray for safety from disasters and epidemics.

The temple area used to be much bigger and splendid, but it burned down entirely in the Tensho era (1573-92) revived in 1632 as a Zen temple, again destroyed in 1832 and was only rebuilt in 1860. The Hondo has a huge dragon painted onto its ceiling by a painter named Unryu.

Fujidera is also a sort of starting point for the hard climb to T12, a last opportunity to use the restroom before the long climb in the forest, but the temple deserves more attention. The Wisteria is all over the temple grounds and can be seen in full bloom in April.

From T11 to T12 – km 38 to km 50

Fascination	***
Walking Distance	11.6 km
Elevation gain	About 1200 m
Difficulty	Very steep, no food
There is no public transportation connecting these two temples, but an easy way to get to T12 by public transportation is to take the bus from Tokushima Station to Kamiyama Koko-mae bus stop and to walk the mountain road up, a 500 m climb over 6.4 km of paved road.	
Points of interest	KM 40 ↗↗ Henro Korogashi KM 41 ↗↗ Chodo-An (Bangai Temple) KM 44 ↗↗ O12 – Ryusui-An 🚻 KM 46 ↗↗ O12 –Joren-An △ 745 m 🚻 KM 48 ↘↘ Bridge, Henro Korogashi KM 50 ↗↗ T12 Shosan-ji △ 712 m
Where to stay	There are no accommodations between T11 and T12. The rest huts on the way do not allow sleeping. Usually, pilgrims continue downhill for another 3 km to stay at Sudachi-an at KM 54, in Kamiyama, or at Moja House, 3 km off KM 56 south of the river.

Carry enough food and drinks, as this stage is one of the hardest parts of the pilgrimage as there are over 1,000 m of elevation gain to master with no restaurants, shops, vending machines or other amenities on the way. Instead, there are thousands of steps and two spots, steep locations, that are particularly hard, called Henro-Korogashi, "Where the pilgrim falls". The first one is in the 2nd km and the second one just before reaching T12.

The entire walk is across the forest, with much to see: three temples and a large Kukai statue at the highest spot, the route continuously ascending or descending. There are different estimations of the time needed. 5 hours is a good time to plan for, which means that you MUST start out in the morning and leave T11 before 9 am to reach the distant guesthouses before it gets dark and T12 temple office which closes earlier than other temples. Check the latest opening times before you go.

The forest has something mystic about it, maybe due to the many little statues that we pass along the way, but we must be sure to be out of the forest before it gets dark.

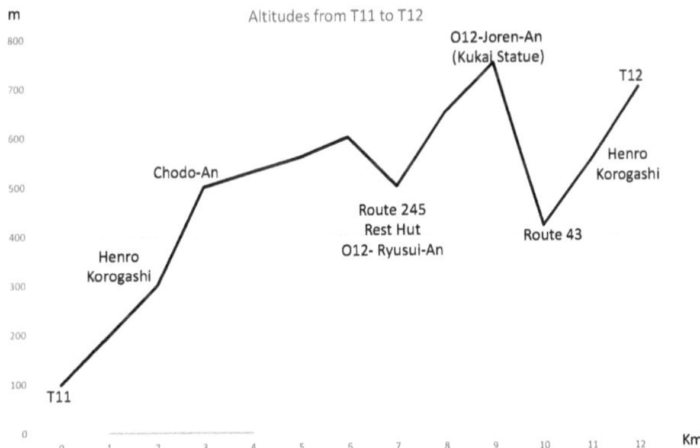

Traditionally, pilgrims eat salty plums at Chodo-An. The Ryusui-An hut is not for sleeping. At Joren-An, we take 42 steps to a huge Kukai statue marking the highest point (750 m) of the stage, after which we head down steep into the valley, passing a river over a small wooden bridge, and this marks the final climb – about 2 km at 13% until suddenly the route becomes flat and we see the lanterns of the temple grounds in a vertical row.

Remember

1. If you want to get the T12 stamp, you need to **leave T11 before 9 am to be at the T12 office before 3 p.m.** Getting lost or simply walking in the forest at night is dangerous. (Imagine slipping and hurting your ankle, on your own, not being able to walk anymore as the sun disappears.) And be sure to allow enough time for rests. It gets dark early and fast

2. **No food and drinks available for the next 2 days,** except the vending machines at T12.

Temple No. 12 – Shosan-ji 焼山寺

Fascination	***
Translation	Temple of the Burning Mountain
Main deity	Kokuzo Bosatsu
Founded in	Konin 6 - 815
Location	KM 50
Distance from last temple	11.6 km
Distance to next temple	22.2 km
Difficulty	Diffficult. Very steep walk across the forest, even worse when wet. Easier from Kamiyama, after coming by bus from Tokushima
Points of interest	50-m tall cedar trees Location on mountain peak Hall with 3-faced Daigokuten left of the Hondo
Okunoin Shosanji has five associated sacred places	Ryusui-An (KM 45) Jyoren-An (KM 47) Ryuo-Kutsu (KM 50) Joshin-An (KM 51) Zao-Daigongen (above the temple)

As mentioned, this temple is hard to reach on foot, and for that reason it is called a Nansho, a "difficult place" to reach. At 706 m altitude, Shosan-ji is the second-highest temple of the 88 temples after T66 and first of 8 Nansho temples on the route. If this temple had nothing in particular to offer, simply reaching it after the hard walk would turn it into a special place, isolated above the clouds. But this magnificent magic place has a lot to offer. The cedar trees, some of them up to 50 m in height and up to 500 years old, have protected the temple from lightnings over the centuries, some of the buildings are above 1000 years old.

For many years, this temple was also a location where ascetic Yamabushi mountain monks practiced Shugendo by running up- and downhill. During the Kamakura period, Shosan-ji became the imperial temple of emperor Godaigo who ruled from 1319 until 1338.

We have passed two of its okunoins on the way up. A third one, Zao-Daigongen, is on the mountain peak which is another 1.3 km-walk with a 230 m climb (18%), a small shrine on the mountain peak. We will pass the other two on the way to T13. The temple runs a little Udon restaurant which is not always open. The stamp fee at T12 was raised to 500 yen in 2023.

The Legend of Emon Saburo

The legend of Emon Saburo is worth mentioning, as it is related to several temples and to the pilgrimage itself: see T12, B9 and T51. The story goes that Emon Saburo was a wealthy man living in Ehime Prefecture at the time of Kukai, around 1200 years ago. Kukai knocked at his door as a begging monk for several days, but every day, Emon Saburo chased him away. The third time Kukai knocked, Emon Saburo even smashed Kukai's rice bowl. In the years that followed, all of Emon's sons died, and he suddenly believed this was related to his mistake of chasing away a holy man. Regretting his deed, he decided to find the holy man, who had continued his journey, but was not able to find him. The legend says that Emon Saburo walked around Shikoku clockwise twenty times, finally deciding to walk in the opposite direction. Old and tired, Saburo finally found Kukai at today's location of O12 Joshin-An (1.7 km downhill from T12). Saburo asked Kukai to forgive him and requested to be reborn as a rich man so he could build temples. He picked up a little stone and died, weakened by his long time on the road. Emon Saburo is considered to have been the first pilgrim.

Years later, a boy was born with a crippled hand. His hand opened one day, holding a stone with the words "Emon Saburo reborn" written on it. This was near Temple 51, which is why that temple is named *Ishiteji* "Stone-Hand-Temple". (Today Temple B9 – Monjuin is considered to be Emon Saburo's former house, and there are some ancient mounds near T47 which are said to be the graves of his sons, however, other theories claim these mounds to be a lot older.)

From T12 to T13 – KM 50 to KM 72

Fascination	**
Walking Distance	22 km
Elevation gain	250 m climb to Tamaga-Toge in the beginning, the rest is downhill
Difficulty	Easy but no food
Public transportation	🚌 from Shosan-ji Station to Kamiyama: 3x per day (or walk 7 km), 🚌 from Kamiyama to T13: 15 x per day.
Points of interest	KM 52 ↘↘ O12 Joshin-An 🚻 KM 54 🛏 Sudachi-an 210 m KM 55 ↗↗ Tamaga-Toge △ 450 m KM 56 Rest Hut KM 57 Kagamishi Daishi (Bangai) KM 58 Prefectural Road 20 KM 65 Pass the bridge KM 66 ⛺ KM 67 Detour to O13 Konji-ji KM 69 Detour to B2 KM 71 🛒
Where to stay	KM 54 🛏 Sudachi-an KM 67 🛏 Yasuragi KM 72 🛏 T13 Temple Guesthouse

This part is not short, but much easier than the way up. First, we head 1.7 km downhill passing Joshin-An, the location where Emon Saburo is said to have met Kobo-Daishi. After another 1.4 km downhill (where our altitude drops by 200 m), after passing a little bridge, we reach Highway 43 where we turn right. Here we find a place to sleep for our 3rd night – Sudachi-an (there used to be two other ones but they closed during corona).

We continue on Road 43 to the right, downhill, and at the exit of the village, opposite the last house on our right, there is a sign to a path on the left. This is the continuation of the main walking pilgrimage route, shown by the little sign post. (If you see another little bridge on your right, you have gone too far.)

We will follow this path into the mountains facing a very tough climb for 1 km as it gets narrower until we reach Tamaka-Toge-Pass at 450 m altitude. From the pass it is a walk of about 4 km downhill until we reach the prefectural road No. 20. Finally, out of the mountains and easily walking along a river bed, we follow this road for 7 km until we cross the river to the other side in the village of Hirono. We turn left after crossing the river and finally follow the river for another 7 km until we reach our next temple.

To Temple B2, stay on Road 20 without crossing the bridge and carry on for 3.4 km, through the tunnel (641 m length). 200 m After the tunnel, Temple B2 is on the left side at the traffic light.

Temple No. B2 – Dogaku-ji 童学寺

Fascination	**
Translation	Temple of Schooling
Main deity	Yakushi Nyorai
Founded in	(not clear) 700-749
Location	1 km away from km 69
Detour from main route	7 km
Difficulty	Easy
Points of interest	Sacred fountain

Legend says that at this temple, Kukai invented Hiragana and Katakana, the Japanese syllable alphabets. The temple was founded by Gyoko-Bosatsu under a different name. Like so many others, the temple has a long history of expansions and destructions, the most recent fire in 2017 having destroyed the main hall and a number of other buildings.

The temple has a holy fountain, where Kukai is said to have taken the water to dilute his calligraphy ink. At this temple, people pray that their children do well at school.

It is allowed to take water for personal use free of charge.

Temple No. 13 – Dainichi-ji 大日寺

Fascination	*
Translation	Temple devoted to Dainichi-Nyorai
Main deity	Juichimen Kannon Bosatsu
Founded in	Konin 815
Location	KM 72
Distance from last temple	22.2 km
Distance to next temple	2.5 km
Difficulty	Easy
Points of interest	Ichinomiya-Jinja
Okunoin	Konjiji (KM 67) Ichinomiya-Jinja, Kuninaka-Ji (Kokuchu-Ji)

T13 is situated on a narrow strip between the road 21 and Akui river. At first it may seem small, but a closer look at the area, especially around the mountain reveals a number of sites and remains from a time when this area was more important than today.

The splitting of temple areas into Shinto and Buddhist areas in the Meiji reformation around 1872 is clearly visible. Ichinomiya-Jinja is located on the south side of the road, and despite its status as prime Shinto shrine in the prefecture, has not been renovated in a long time, but you can feel a special aura when walking among its little buildings, rocks and horse statues. While Dainichi-Ji, the temple, is in good shape, Ichinomiya-Jinja is not, but it has a charming aura of patina.

Close to Ichinomiya-Jinja, a road leads uphill to the ruins of Ichinomiya Castle, just a steep 500 m away with a 150 m climb. The foundations are still visible. Apart from Ichinomiya-Jinja, T13 has two other sacred places: Konjiji, which is 1 km away from the main route (we passed it at KM 67) and probably owes its presence to the nearby waterfall, and Kuninakaji which is 2 km east of T13 and has on its grounds another shrine by the same name, Kuninaka-Jinja. There are several other smaller temples and shrines in the area near the castle mountain, for instance Jishoin, a Bangai temple hidden only 200 m west of T13.

From T13 to T17 – KM 72 to KM 80

Fascination	**
Distance	8 km
Elevation gain	50 m in the beginning, rest is flat
Difficulty	Easy
Public transportation	By railway from Tokushima to Koo (or Kou)
Points of interest	KM 73 Bridge over Akui River **KM 74 T14** and O14 Jigenji **KM 75** Hasso Daishi and **T15** **KM 78 T16** 🛒 KM 79 🚂 Kou Station
Where to stay	🛏 Matsumotoya near T17, or in Tokushima

T13 is the beginning of our second group of five temples near Tokushima (T13-T17) over only 8 km returning northbound to the western part of the city. After visiting T17, we can stay in Tokushima or – at KM 83 – head south for the shortest way to T19 which is 19 km from T17 (this route is called the Jizo-Goe Route as it passes a Bangai temple called Jizo-in). The route crosses the railway to Tokushima between T16 and T17 making this group of temples easily accessible by public transportation.

Temple No. 14 – Joraku-ji 常楽寺

Fascination	*
Translation	Temple of Everlasting Peace
Main deity	Miroku Bosatsu/Maitreya
Founded in	Konin 6, 815
Location	KM 75
Distance from last temple	2.5 km
Distance to next temple	1 km
Difficulty	Easy
Points of interest	Tree in front of the main hall

This little temple is situated on top of a rock, the area is called "garden of water rocks". It was moved to this place in 1818. People come here to drink the water and pray for a cure against diabetes and to pray for children's sleep. The temple runs a childcare facility.

Temple No. 15 – (Awa) Kokubun-ji 國分寺

Fascination	**
Translation	Main Temple of Awa Prefecture
Main deity	Yakushi Nyorai
Founded in	Tenpyo 3, 741
Location	KM 76
Distance from last temple	1 km
Distance to next temple	2 km
Difficulty	Easy
Points of interest	2-Story main hall, garden

Every prefecture has its main temple, this is the main temple of Tokushima prefecture, formerly called *Awa*. The other prefectural temples – *Kokubun-ji* - are T29, T59 and T80.

This temple must be approached from the south, not from the road coming from T14 and continuing to T16, which would be east. As we approach the temple, look for the sign indicasting the parking lot on your left after passing Hasso Daishi.

The temple was founded by Gyoki Bosatsu, destroyed in the Tensho era and only rebuilt 150 years later, in 1741. Like many other temples, this one was destroyed several times. The tall, 2-story main hall from 1810 was under renovation in 2020 after being destroyed in a fire in 1999.

Formerly, the temple area was much larger and included the fields next to the temple, its surface measured 47,000 sqm. You can still see the foundations of a 7-story pagoda left of the main gate.

This temple is not run by Shingon, but, like T11, by Zen Buddhists of the Soto-school.

Its arrangement of buildings is in a classical Shichido-garan (7 buildings) arrangement. The temple has an impressive Zen garden on the right of the Hondo with stones up to 4 m high.

Temple No. 16 – Kannon-ji 観音寺

Fascination	*
Translation	Kanon Temple
Main deity	Senju Kannon Bosatsu
Founded in	Tempyo 13, 741
Location	KM 78
Distance from last temple	2 km
Distance to next temple	2.9 km
Difficulty	Easy

Kannon-ji was founded by Gyoki but renamed by Kukai when he visited the temple. A smaller temple, but with a large wooden gate that includes the bell tower. After the destruction by Chosokabe Motochika, today's buildings were built in 1659. People visit this temple to pray for the well-being of their young children. There is a statue of Yonaki-Jizo with babies at his feet, who takes care of small children crying at night.

Temple No. 17 – Ido-ji 井戸寺

Fascination	**
Translation	Temple of the Well Door
Main deity	Shichibutsu-Yakushi-Nyorai
Founded in	Hakuho 2, 673
Location	KM 80
Distance from last temple	2.9 km
Distance to next temple	18.7 km
Difficulty	Easy
Points of interest	Omokake-no-ido well

Located 1.5 km north of the railroad (Kou Station), the entrance to this temple is on the south side and it is hidden in an urban area on its other sides.

The temple was founded on behalf of emperor Temmu and designed as a Shichido-garan in 673, destroyed in a war in 1362 and again by Chosokabe Motochika in 1582 and finally rebuilt in 1661. It is famous for its well, which is inside a little house. The legend says that people who can see the reflection of their face in the water of the well, will have good luck.

From T17 to T18 – KM 80 to KM 100

Fascination	*
Walking Distance	19 km
Elevation gain	77 m at the end
Difficulty	Easy
Public transportation	Train from Kou to Minami-Komatsushima via Tokushima, 2 km walking.
Points of interest	KM 83 , KM 83 alternative route to T18 KM 88 Tokushima Station KM 89 KM 90 Nikenya-Station KM 91 KM 94 alt. route meets main route KM 95 Chuden-Station, hut KM 96 KM 98 Turn right, leave the highway
Where to stay	Tokushima

On this stage, the route passes the city of Tokushima. After 3 km, if we turn right at the 7-Eleven at km 83, there is an alternative route to T18 of the same length, which lets us avoid the city. The alternative route is the much prettier walk, passing a Bangai temple, a cemetery and an onsen, but includes a climb as we need to cross a pass at 140 m altitude. The main route is mainly along noisy highways. The Route Guide lists another Bangai near KM 97 named Kobo-Daishi Otsui-no-mizu, which is actually a tiny shrine in a rice field.

The return to the city is a convenient solution because it allows us to walk our first 3 days (the first one staying at T6, the second one staying in Kamojima and the 3rd one staying at Sudachi-an just after T12) carrying a minimal amount of luggage, as we can leave the rest in our Tokushima guesthouse or at a locker in the train station. The fourth night can be back in Tokushima. Also, it is a good opportunity to enjoy city life and shopping opportunities, as the next larger city, Kochi, is 270 km away.

Temple No. 18 – Onzan-ji 恩山寺

Fascination	**
Translation	Gratitude-Mountain Temple
Main deity	Yakushi-Nyorai
Founded in	729-749
Location	KM 100
Distance from last temple	20 km
Distance to next temple	4 km
Difficulty	Medium, 77 m elevation gain
Points of interest	-
Okunoin	Benzaiten

As we approach the temple going uphill, we first see the temple gate on the side of the road. The old route did not follow today's road.

Early on, women were not allowed in this temple. Kukai changed that after 17 days of waterfall meditation and his mother stayed at this temple as a nun. This temple is dedicated to gratitude to parents, hence the name. Today's buildings were built in the beginning of the 19th century.

Its okunoin, Benzaiten, is a Shinto shrine located in a beautiful location 4 km east on a coastal rock.

The old gate to T18, no longer in use

From T18 to T19 – KM 100 to KM 103

Fascination	*
Distance	About 4 km
Difficulty	Easy
Public transportation	T19 is located 0.5 km from Tatsue Station. The 4 km stage could be done by train from Minami-Komatsushima to Tatsue, but that would involve 2.5 km walking back to the station from T18.
Points of interest	KM 101 Shakaan (Bangai) KM 103 Okyozuka (Bangai) Rest hut
Where to stay	KM 103 Funa-no-Sato KM 103 Guesthouse T19 KM 105 Henro House Fun Farm

Easy to find: After a short but steep descent down to Road 136 we take a right turn and follow the road for 2.6 km. After 2.4 km we will see Okyozuka, a little Bangai temple and Henro-Goya rest hut. The Henro Goya Project is a privately funded project committed to building open rest huts along the pilgrimage route. All huts are made of wood, designed by an architect and usually built in a way that you can stop there for a rest is possible but there is no space for sleeping. This one offers more space.

We are now in a particular location, where the route meets the Tatsue river, just 100 m down the road.

It would not be a detour to cross the river at this bridge, but the main pilgrimage route continues along the road for another 400 m until reaching Shirasagi-bridge, more distinctive due to its red and golden rails, which we cross and head on straight to T19. Many of the bridges related to the pilgrimage are red. This area's guest houses are a good place to spend the 5th night.

Temple No. 19 – Tatsue-ji 立江寺

Fascination	**
Translation	Tatsue Temple
Main deity	Enmei Jizo Bosatsu
Founded in	Shomu Era 724-749
Location	KM 103
Distance from last temple	4.2 km
Distance to next temple	13.2 km
Difficulty	Easy
Points of interest	Paintings on the Hondo ceiling
3 Okunoins: Seisuiji (KM 104) Shushoji (6 km detour from T19) Hoshino Iwaya (4 km from KM 112, see Route Guide Map 25a)	

T19 is named after the Tatsue-river flowing nearby. The temple used to be appr. 400 m west of today's location, which would be near its okunoin Seisuiji.

A legend says that a woman who had run away from her husband with her lover got her hair entangled in the temple's bell rope, which is now kept as a relic. The massive rope next to the Daishi-do refers to this legend. This is said to have happened in 1803.

The paintings on the ceiling of the main hall were donated by Tokyo University of Arts in 1977, when the temple was restored after a fire in 1974.

This temple has a guesthouse (Shukubo).

Tatsueji has three okunoin, all located (some with detours) along the route to T20.

From T19 to T20 – KM 103 to KM 116

Fascination	**
Distance	13 km
Elevation gain	480 m
Difficulty	First 14 km easy, but very steep towards the end: Henro-Korogashi – a climb of 480 m over 2.9 km (16%)
Public transportation	Only possible by train back to Tokushima an from there by 🚌 to Ikuna (KM 113), not recommended
Points of interest	KM 104 O19 Kyosuiji/Seisuiji KM 106 road to 🛏 Henro House Fun Farm KM 109 Rest hut 🛒 Katsuura River KM 112 Detour to O19 Hoshino Iwaya KM 113 Ikuna 🚌. Rest area. Detour to B3 and/or O19 Hoshino Iwaya KM 114 Rest hut 🚻 ↗↗ Henro Korogashi KM 115 ↗↗ Panoramic view
Where to stay	KM 106 🛏 Fun Farm KM 113 🛏 Kanekoya or Kakufutei

This is an interesting stage: The first 6 km of this stage is flat along country roads, where we pass a number of smaller temples and shrines. Ikuna 🚌 at KM 113 is a large rest area with good infrastructure, a place where we need to make a decision regarding our options:

1. Visit O19 Hoshino-Iwaya, a beautiful, almost magic temple for waterfall meditation, a detour of about 6-7 km (2 hours) but worth it. Cross the river to get there.
2. Include B3, an impressive Bekkaku temple located higher in the mountains, which might take an additional day, but you will not regret it. For this one, continue along route 16 for another 6 km (see B3 for further details)
3. To T20, either along Road 283 or taking the steep path.

At the final climb, we need to decide between the road and the path. As so often, the road is a bit longer but might be the better choice especially when it is wet or when travelling with a heavy backpack, avoiding slippery surfaces. Along the route you will find 21 traditional Choseki-stones on the last 2.2 km. These are distance markers, one Cho every 109 m. Each stone bears the name of an imperial era, the path is classified as a national historic site.

The rest hut at KM 114 has enough space to lie down and roll out a sleeping bag but it is completely open to the sides and not recommended for an overnight stay. In 2023 the roof was redone and the thatched roof unfortunately disappeared.

Be sure to have some food with you once you leave the rest area at KM 109 since there will be **no shops** until you reach T22 after 23 tough kilometers.

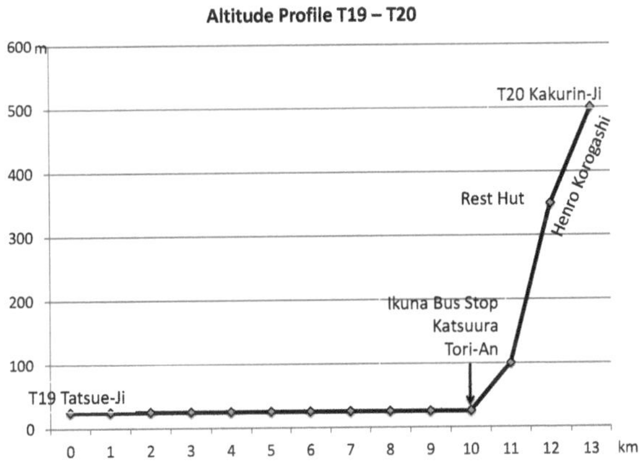

Temple No. B3 – Jigen-ji 慈眼寺

Fascination	***
Translation	Temple of the Merciful Look
Main deity	Juichimen Kanon Bosatsu
Detour from main route	20 km
Difficulty	530 m climb, paved
Points of interest	Waterfall Kanjo-ga-daki Ana-Zenjo Cave
Where to stay	🛏 Sakamoto

Some of the Bekkaku temples are hidden gems. B3 Jigen-ji, which is also classified as an okunoin of T20, is one of those. Located at 560 m altitude and requiring a detour of 20 km from KM 133 westbound, visiting this temple will require adding an extra day in your schedule. But it is worth it, especially because you might include two waterfalls and two Bangai Temples on the way, close to the highway station: Hoshi-no-Iwaya and Buddha-Ishi are close to the route to B3. The second waterfall Kanjo-ga-daki is to our left just one km before arriving.

The cave temple, called Ana-Zenjyo, is another Bangai. The entrance to the cave is very narrow and to avoid difficulties crawling into the dark cave, your "diameter" will be checked between two walls to make sure you will not get stuck. This is not for the faint of heart, but entering this cave through a small hole and tunnel in the mountain is a mythical experience.

Temple No. 20 – Kakurin-ji 鶴林寺

Fascination	***
Translation	Temple of the Crane Forest
Main deity	Jizo Bosatsu
Founded in	798
Location	KM 116
Distance from last temple	13.2 km
Distance to next temple	6.1 km
Difficulty	Very steep climb (2 km at an average of 16%) with a Henro-Korogashi
Points of interest	Panorama on the way up Choseki stones Triple-story Pagoda

T20 and T21 are two highlights of the pilgrimage, both challenging *Nansho* places, situated on opposing mountain peaks. Kakurinji is devoted to cranes, the big birds can be seen in many places in the decoration. The main hall is guarded by two huge bronze cranes, and the crane motif can also be seen printed on the curtains.

This temple has some of the oldest buildings along the pilgrimage and was given the title "official imperial temple" by emperor Kanmu upon its completion. Today, it is considered a cultural treasure of Tokushima prefecture. The main hall was completed in 1604, the three-story-pagoda was built in 1827, the only one in Tokushima prefecture.

Its 470 m altitude offers an impressive panorama over a large part of Shikoku.

From T20 to T 21– KM 116 to KM 122

Fascination	**
Distance	5.6 km
Elevation gain	460 m
Difficulty	Short but hard. A steep descent of 2 km followed by a tough climb after crossing the river. No food.
Public transportation	Not available
Points of interest	KM 118 ↘↘ Bridge KM 120 Ancient mercury mine KM 121 ↗↗ Henro Korogashi
Where to stay	Difficult. If you walk, it is best to stay in Katsuura (KM 109) and try to walk all the way to T22. Or at Aoi, 3 km off the bridge in Kamodani village near an alternative way to T21 called Kamo trail

A short but difficult stage. 2 km steep downhill, crossing the river and 3 km steep uphill including a Henro Korogashi stretch where the pilgrim is again challenged by a particularly hard climb.

Since there are no accommodations along this route (as of May 2024, there are rumours of the guesthouse next to the bottom ropeway station reopening), walking the entire stretch from Katsuura to T22 would be either

- 20 km including two climbs of each 450 m, or …
- after T20, continuing along the river and taking the ropeway to T21 which would sum up to 3 km uphill to T20, 3 km downhill to the bridge, 7 km along the river to the ropeway, up to T21 and finally 10 km downhill to T22. 23 km in total but with just one heavy climb. This one would be my choice.

The bridge, Suii-Bashi, has not always been there. In the old days, pilgrims had to follow the river to the left for 4 km until the next bridge in the village of Kamodani.

From there, the Bangai Temple of Isshukuji was the starting point of one of the earliest parts of the pilgrimage, (4.2 km uphill along the Kamo Trail to T21), which can still be walked, and this is a longer but more gentle way to get to the temple. . At KM 120 during the final climb, there is an ancient entrance to a mercury mine.

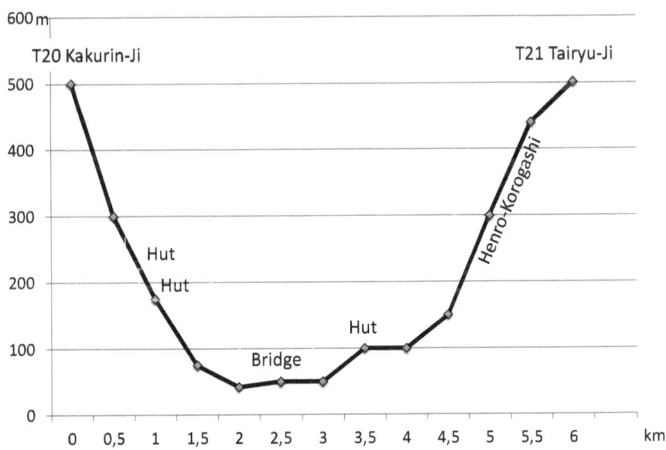

The replica of the mausoleum at T21

Temple No. 21 – Tairyu-ji 太龍寺

Fascination	***
Translation	Temple of the Big Dragon
Main deity	Kokuzo Bosatsu
Founded in	793
Location	KM 122
Distance from last temple	6.1 km
Distance to next temple	10.2 km
Difficulty	Tough, last 3 km has 460 m climb (average 15%)
Points of interest	Northern and southern shashin Trees, mausoleum replica
Okunoin	O21 southern Shashin

We have arrived at another highlight of the pilgrimage. Tairyu-ji, situated at almost 600 m altitude.

Tairyu-ji itself has its name from a legend about Kukai fighting a dragon and locking him up in a cave inside the mountain. It is not only a beautiful temple on a plateau close to the peak, and a favorite of many Henro, but it is also worthwhile to look at the surroundings and other sacred places on its mountain which is about 3 km x 3 km.

The gate was built in the Nyomon period (1192-1335). Apart from the temple itself, there are two particular locations nearby that deserve a visit: The Northern Shashin, a rock with a panoramic view just about 200 m northeast of the temple, which can be climbed via permanently installed ladders, and Southern Shashin which is a scenic view point with a Kukai statue, near the ropeway. Kukai meditated here. The climb up to the rock is just a few meters, and you can sit in Kukai's lap and share his view over the mountains. A beautiful stop before continueing to T22.

The temple, situated under enormous cedar trees, is large enough for a stroll around, and it has a small building behind its main hall which is a copy of Koya-san's Kukai mausoleum. This is one of the few places in Shikoku which has proof of Kukai's stay as he mentions it in his own books as a site he visited for meditation.

The mausoleum replica and the temple's remote location are the reason why people call it the "Western Koya-san".

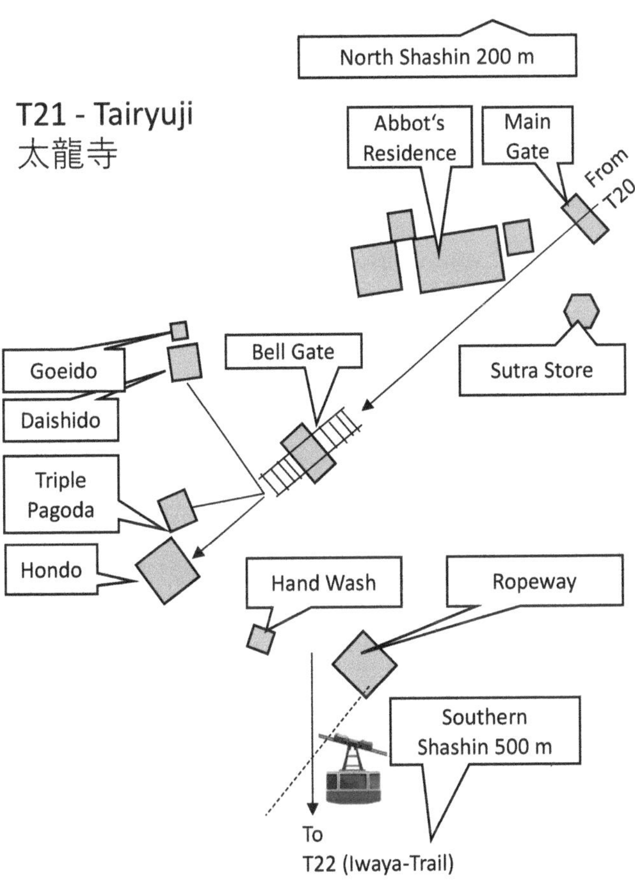

From T21 to T22 – KM 122 to KM 132

Fascination	***
Walking Distance	10.2 km
Elevation gain	110 m
Difficulty	Medium: Easy hike mostly downhill but a 110 m climb in the middle. No food.
Public transportation	Ropeway down, walk 1 km, bus from Naka police office every 2-3 h to Asebi, walk another 3.5 km.
Points of interest	KM 123 Southern Shashin KM 128 Asebi 🚌 rest hut
Where to stay	Several options near T22 in Aratano

After two Nansho temples, it feels good to have a hike that goes smoothly downhill across the forest. One km after leaving T21 we can enjoy the panorama on Southern Shashin from Kukai's lap after climbing the rock on which he is sitting. There are aluminum ladders to make it easy, but if you want to avoid risks, pass the rock on its right side. This is where Kukai is said to have meditated.

We continue along the path across the forest for another 5 km, reaching the road at a bus stop. Another 4 km (2 km at 6%) over One pass, and we arrive at a river where we take a left turn. T22 is located near the river in the valley at the village of Aratano.

Instead of the forest hike, you can also take the ropeway downhill and hike 7 km along route 195, or take the bus from the bus stop on the other side of the river from Naka village to Asebi bus stop at KM 128, but it only goes every 2-3 hours. There are several bus stations in the village, the closest one is 1.2 km from the ropeway station.

This may also be an option in case you have blisters, if you are tired or if you have run out of food as there is a Lawson's convenient store right at Wajiki-Higashi bus station.

Temple No. 22 – Byodo-ji 平等寺

Fascination	**
Translation	Temple of Equality
Main deity	Yakushi Nyorai
Founded in	814
Location	KM 132
Distance from last temple	10.2 km
Distance to next temple	20.2 km
Difficulty	Easy
Points of interest	Fountain left of the stairs Painted ceiling at the main hall
Okunoin	Iyadani Kannon KM 139

Byodoji is a smaller temple that is famous for its well. Its water is said to cure walking ailments. (Maybe just the right thing after the first week of pilgrimage and two Nansho temples.) Some wheelchairs, no longer needed, are at display.

One of its characteristics is the long colorful ribbons in the colors of Buddhist prayer flags that connect the gate to the elevated main hall, built in 1737. The hall itself and the gate are decorated with flags of the same color. The Daishido is from 1824.

The sacred well is located just left of the stairway leading to the main hall

At each 8th, 18th and 28th of a month at 3 p.m. pilgrims can participate in a temple ritual, taking pictures is permitted.

From T22 to T23 – KM 132 to KM 153

Fascination	Minimal, just a 20 km walk along Highway 55, several tunnels
Distance	20.2 km
Elevation gain	No major climbs, but the first half has a hidden climb of 2% over 5 km.
Difficulty	Easy but no food
By public transportation	Easy: from Aratano Station to Hiwasa Station, 20 minutes, 5 stops, 360 yen.
Points of interest	KM 136 Tsukiyo Omizu Daishi (Bangai) KM 138 Hut 🚻, Fukui river KM 138 O22 Iyadani Kannon KM 143 △Pass 132 m, tunnel 🚻 KM 144 🚻 KM 146 Kubo tunnel, hut KM 147 Ichinosaka tunnel KM 150 Kaizokusen rest area, 🚻 🍽 KM 151 🚂 Kitagawachi Station KM 152 🛒 first sea view KM 153 🚂 Hiwasa Station
Where to stay	Several options in Hiwasa 🛏 Ichi the Hostel, 🛏 Oyado Hiwasa

Before starting the journey, take a 2 km detour to pick up some food at Lawson's near Aratano Station, as there will be none for 20 km. No convenience shops, no supermarkets and almost no restaurants.

The route is simple: From T22, we will follow Road 284 south (or Road 24 from Aratano) until the road meets Highway 55 and we continue for about 6 km to cross the bridge over Fukui-river. From there, we follow the major road to the right for another 14 km until we reach the pretty coast town of Hiwasa. From a distance, we will be able to see T23 with its distinctive red and white pagoda.

Hiwasa is a good place to stay for a night, there are several guesthouses and traditional hotels. In case your feet need a rest or needing to gain some time, this is an easy stage to do by train.

Temple No. 23 – Yakuo-ji 薬王寺

Fascination	***
Translation	Temple of the Medicine King
Main deity	Yakushi Nyorai
Founded in	726
Location	KM 153
Distance from last temple	20.2 km
Distance to next temple	75.7 km
Difficulty	Easy, close to the station and the highway
Points of interest	Yugito pagoda at the highest level of the temple grounds. Fountain left of the main hall
Okunoin	Taisenji (4 km off KM 159)

T23 is a popular temple, conveniently and beautifully located. Like many of the temples in Tokushima, this one was also founded by Gyoki.

This temple is impressive, and spread out over several levels up the hill overlooking the town. It is the last temple of Tokushima prefecture and the only one in the prefecture from which we can see the ocean. From this slightly elevated location, we have a painting-like panoramic view of the town, the water and two huge rocks "protecting" it.

On the stairs, people leave small coins as donations, there is one staircase for women with 33 stairs, and one for men with 42 stairs to protect from bad luck.

Under the emperors Heisei, Junna and Saga, the temple's function was to ward-off misfortune.

The Yugito tower can be seen from far, it was completed in 1965. The Daishido is on the left side of the main hall.

From T23 to T24 – KM 153 to KM 228

Fascination	***
Distance	75 km, about 3 days
Elevation gain	100 m
Difficulty	long distance and lack of infrastructure
Public transportation	Relatively easy: 🚃 from Hiwasa (KM 154) to Kannoura (KM 190), 840 yen. 🚌 from Kannoura to Cape Muroto (KM 230) 1710 yen.
Points of interest	KM 154 road to alternative coastal walk KM 157 rest hut, Hiwasa tunnel KM 159 rest hut, temple 🍽️🍽️ KM 165 🚃 Hegawa Station, Komatsu Daishi (Bangai), 🛒 KM 168 🚃 Mugi Town, Tebajima Island KM 174 🚃 B4 Saba-Daishi 🍽️ KM 176 🚃 Asakawa Station, rest huts 🚻 KM 179 🚃 Awa-Kainan Station KM 181 🚃 Kaifu Station, huts KM 187 🚃 Shishikui Station 🛒 KM 190 🚃 Kannoura Stn. (Railway ends) KM 194 🛏️ Ikumi Village (Hotels) KM 195 Myotokuji (Bangai) 🚻 KM 202 🚻 KM 206 Bukkaian (Bangai) KM 210 Sakihama village, stores 🍽️ KM 215 Meoto Rock 🍽️ KM 227 Path to T24, Raieiji, Mikuroji
Where to stay	🛏️ KM 168 Tebajima Shanti Guesthouse 🛏️ KM 187 Shishikui (several hotels) 🛏️ KM 194 Ikumi (several beach hotels) 🛏️ KM 213 Lodge Ozaki 🛏️ KM 223 Sea and Sky Hostel 🛏️ KM 227 El Flamenquito 🛏️ KM 228 T24 Guesthouses and ryokans

The stage to T24 is the second-longest distance between two main temples (it passes B4), and it will take us to Cape Muroto, the first of Shikoku's two southern capes. It is also a stage passing different landscapes, going from forests to tropical beaches, and it offers some wonderful detours. The main route basically follows Highway 55 over the entire distance, so there is no risk of getting lost. The first part, until Mugi, is not very interesting and includes some annoying, noisy tunnels.

I recommend a detour that is just 4 km longer and offers an unforgettable experience: The coastal route along the Minami-Awa Sun Line. Just 1.5 km after leaving T23, leave the highway to your left on route 147. Instead of noisy tunnels, you will have 20 quiet kilometers with amazing views on an empty road all the way to Mugi. There is only one public toilet and one vending machine, on the parking lot 3 km after that left turn, so make sure to be prepared with enough liquids for the next few hours.

Mugi is a "well-kept secret" on the route: a quiet little town with a port, a temple, a train station and a supermarket. Tebajima island is just 20 minutes away by ship and has a tiny village with a guesthouse, there are five ferries per day. Staying there for two nights and visiting B4 6 km down the coast is a good option and you might choose to continue by train the day after, if you want.

The train stops close to B4, in Sabase, and the main JR line only continues to Awa-Kainan, from where a small private line, named Asakaigan adds another 11 km until the tracks end in Kannoura. Public transportation along the coast continues from here (km 190) by bus a little over 50 km until the train line begins again near T27 at Nahari (KM 242). Sometimes this connection is served by a hybrid train/bus vehicle.

Between B4 Saba-Daishi and the cape, the only location with some infrastructure is Ikumi (KM 194), a popular place for surfers, followed by a Bangai temple named Myotokuji or Meitokuji (Km195), accentuated by high trees and colorful ribbons. This place was already a rest stop for pilgrims in the 17th century.

Meitokuji is followed by a rather monotonous 10 km stretch along the coast named the Goro-goro-ishi-Section, the "section of rumbling rocks". Today, pilgrims walk on the sidewalk of Highway 55, called Eastern Tosa Highway in this area, reaching the next Bangai, Bukkai-an, after a good two hours. This temple is dedicated to Bukkai, a monk who lived in the 18th century and made many improvements to the pilgrimage, building shelters and adding road markers. Unlike Myotokuji which is a temple, Bukkaian just a place of worship under pine trees on the roadside.

After another quiet hour of walking and crossing the Sakihama river, we enter the village of the same name where we find several convenience stores and snack bars located off the main road towards the seaside.

But we still have 17 km to go, 4 hours. After 5 km we reach the characteristic rocks of Meoto, standing like pyramids between the road and the sea. From here, the particular rock formations become more visible, and gradually the temple density increases as we get closer to the cape.

Raieiji is the next Bangai, a 21 m tall, white ceramic statue of Kukai, followed by Mikuro Cave, the location where Kukai might have lived for a while and found enlightenment. Other sources challenge this, as 1200 years ago the entire area was 6.4 m lower and the cave would have been at water level. And of course, we will never find out. Apparently, Kukai wrote that he was meditating near Muroto in a cave where he had an unobstructed view of the sky and the sea. There might be a number of places where this might fit. Other sources claim it was on Fudo Iwa Rock, O26 at KM 241.

Finally, just before reaching the cape, we get to a parking lot with a public toilet and a pedestrian crossing. There is a paved ramp going uphill, with a sign saying Muroto Misaki Light House. Following the ramp, the path leads us uphill to T24 after about 10 minutes.

Temple No. B4 – Yasaka-ji (Saba Daishi 鯖大師)

Fascination	**
Translation	Temple of Eight Slopes Mackerel Temple
Founded in	1945
Main deity	Kukai
Location	KM 174
Detour	-
Difficulty	Very easy
Points of interest	Cave

Saba Daishi, as B4 is commonly called, received its name from a legend involving Kukai and a wagonload of mackerel which he brought back to life. Mackerels are the main object and symbols all around the temple grounds, and the signature dish of the restaurant nearby.

Visiting requires no detour as it is located along the main pilgrimage route just a few km after Mugi.

According to "Japanese Pilgrimage" by Oliver Statler, there had been a hermitage in this place for centuries, but it only started as a temple as late as 1945.

The temple runs a small pilgrimage guesthouse, and the temple's cave and inner-mountain sanctuary are worth a visit. The entrance is in the central part of the temple ground but hardly visible.

Temple No. 24 – Hotsumisaki-ji 最御崎寺

Fascination	***
Translation	Cape Temple
Main deity	Kokuzo Bosatsu
Founded in	807
Location	KM 228
Distance from last temple	75 km
Distance to next temple	6.8 km
Difficulty	Short but hard path uphill when coming from the east, from the west follow the serpentines of road 203
Points of interest	Caves, Bangai, Panorama Cape Muroto
Okunoin	Kannon Kutsu

Obviously, this place, elevated at the tip if the peninsula, with its caves and strange rock formations, must have been a place for worship since the beginning of humanity, and it used to be a Shugendo temple, run by the Yamabushi mountain ascetics whose traditions go back further than Buddhism and includes many Shinto elements.

At this point, we have covered the longest distance between two main temples and arrived one of the most exposed, locations. Walking clockwise, access to the temple is from the ramp on the coastal road on the east side of the cape. The temple can be accessed from a larger road from the west side going uphill in serpentines, offering amazing views over the cape area and the large bay of Tosa.

Among the several caves, Kannon Kutsu, which we pass following the footpath from the east side, has the status of an okunoin of T24. The samurai statue which is easily visible on the cape, is Shintaro Nakaoka, one of the local heroes of Shikoku. Together with Ryoma Sakamoto, who was from Kochi, Nakaoka was fighting against the shogunate intending to reestablish the power of the emperor, Emperor Meiji in this case. Both were murdered in 1867, but that did not prevent Emperor Meiji from taking power the following year.

Ichiki & Inari Shrine
Sky and Sea Guesthouse
Base 55 Hotel
T25 Shinshoji
Muroto Skyline Observation Deck
Sakura Home & El Flamenquito Guesthouse
5 km
Umamenoki
Raieiji
Mikurodo Cave
T24 Hotsumisakiji

Cape Muroto

Umamenoki Hotel
Raieiji
Bishagoiwa Rock
Observatory
Kukai Cave
1 km
Temple Parking, Toilet, Pilgrim Hostel
T24 Hotsumisakiji
Misaki Kanko Hotel
Path to T24
Toilet, Parking
Lighthouse
Nakaoka Statue
Akou Tree
Minshuku Muroto so
Cape

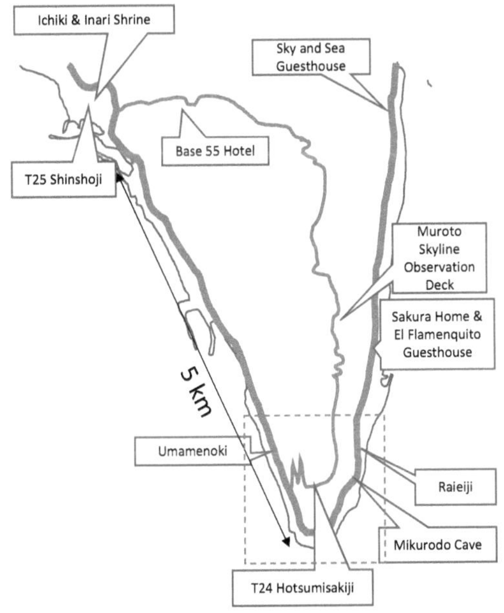

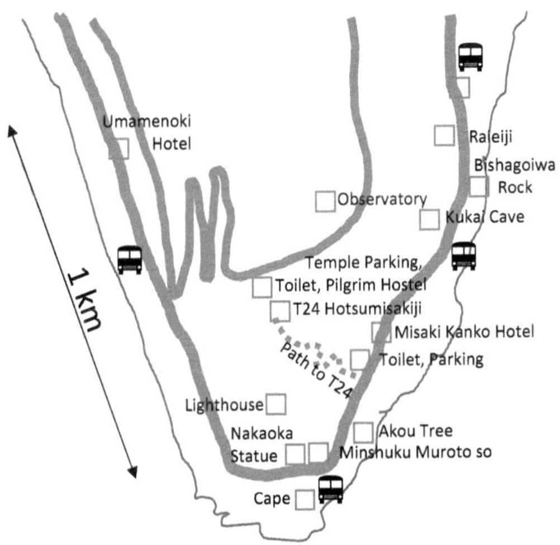

From T24 to T25 – KM 228 to KM 235

Fascination	**
Walking Distance	6.8 km (1.5 - 2 hours)
Difficulty	Easy
Public transportation	🚌 from Murotomisaki to Muroto village, 320 yen, 17 minutes
Points of interest	🍴🍴 in Muroto village
Where to stay	Several places around the cape

This stage is an easy one. It is short, flat and easy to find. We just is continue along the coast for two hours until we reach Muroto village. T25 is located on a little hill in the center.

Temple No.25 – Shinsho-ji 津照寺

Fascination	**
Translation	Temple of the Illuminated Port
Main deity	Kajitori Enmai Jizo Bosatsu
Founded in	807
Location	KM 235
Distance from last temple	6.8 km
Distance to next temple	3.9 km
Difficulty	Easy, stairs upon arrival
Points of interest	Thousands of little Jizo

The temple has long been dedicated to the fishermen, maybe ever since people began fishing in this area, allowing the ones at home to look out for the boats of the family member, and for the boats out on the sea to serve as an orientation point.

Formerly the temple area was much larger but it lost most of its property in the Meiji era when its grounds were given to the local community. After that, it was abandoned for several years. In 1883 it was rebuilt.

The way up is a long stairway and we will pass the temple gate with the bell in the middle in the middle of our steps. Due to lack of space, this temple has an unusual arrangement: While the Daishido and the office are on street level, the Hondo is on top of the hill. The current Daishido was built in 1963, the Hondo as late as 1975.

From T25 to T26 – KM 235 to KM 239

Fascination	*
Walking Distance	3.9 km
Elevation gain	140 m
Difficulty	3 km flat, last km with a 14% climb, no food
Public transportation	🚌 from Muroto village to Motohashi, 200 yen
Points of interest	KM 237 ⛩ Iwato Shrine
Where to stay	Several traditional hotels in Muroto 🛏 Henro House KM 244 🛏 Shukubo Temple 26

Another easy one. About 4 km, or 5 km if you take the road uphill. You can basically walk along Highway 55, but it is nicer, once you leave town after 1 km, to cross Highway 55 at the traffic light and follow the little road that runs parallel.

Once we get to the bridge, which is after about 2.5 km, turn right and follow the little country road up the hill. Where the country road veers right at the white garages, you can continue straight for the shorter, very steep walk - look for the signs, it is 1.5 km with 10%.

The next convenience store after visiting T25 is 24 km away, if necessary buy some food at one of the shops near T25.

Temple No. 26 – Kongocho-ji 金剛頂寺

Fascination	**
Translation	Temple of the Vajra Arrow Point
Main deity	Yakushi Nyorai
Founded in	807
Location	KM 239
Distance from last temple	4 km
Distance to next temple	28.5 km
Difficulty	Easy but very steep at the end
Okunoin	⛩ Fudo-Iwa (at the coast as we continue) Formerly Ikeyama-Jinja, not accessible anymore. Now moved to Iwato Jinja, KM 237, near T25

The stage is flat until we climb a long flight of stairs to T26 which is located in the forest at 130 m altitude.

This temple is also called the Western Temple (referring to Cape Muroto, T24 being the eastern temple). It was forbidden for women until 1872 and it burned down in 1899. It is said that this temple was founded by Kukai in 807. The Hondo was built in 1984

Its original okunoin used to be 5-8 km north in the mountains, but it is now in disuse and its objects of worship have been moved to Iwato-shrine, which we passed coming from T25 at KM 237. This former temple located nearby is associated to T26, but not considered an okunoin.

This area used to be a place for whaling.

Fascination	**
Walking Distance	28.5 km
Elevation gain	400 m
Difficulty	Easy but long, 3 km with a 13% climb at the end, no food shops during the first 20 km.
Public transportation	🚌 from Motohashi to Yasuda Myojin
Points of interest	KM 241 Fudo-Iwa KM 242 🚻 🍴 KM 244 Kiragawa antique street KM 247 🍴 KM 250 🚻 KM 254 Goreiseki Daishido (Bangai) KM 259 Nahari, 🚂 🚻 🛒 Monet's Garden KM 263 Bridge over Yasuda river 🚻 KM 265 pass under railway near 🚂 Tonohama, 3 km of climb with 13% gain KM 268 ↗↗ Henro Korogashi, hut, 🚻 △450 m
Where to stay	🛏 KM 244 Henro House Himitsukiji 🛏 KM 254 Henro House Karyogo 🛏 KM 265 3 hotels near Tonohama

This is more than a one-day stage, since we cannot stay at T27, so in addition to the distance, we need to consider the hard climb and that we need to return down after the temple visit.

Upon leaving T26, be sure to visit O26 Fudo-Iwa. When T26 was open to men only, Fudo-Iwa was the women's temple no. 26. Its exposed location and the unusual rock formations suggest that this might have been a place of worship even before Buddhism. Before heading for the 450 m up to T27 and back, to travel lightly, find a place to leave your backpack. Either at a restaurant or a place to sleep, or you can just hide it somewhere. This is quite common and the crime rates are very low.

Temple No. 27 – Konomine-ji 神峯寺

Fascination	***
Translation	Temple of the God's Peak
Main deity	Juichimen Kanzeon Bosatsu
Founded in	809
Location	KM 268
Distance from last temple	28.5 km
Distance to next temple	38 km
Difficulty	Difficult, very steep.
Points of interest	Garden arrangement uphill Fountain, Stairs
Okunoin	Konomine Jinja (nearby)

The steep climb is a Sekisho, (spiritual checkpoint) but once we made it, we are at one of the most fascinating temples, as its arrangement is vertical up the hill on an altitude of 450 m.

The legend of this sacred place goes way back to the year of 207 A.D. when empress Jingu requested for a shrine to be built on this location. In 730 this became one of the first Buddhist sites in Japan when emperor Shomu ordered Gyoki to carve and enshrine a statue of Juichimen Kannon Bosatsu marking a beginning of Shinto-Buddhist syncretism. However, the temple lost its status during the period of temple separations in 1868. It remained a Shinto shrine and a less important Buddhist temple, left idle for 20 years in the early Meiji period, until it became famous as the family temple of the family of Iwasaki Yataro, the founder of the Mitsubishi Company which might explain why the temple did so well from the 19th century onwards.

Konomine Jinja, on top of the hill, 130 m higher up, is its okunoin. This was probably the original place of worship.

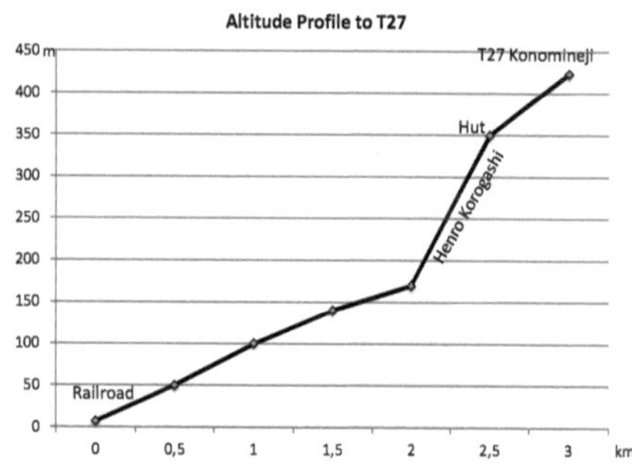

From T27 to T28 – KM 268 to KM 306

Fascination	**
Distance	38 km
Difficulty	Long distance but no climbs
Public transportation	🚂 Tonohama to Noichi 32 minutes, 920 en
Points of interest	KM 271 ↘↘ 🚉 Tonohama Station, 🛒
	KM 272 🚻 🍴
	KM 274 🚉 Shimoyama Station
	KM 279 🚉 Ioki Station, 🛒
	KM 280 Aki Town
	KM 282 - 297 Cycling Road
	KM 290 🚉 Akano Station.
	KM 297 🚉 Yasu Stn., end of cycling road
	KM 298 🛒
	KM 300 🚉 Akaoka Stn., route leaves coast
	KM 303 🛒 Route 22
	KM 304 🚉 🍴 Noichi Station
Where to stay	🛏 KM 275 Henro House Cosumo
	🛏 KM 294 Henro House

This stage takes us to the first temple near Kochi, the big city on the south side of Shikoku. The walk is mostly along the coast, parallel to the railway line. Near the end, there is a 3 km section along large highways which is less attractive. After 12 km, we reach the town of Aki which is the birthplace of Iwasaki Yataro, the founder of Mitsubishi.

About 1 km outside Aki, where the port infrastructure ends, we enter the bike path which we can follow for 15 km parallel to Highway 55. After the end of the bike path, we continue along Route 55 to KM 303, the highway onramp. There is a Family Mart to our right and a "Kochi 17 km" marker. Here, we leave Highway 55 and continue on Route 22 for another 2 km across Noichi to T28. There will be a footpath uphill up the little hill to our right as we arrive.

Temple No.28 – Dainichi-ji 大日寺

Fascination	**
Translation	Temple devoted to Dainichi Nyorai
Main deity	Dainichi Nyorai
Founded in	806
Location	KM 306
Distance from last temple	38 km
Distance to next temple	9.2 km
Difficulty	Easy, a short but steep ramp
Points of interest	Garden, Statues, Fountain
Okunoin	Tsumebori Yakushido on the temple grounds

The name sounds familiar, Dainichiji is also the name of T4, they are devoted to the same deity – Dainichi Nyorai.

Approaching from the main road, take the path uphill or take a right turn at the bus stop and head up the ramp and 2 serpentines, about 300 m with a 10-12% climb. The first temple gate will be on your left. You can reach the okunoin by continuing straight, crossing the parking lot and heading 100 to 200 m into the forest.

Dainichiji formerly had 7 okunoins before its destruction in the unrests during the Meiji era (these might be some of the shrines on the same mountain). After the Meiji era unrests, the temple fell into disuse for 16 years but it was revived in 1884. The Hondo was built in 1997. In 2024, the bell tower was under renovation.

Today, it is a small but beautiful temple. The garden in which the temple office is located is particularly pretty. The seated Dainichi Nyorai statue measures 146 cm and was carved by Gyoki. There is also a Henro gear shop on the premises run by a very kind lady.

Here, we are about 18 km from the center of Kochi, and we can feel the traffic getting busier.

From T28 to T29 – KM 305 to KM 315

Fascination	*
Walking Distance	9.2 km
Elevation gain	-
Difficulty	Easy 2-hour walk
Public transportation	Train from Noichi to Gomen and on to Tosa-Ikku, 2 km walking at either end, so the train saves 5 km
Points of interest	KM 310 Daishido (Bangai), hut KM 311 Tosa Nagaoka Station KM 313 Railrod crossing KM 314 Walk across the fields KM 315 Log Café
Where to stay	KM 305 2 guesthouses near T28 KM 306 HH Guest House Suisen

It is an easy walk of about 2 hours across the fields, only interrupted by a Bangai called Matsumoto Daishido and a railway crossing. The Daishido also has a larger rest hut, big enough to take a nap but not meant for staying overnight.

As we get closer to T30, passing the Kokubu river, we have the choice for the last 700 m to continue straight on the road or to approach the temple along the riverside, passing a shrine called Jizo-Watashi and walking through the fields which is the nicer option.

The rest hut at KM 310

Temple No. 29 – Kokubun-ji 国分寺

Fascination	***
Translation	Main Temple of Kochi Prefecture
Main deity	Senju Kannon Bosatsu
Founded in	741
Location	KM 315
Distance from last temple	9.2 km
Distance to next temple	6.9 km
Difficulty	Easy
Points of interest	2-story gate, roses, cedar trees
Okunoin	Bishamondo (Waterfall) on the way to T30

This beautiful temple is located between two rivers in an area covered by high cedar trees. The arrival is impressive as we follow the path under the trees.

For many years, this temple was supported by members of the imperial family and by local aristocrats.

The Chosokabe clan destroyed many temples in Shikoku, but after converting to Buddhism, this was one of the temples they rebuilt. The gate and the pathway to the main temple were built at the request of Tadayoshi Yamauchi (1592-1665), a ruler of Tosa. In 1922, the entire temple received the status of "important cultural heritage of Japan". This temple is also called the "moss temple of Tosa". The main hall was built in 1558, the Daishi-do in 1634.

There is a much smaller Shinto shrine on the same area called *Kokubusosha,* the entrance is just 50 m left of the main gate. Another example of shrines and temples sharing spaces. T29 also has a beautiful 100kunoin, which we will pass on the way to T30: *Bishamondo,* just 500 m off KM 319, a temple for waterfall meditation.

Opposite the main gate there is a shop for pilgrimage gear.

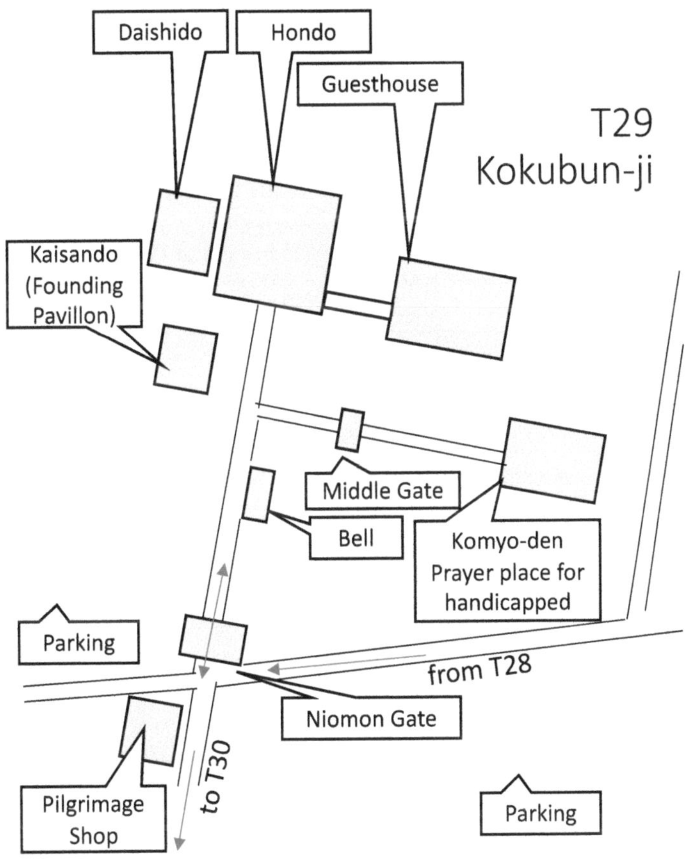

Daishido
Hondo
Guesthouse
T29
Kokubun-ji
Kaisando
(Founding
Pavillon)
Middle Gate
Bell
Komyo-den
Prayer place for
handicapped
Parking
from T28
Niomon Gate
to T30
Pilgrimage
Shop
Parking

Fascination	●
Walking Distance	6.9 km
Difficulty	Easy
Public transportation	Would involve 3.2 km walking, train from Gomen to Tosa-Ikku
Points of interest	KM 317 Pref. Museum of History KM 318 KM 319 O29 Bishamondo Waterfall
Where to stay	KM 322 Guesthouse Kacho-Fugetsu. After T30, staying in one of the hostels in Kochi, T31-T33 can be done as a day trip.

This is short stage of less than 2 hours, but the detour to the 102kunoin of T29 is recommended, it is just about 500 m off the main route, so it will be an extra half hour to visit it. A red bridge will take us there, over a little pond to the waters pouring down from 20-30 m above. The place is usually very empty.

The main route will lead us to the back entrance of T30. If you are interested in a splendid approach, follow the main road, along the temple on your right, take a right turn at the traffic light and enter the area from the south side, walking 300 m on the Sando avenue leading to the Torii gate of the adjacent Shinto shrine, whereas T30 itself is on the right. The beautiful alley with its old cobblestones and its canal has been preserved and cars are not allowed.

There is an alternative route from T29 to T30: After about 2 km, after crossing the river at Km 317, continue left, along the north side of okubu river. This route is less monotonous and quieter, but it does not pass the waterfall and the convenience stores. It is just 200 m longer.

Temple No. 30 – Zenraku-ji 善楽寺

Fascination	**
Translation	Temple of Eternal Joy
Main deity	Amida Nyorai
Founded in	Daido Period (806-810)
Location	KM 322
Distance from last temple	6.9 km
Distance to next temple	6.4 km
Difficulty	Easy
Points of interest	Sando (Avenue to shrine gate) Tosa Jinja
Okunoin	Tosa Jinja next to the temple, Anrakuji (in Kochi, near Iriake stn.)

Like T29, T30 is also a shared between a Shinto shrine (Tosa Jinja) and a Buddhist temple (T30 Zenrakuji), but this time, it is the Shinto area that is more impressive, so after your temple rituals, take some more time to walk around the entire area, you will be surprised. There are 6 shrines and the Shinto part is over four times as big.

During the time of the temple destructions (1868-72), the bell and the Amida-Nyorai statue of T30 were taken to another temple, Anrakuji, in the center of Kochi, which then became T30. Zenrakuji was only rebuilt in 1929. For a while, there were two temples claiming to be T30, one, because it had the bell and the statue, the other one because it was still in its original location. The dispute was only settled in 1995, when Anrakuji and Zenrakuji merged. In 1994, Zenrakuji was reassigned its old status as T30 and Anrakuji became its okunoin.

The statue was returned, but the bell ended up in the Prefectural Museum of History, located near KM 317.

Should you be staying at the wonderful Kochi Youth Hostel Sakenokuni, the okunoin Anrakuji is just 1.6 km away to the east, south of the railway line, or 800 m north of Hirome Ichiba, the food market.

From T30 to T31– KM 322 to KM 329

Fascination	**
Walking Distance	6.9 km
Elevation gain	100 m at the end
Difficulty	Flat walk of 2 hours across urban areas, 1 km climb of 10% at the end
Public transportation	Possible but would not give any major benefit as it would involve 1h of walking: Train from Tosa-Ikku to Kochi, 🚌 from north exit, direction Katsurahama, 4 stations to Chikurijin-mae
Points of interest	KM 323 🚂 Tosa-Ikku Station 🛒 KM 324 Bridge over Kokubu River KM 325 🛒 🍽 KM 326 Kochi Art Museum KM 328 ↗↗ Climb up Mount Godaisan △ 105 m
Where to stay	Kochi

This stage takes us from the north-east to the south-east suburbs of Kochi. The walk is mostly unspectacular, but it becomes beautiful at the end, as we reach Godaisan, the hill on which T31 is located. The temple is next to the Makino Botanical Gardens and the noisy, bustling ambience of the route suddenly changes to a green but steep environment with occasional panoramic points.

KM 330: Looking back at T31 on the hill, from Shimoda-river

Temple No.31 – Chikurin-ji 竹林寺

Fascination	**
Translation	Temple of the Bamboo Forest
Main deity	Monju Bosatsu
Founded in	Jinki 1 - 724
Location	KM 329
Distance from last temple	6.9 km
Distance to next temple	6.1 km
Difficulty	Steep but paved 1 km at 10% up to Godaisan
Points of interest	Botanical Garden

Godaisan mountain with its peak at 105 m altitude overlooking the bay must have been a place to worship since the early days, and it is no surprise that the hill and the areas near the waters have numerous Shinto shrines. (I counted 8 Shinto shrines on an area of 500 x 700 m).

Chikurinji itself is a large temple spread out on the top plateau of the hill over an area of about 200 x 300 m. The 5-story Pagoda was only built in 1980, as the former 3-story pagoda on that at this site had been destroyed by a typhoon in 1899. It is the only 5-story pagoda in Kochi prefecture, its height is 31 m.

This temple has been an important place for religious studies since centuries, also historically a temple of the lords of Tosa.

If you visit the place after some rainfall, you can experience wide parts of the area covered under green moss.

Kochi 高知

Kochi (population 328,930) is the only larger city on the south coast of Shikoku. If we look at the map, we can see that the shape of the bay provides an ideal port protecting the ships and the city from storms and tsunamis. The opening "gate" to the sea is only about 200 m wide at Urado Bridge, while the protected bay is about 2 km wide (we will cross the gate by ferry on our way from T32 to T33) and opening to the east, even though this is technically the south coast. This explains the origin of Kochi, an ideal port location.

Unless you insist on following the main trail on foot without exceptions, Kochi is a place where you could stay for several nights and visit some temples with a daypack, taking a bus to the first temple and returning to the same hostel every night. Three days could be split into

        Day 1 T28-T29-O29-T30 staying in Kochi
        Day 2 T31-T32-T33 staying in Kochi
        Day 3 T34-T35-T36

In the past, pilgrims disliked the southern coast and Kochi. The area was poor, Buddhism was never widely accepted, and its inhabitants had the reputation of making a living from fishing or piracy, or by ripping off the pilgrims for their own survival.

Today, Kochi is a welcoming city with wide streets and good food. I found the people to be open and friendly, less formal and more relaxed than in other cities. Kochi has a lot to offer

- Hirome-Ichiba, a foodie paradise
- A long shopping street for rainy days
- A city beach called Katsura-hama
- Kochi Castle
- A Sunday-market offering local street food
- Makino Botanical garden (See T31)
- For a day or two, relax your feet. You can rent a bike at the tourism office near the station.

Kochi is also the birthplace of Sakamoto Ryoma, a samurai who played an important role in the Meiji restauration. He was murdered at the age of 31. His statue is one of the three next to the train station, with two of his companions (see T24).

From T31 to T32 – KM 329 to KM 335

Fascination	*
Walking Distance	6.1 km (90 minutes)
Elevation gain	89 m
Difficulty	First downhill, then with a short climb at the end (500 m at 10%) No food
Public transportation	Not available, or 🚌 back to Kochi center (Harimaya Bashi) and from there 🚌 #J2 direction of Gomen Machi.
Points of interest	KM 329 ↘↘ walk along Shimoda-river KM 330 detour to O32 Yakushiji KM 334 walk along Sekido pond KM 335 ↗↗△ 85 m
Where to stay	Kochi

It is just a short walk, down the hill from one temple, 1.5 hours along a river, over a small hill, along a pond and finally up a little hill. But be prepared to reach another highlight, one of the prettiest spots of the pilgrimage.

After the descent from Mount Godaisan, turn left when you reach the river. You can follow the river along the dam in the middle until you reach the next bridge and heading south from there unless your intention is to visit the okunoin of T32, Yakushiji which would add a detour of 3 km to the route.

Temple No. 32 – Zenjibu-ji 禅師峰寺

Fascination	**
Translation	Temple of the Zen Master's Peak
Main deity	Juichimen Kanzeon Bosatsu
Founded in	Daido 2 (807)
Location	KM 335
Distance from last temple	6.1 km
Distance to next temple	8.1 km
Difficulty	Short but hard climb, about 500 m at 10%
Points of interest	Panorama
Okunoin	Yakushiji, 4 km north

Also known as Mineji ("peak temple"), this temple is in a beautiful location: It is located on a terrace at about 85 m altitude overlooking Tosa-bay to the east and the west and the entrance to Urado Bay. Due to its altitude, on clear days, we can see Cape Muroto (60 km away) as well as the mountains near Cape Ashizuri (100 km away) from this elevated location.

The Hondo was built In the 19th century, the Daishido only in 1984, but the statues in the Niomon gate were carved in the 13th century. In front of the Hondo, one of the stones bears a winter Haiku written by Basho.

There is a comfortable little spot for pilgrims to relax just in front of the temple office, which displays Osamefuda from pilgrims who completed the route over 100 times.

Just like at T25, locals prayed for safety at sea at this temple. Even the lords of Tosa did so, especially when their travels involved longer distances by ship.

From T32 to T33 – KM 335 to KM 343

Fascination	**
Walking Distance	8.1 km (2 hours)
Elevation gain	-
Difficulty	Easy
Public transportation	-
Points of interest	KM 336 ⛩ Sumiyoshi Jinja Km 338 🚻 KM 339 🍽 Katsuo Bune KM 340 🛒 ⛺ 🚻 O33 Goza Daishi Ferry across the bay KM 342 🚻 🚌
Where to stay	🛏 Kochiya, opposite T33

The next two hours are an easy walk across the fields of the flatlands along the coast. Some parts are below sea level which explains the many tsunami shelters and warning signs. It also explains why we cannot see the ocean that is hidden on our left, beyond the fields and behind the dam.

After 4 km, as we get to the outer parts of the peninsula, there is an opportunity to have a local specialty for lunch, Katsuotataki (barbecued bonito), at the Katsuobune barbecue restaurant on the parallel road to out left.

The distance between the two peninsulas embracing Urado bay is barely 500 m at this location. We either pick the bridge to Katsurahama, the local beach of Kochi, or we take the more direct way hopping on the free-of-charge ferry. After leaving the ferry, it is just a 20-minute walk across the fishermen villages to T33.

Temple No. 33 – Sekkei-ji 雪蹊寺

Fascination	**
Translation	Temple of the Snowy Cliff
Main deity	Yakushi Nyorai
Founded in	Konin 6 (815) or 1225
Location	KM 342
Distance from last temple	8.1 km
Distance to next temple	6.4 km
Difficulty	Easy
Points of interest	2 Shinto shrines, Tombs of Yamamoto Genpo, a famous blind priest who consulted the Japanese prime minister at the end of WWII, and of Taigento, his teacher.
Okunoin	Goza Daishi (KM 340) Nakatanido (2 km north)

The name of the temple refers to Motochika's posthumus name Sekkei Josandaizen Jōmon (雪蹊恕三大禅定門). There is contradicting information about the temple's founding date. It was rebuilt in 1880 after it had suffered from the destructions that affected many temples in the early Meiji period, but its sacred statues date back to the 13th century, carved by famous sculpturer Unkei and his son. The temple houses several statues carved by Unkei in its treasure hall.

This temple has gone through several phases of destruction, several names and through several Buddhist sects, until the Zen Buddhists took care of it. After T11 and T15, it is the third of the three Zen temples on the pilgrimage. It shares its grounds with two Shinto shrines, Inaridaimyoin, and Hada shrine, hidden 50 m north of the main temple.

We already passed its first okunoin just before reaching the ferry, Goza-Daishi. We did not notice it: A tiny shrine with a palm tree, too small for anyone to enter, like many Daishi places. The other one, Nakatanido is equally unspectacular, situated about 2 km north next to Highway 34 on a little hill.

From T33 to T34 – KM 343 to KM 349

Fascination	*
Walking Distance	6.4 km, 90 minutes
Difficulty	Easy but no food
Public transportation	Only by bus with transfer in central Kochi, will take longer than the walk
Points of interest	KM 343 🚻 KM 346 detour to O34 Motoozan after crossing the river, 5 km detour
Where to stay	🛏 Kochiya, opposite T33

Short but monotonous walk out of Kochi city to the countryside without any major infrastructure on the way.

Temple No. 34 – Tanema-ji 種間寺

Fascination	**
Translation	Temple of the Seeds
Main deity	Yakushi Nyorai
Founded in	Konin Period 810-824
Location	KM 349
Distance from last temple	6.4 km
Distance to next temple	9.8 km
Difficulty	Easy
Okunoin	Motoozan (off km 346)

The temple's name refers to the legend that Kukai had brought different types of seeds upon his return from China, which he planted nearby: rice, wheat, beans and millet. At this temple, people pray for safe child-birth, hence the stuffed animals that are kept in one of the side-buildings.

The Hondo was rebuilt in 1970 after the old one had been destroyed in a typhoon. In May, the street leading to the temple celebrates its hydrangea in full bloom.

From T34 to T35– KM 349 to KM 359

Fascination	**
Walking Distance	9.8 km
Elevation gain	130 m
Difficulty	Flat 2.5 hour walk but with an arduous climb at the end (1 km at 13%)
Public transportation	Not available
Points of interest	353 Bridge over Niyodo river 354 356 358 ↗↗ Hachosaka climb
Where to stay	KM 352 Haruno Guesthouse KM 359 Onkosha

The first few kilometers are flat across the fields. After crossing Nyodo river, we pass Tosa city which offers some choice of convenience stores, shops, restaurants, and places to stay.

The temple itself is located 130 m above the city, the hard climb offering us a wonderful panorama of Tosa-bay.

The climb is called Hachosaka, the slope of eight cho (One cho is a distance of 109 m, eight cho is about 900 m, and the distance is counted down during the climb, with a choseki stone every 109 m)

Temple No. 35 – Kiyotaki-ji 清瀧寺

Fascination	**
Translation	Temple of the Clear Waterfall
Main deity	Yakushi Nyorai
Founded in	Yoro 7- 823
Location	KM 359
Distance from last temple	9.8 km
Distance to next temple	14.5 km
Difficulty	Steep climb towards the end
Points of interest	Panorama, okunoin, well
Okunoin	Akai, above the temple

The temple is located on a hill overlooking Tosa-bay, we can see as far as 20 or 30 km. The temple can be seen from far as we approach it passing Tosa city.

Its old buildings were not destroyed by Chosokabe or during the early Meiji era. The fish pond receives its water from a well that according to the legend was drilled by Kukai. The fire engine next to the Hondo is an unusual sight.

T35

From T35 to T36 – KM 359 to KM 374

Fascination	**
Distance	14 km
Elevation gain	About 200 m
Difficulty	3-4 hours with one 170 m climb that can be avoided, another 40 m at the end
Public transportation	🚌 Takaoka Town to Ryu (Usa Ino Line) several times per day. Bus stop is 850 m from T36
Points of interest	KM 361 ⛩ Mishima Jinja KM 362 🛒 🚻 KM 363 ⛩ Takaishi Jinja KM 365 Rest hut 🚻 Shoryuji trail, pass with 202 m altitude or tunnel KM 369 Usa village, coast 🛒 KM 370 Usa bridge KM 373 🚻
Where to stay	🛏 KM 368 Hostel Utage 🛏 KM 372 Sanyo-So

Down the hill back into Tosa city, but from there we continue south. At Takaishi Jinja, we follow Route 39, crossing the river. After 2.5 km along the road, we have the choice between the pass and the tunnel. Tsukajizaka tunnel is 830 m long and can be passed on foot. If you can stand the noise for ten minutes, it will save you 170 m climb.

When reaching the port town of Usa, we will turn right, follow the coast and cross the big bridge to the tip of the peninsula. The walk on the narrow bridge may seem a bit scary at first but there is a sidewalk and the Japanese are careful drivers. (Until 1975, before the bridge was built, pilgrims had to take a ferry to reach T36).

After two beautiful kilometers along the water, the temple is to the right and we need to walk another 500 m away from the coast on a footpath with a climb of 40 m.

Temple No.36 – Shoryu-ji 青龍寺

Fascination	**
Translation	Temple of the Blue Dragon
Main deity	Nakiri Fudo Myoo
Founded in	Konin 6 (815)
Location	KM 374
Distance from last temple	14 km
Distance to next temple	56.6 km
Difficulty	Mostly flat with a short, steep climb of 40 m at the end
Points of interest	Waterfall, 3-story pagoda
Okunoin	Fudodo, nearby on the cape

The name of this temple refers to a temple in Xi'an written the same way in Chinese, China, where Kukai studied esoteric Buddhism from 804 to 806. He founded this temple upon his return. Until the Meiji era, this temple was one of the seven largest temples of Tosa prefecture.

A pretty temple dedicated to the fishermen with a pagoda, beautiful carvings, and a waterfall. Usa used to be a town active in bonito fishing.

The temple is split into two areas: the lower part is situated next to the pond; it has the abbey and the triple pagoda. A long stairway leads to the main hall, which has a beautifully decorated Chinese-style gable, and the Daishi-Do.

Do not be fooled by the short distance of Fudodo, the okunoin on the map. The okunoin, a Shinto shrine located in the forest on top of a cliff 100 m above the sea, just 200 m away, can only be reached following the panoramic road which requires another 2 km of walking.

Probably the exposed location at the tip of the peninsula might explain the temple's location, or rather, the location of the okunoin.

T36 – Shoryu-ji

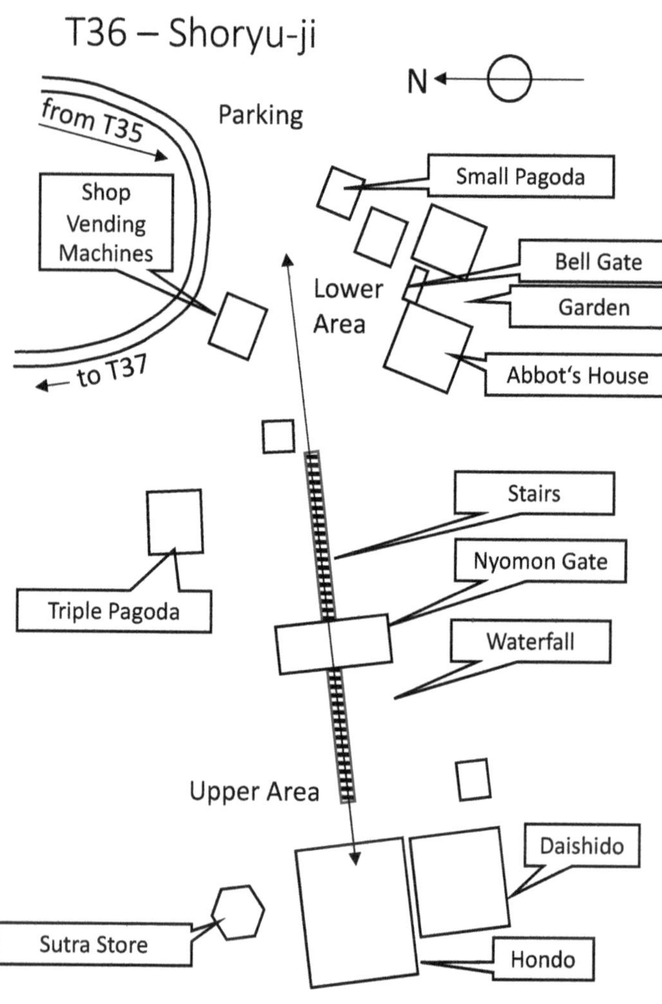

From T36 to T37 – KM 375 to KM 430

Fascination	***
Distance	56 km
Elevation gain	523 m
Difficulty	Very long stage, 2 days walking, some climbs
Public transportation	Part 1 by 🚌 and 🚂 via Kochi Part 2: 🚂 Susaki (KM 398) - Kubokawa
Points of interest	KM 376 Ferry Station (start) KM 384 Tunnel KM 387 🛒 KM 389 Ferry Station (end) Uranouchi KM 390 meeting point of Route A and B KM 392 Hut 🚻 🛒 KM 395 🛒 KM 397 🚂 🛏 🛒 🍴 Susaki KM 398 B5 Daizenin KM 403 🚂 🛒 Awa , 2 alternate routes (pass or tunnels) KM 404 Beginning of difficult part ↗↗ KM 405 ↗↗ Yakezaka-Toge pass KM 407 pass and tunnel routes meet again KM 410 🚂 Tosa-Kure Station KM 415 ↗↗ Nanako-Toge Pass △ 409 m KM 416 🚻 KM 420 🚂 Kagano Station, hut KM 429 🚂 Kubokawa Station 🛏 🛒 🍴 KM 430 Old House Hanpei Café
Where to stay	🛏 KM 397 Several options in Susaki city 🛏 KM 410 Several options in Tosa-Kure 🛏 KM 425 Shimanto Guesthouse 40010 🛏 KM 429 Several options in Kubokawa 🛏 KM 430 T37 Guesthouse

This is the third-longest stage on the pilgrimage. Since T37 is located at an altitude of 200 m, some climbs are unavoidable, no matter which route you pick. The stage can be split into two parts.

- Part 1: 25 km from T36 to Susaki with B5 (KM 397)
- Part 2: 32 km from Susaki to T37 in Kubokawa

Part 1 to Susaki is a beautiful day's walk of around 25 km to Susaki, either along the coast of the mainland or along the coast of Yokonami peninsula. Upon leaving T36, we have a choice of two routes:

1. Route A in the Route Guide - heading left on the coast, walking the original route back over the bridge and left along Uranouchi bay, where we can do a part by ferry if we want (one hour, saves us 11 km), or
2. Route B in the Route Guide: heading right and following Yokonami skyline, a beautiful walk above the coast of the peninsula, which is about 1 km shorter, but without infrastructure (no public toilet for 16 km)

Both routes meet at KM 390. From there, we walk another 9 km to Susaki (KM 399) where we can spend the night. In any case, the distance is 24 or 25 km and a beautiful, coastal walk, no matter which one we pick.

Susaki is a busy city with several shipyards. The city is a good location to stay for the night unless you want to continue to Kubokawa (T37) by train.

Usa – T36 - Susaki

Part 2 to Kubokawa is a longer hike of around 32 km which can easily be done by train as well. After Route 56 passes underneath the railway at Awa Station (KM 403), we have another choice to make at the traffic light: how to tackle Yakezaka pass and get to Tosa-Kure (KM 410):

1. Option 1: <u>Walking the pass</u>. 7.7 km with a 200 m climb. This is the common route which includes a climb on a mountain path and can be challenging in wet conditions. For this option, we take the first road left after the traffic light.
2. Option 2: <u>Taking the tunnel</u>, in this case, after the traffic light we continue along Route 56. This option is 6.4 km and still includes a climb of 93 m.
3. Option 3: Walking <u>along the panoramic coast</u>, 8.2 km with a 40 m climb. For this one, follow Route 59 for another 400 m and turn right at the Lawson's following the "Awa Seaside" sign. The slightly longer distance is easily compensated by the less climbing and the wonderful views.

No matter which option we pick, we will end up in Tosa-Kure, a good location to take a rest at the seaside. Here again, we have two options to continue to Nanako-Toge pass (KM 416) which is at 287 m altitude:

1. Soemimizu Trail, 6.9 km with a 409 m climb, which is the main Henro route. Take the narrow road to the right after crossing Kure-river, at the narrow white house on the right, or…
2. Osaka Henro Trail, 7.8 km 287 m climb. Continue along Route 56 for another 1 km, passing Tosa Kure Station. After crossing Osaka-dani-river, head right and follow the river. This option is easier to walk and has less of a climb. It is mostly paved except the last kilometer.

Both routes meet at the parking of Nanako-Toge pass. From here we need to walk another 13 km gently downhill without climbs to Kubokawa/T37.

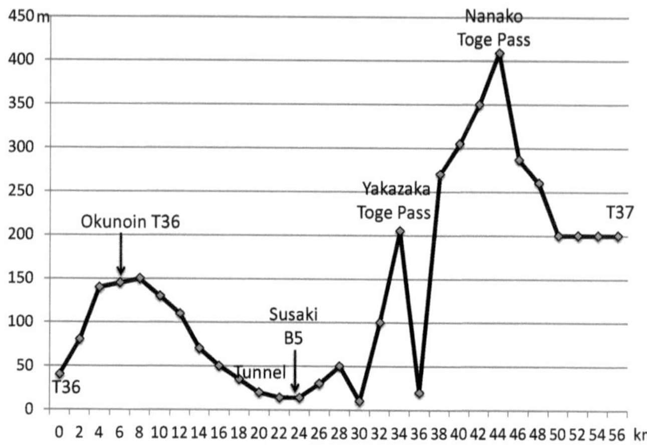

Temple No. B5 – Daizenji 大善寺

Fascination	*
Translation	Temple of Great Kindness
Main deity	Kukai
Location	KM 399
Detour	0.5 km, almost on the main route
Difficulty	Easy, a short set of stairs as you arrive
Points of interest	View over the bay of Susaki

Small temple at an elevated location in the city of Susaki. The temple office is next to the temple grounds. At this temple, people traditionally pray for the prevention of drowning and for safety on the water.

B5 is located in the center on a little hill, the stamp office is not on the temple area, but in the house nearby.

Temple No. 37 – Iwamoto-ji 岩本寺

Fascination	**
Translation	Temple of the Petrified Root
Main deity	Fudo Myoo, Kanzeon Bosatsu, Amida Nyorai
Founded in	Tempyo era 729-749
Location	KM 430
Distance from last temple	56 km
Distance to next temple	82.7 km
Difficulty	Easy, temple located next to road
Points of interest	Pictures on the ceiling of the main hall
Okunoin	Takaoka Jinja (2 km NW)

At first, this temple does not seem impressive. The reason is that during the Meiji restauration and the period of temple separations, this temple had to move from its original location on the other side of the plain. The okunoin Takaoka-Jinja used to be the former main hall. It is about 2.5 km to the northwest, on the other side of the Shimanto river, an area where in the forest there are a dozen of other shrines. The detour takes about 2 hours, it is an enjoyable walk along the river.

After being forced to leave, the temple grounds were rebuilt in their current location in 1890, the current main hall was built in 1974. The ceiling displays 575 paintings.

The entire area of Kubokawa, especially the northwest, has plenty of Shinto shrines. All in all, zooming in on Google maps, I counted close to 30 shrines and temples around Kubokawa, most of them 1-2 km north of T37 near the Shimanto river.

Iwamotoji runs a guesthouse.

There is a nice café in a traditional house just 100 m from the temple, called "Old House Hanpei Café".

From T37 to T38 – KM 430 to KM 512

Fascination	***
Distance	82 km
Elevation gain	A total of 512 m climbs along the distance, no major challenges
Difficulty	Very long distance
Public transportation	🚂 from Kubokawa to Nakamura 🚌 from Nakamura to Ashizuri Misaki

Points of interest:
Part 1: Kubokawa to the outskirts of Kuroshio town (30 km)
KM 430 Kubokawa (210 m)
KM 434 Mt. Gozaisho △ 290 m
KM 435 Ichinose trail 🚻, hut
KM 445 🚂 Iyoki Station, tunnel
KM 449 🛒 🚻
KM 450 🚂 Tosa-saga Station, Yokohama tunnel, seaside
KM 459 🚂 Ariigawa Station 🛏

Part 2: Kuroshio to Tosa-Shimizu (about 30 km)
KM 471 🚂 Kotsuka Station, pass the railway, leave
Highway 56 and head for the riverside
KM 473 🚂 Nakamura Station 🛏
KM 476 Shimanto bridge, turn left follow Highway 321
KM 479 🚻 🍽 Bird Park, 🚻
KM 484 Shin Izuta Tunnel (1610 m)
KM 490 Bridge 🛒
KM 492 🛏 Several

Part 3: Tosa-Shimizu to Ashizuri and a little further (20-30 km)
KM 496 Okinohama Beach
KM 500 follow the coastline

Where to stay	🛏 KM 460 Several guesthouses Kuroshio
	🛏 KM 475 Several guesthouses Nakamura
	🛏 KM 495 Minshuku Okinohama
	🛏 KM 512 Several Guesthouses near T38

We are now facing the longest stage of the pilgrimage, which will take three days to walk, but compared to the 75 km from T23 to T24 on Cape Muroto, this one is less lonely as there is more variety along the way. Let us divide the stage into three parts (for three days, assuming we have stayed in Kubokawa the night before):

Part 1: On the first day, we follow Route 56, or we walk smaller roads parallel to it. The first 4 km take us uphill but only with a moderate climb until we reach the highest point at Mount Gozaisho. From then on, we walk downhill or on flat terrain for the rest of the day, and we will follow the Iyoki river bed until it flows into the sea 500 m past the Lawson's convenience store. We follow Route 56 to the right, heading south for another 10 km, crossing a vacation area with public toilets, beaches, camping grounds and several places to stay, about 10 km before Nakamura.

Part 2: Nakamura, near Kuroshio, is where the Shimanto river flows into the sea. After crossing the railroad tracks near Kotsuka Station, we leave route 56, head for the river banks and cross the river on the big bridge. We are now at KM 476, following Route 321 south, (the sea is on our left side). At the restaurants and the wild bird park, the road takes a right turn and leaves the coast across the hills for 5.5 km. We have the choice between 1,610 m of tunnel and taking the mountain path, which is 700 m longer, has 200 m more climb but we are not exposed to the noise of the cars and trucks in the tunnel. At the Family Mart, we cross the bridge. We can stay at one of the places 2 to 3 km farther down the coast. By now, we can feel and smell that we have reached a tropical latitude, being as far in the south as Morocco or Florida.

Part 3: Depending on where we spent our second night, it is now only another 15 or 20 km to the cape and T38, where there are a large number of guesthouses and hotels. The main route will make a U-turn at T38 and take us back to KM 490 (which becomes KM 539 on the way back), so we might try to find an option where we stay 2 nights at the same place and leave a part of our luggage there when visiting (and maybe staying) at T38.

Temple No. 38 – Kongofuku-ji 金剛福寺

Fascination	***
Translation	Temple of Eternal Happiness
Main deity	Senju Kannon Bosatsu
Founded in	Konin 13 (822)
Location	KM 512
Distance from last temple	82 km
Distance to next temple	53 km
Difficulty	Easy
Points of interest	Location, coast, panorama The seven wonders of Ashizuri
Okunoin	Shirao Jinja Okunoin near Ishizuchi Jinja

T38 represents another highlight in our pilgrimage, being the most remote temple. It is located in a beautiful location on Cape Ashizuri, the southernmost point of Shikoku Island. Unlike T24 at Cape Muroto, T38 offers a view onto the cape and the sea. This temple, too, was used by Yamabushi mountain monks for Shugendo ascetic practices.

The temple was never destroyed and is situated in an array of stones and little gardens. It has two okunoins: Shirao-Jinja, just 500 m west, named after mount Shirao, the highest mountain on the peninsula. The other okunoin is located near the mountain peak. It is in ruins today, deep in the forest and difficult to find. T38 itself is an impressive area characterized by a fish pond and many colorful stones all around the area. Near the temple, there are a number of other landmarks.

In front of the temple, John "Nakahama" Manjiro stares at the sea, his statue is located near the lighthouse. Manjiro was a person with an impressive life. As a fisherman at 14, he was washed ashore a deserted island far away from the coast of Japan. Saved by an American fleet of whale ships, he was adopted by the fleet's captain, taken to New England and baptized. After making a small fortune during the gold rush, Manjiro insisted on returning to Japan, taking the risk of a death penalty (in the Edo era, when Japan was self-isolated for 250 years, it was forbidden to leave or return to the country). The government, convinced his knowledge might be important, decided to hire him. At the time of the negotiations with the United States when Colonel Perry landed in Tokyo and insisted that the country open, Manjiro was about the only Japanese who could speak English, probably the only one who was really fluent and he played an important role in the negotiations which ended peacefully. Later Manjiro founded the English faculty at the University of Tokyo and accompanied the first Japanese delegations to Europe in the 19th century. Nakahama Manjiro was born near this temple, in Nakanohama, at KM 520, and his birthplace can be visited. He is buried at Tokyo's Mejiro Cemetery.

The cape itself has an interesting path through the forest which goes straight to the cliffs, with panoramic views over the sea and the rocky coast. The coastal road is more than 100 m above sea level. It is quite probable that the exposed position and the unusual landscape made Cape Ashizuri a spiritual location with shrines before the temple was founded. Hakusan Shrine (Shirao Jinja) is located about 300 m west of T38 and consists of several buildings. There are at least two other shrines on the cape: Isemiya (200 m north of T28) and Gogoku-Jinja, opposite Hakusan Shrine.

The wonders of Ashizuri are a number of natural sites on the cape
1. The hell hole, an underground cave into which people throw coins and make a wishing
2. The fingernail rock, a rock into which according to legend some sutras were scratched were scratched by Kukai
3. The tortoise calling place, where Kukai is said to have called sea turtles to cross the sea on
4. Kame-Ishi, a turtle-shaped rock at the end of a little footpath that crosses the forest.
5. The torii gate that wasn't built in one Night
6. The tide pool
7. The swaying rock

T38 and Cape Ashizuri

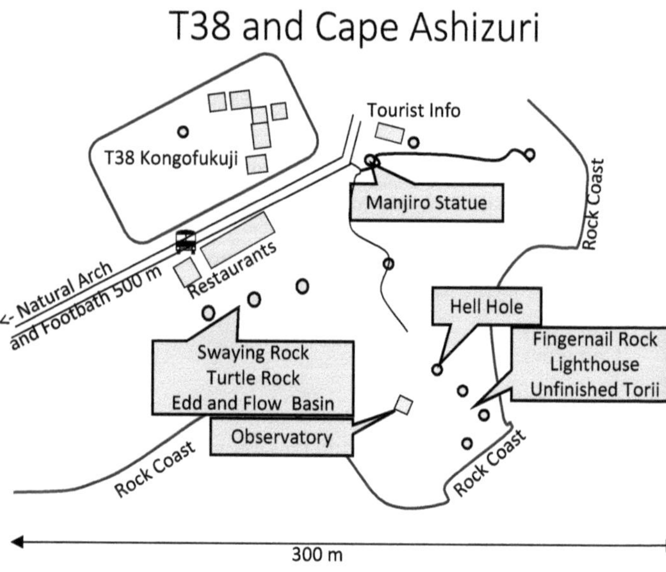

There are some more interesting nearby places to visit:
- The lighthouse,
- Hakusan-Domon, a natural arch at sea level which has a height of 17 m during low tide.
- Ashizuri-Manjiro-Footbath, a hot spring where the view over the sea can be enjoyed while relaxing one's legs in the foot bath.

From T38 to T39 – KM 512 to KM 565

Fascination	**
Distance	53 km
Elevation gain	400 m in total but no major challenge
Difficulty	Easy to walk but long (2 days)
Public transportation	🚌 From Shimanto city to Sukumo, 🚃 to Hirata Station, walk 2.7 km
Points of interest	KM 517 🚻 🚌 KM 520 🚻 🚌 Nakanohama KM 524 🛒 🍴 🛏 Tosa-Shimizu Town KM 532 🚻 🚌 Okinohama KM 538 🛒 🚌 🚻 Shimonokae bridge, split of Route A and B KM 543 Bangai Temple Shinnen-anan KM 554 Miyanokawa Tunnel, merging of Routes A and B KM 555 🛒 🚻 🍴 🚌 Mihara Village KM 560 🚻 Umenoki Park, Nakasuji Dam KM 564 🚃 🚌 Hirata Station
Where to stay	🛏 KM 525 Several in Tosa Shimizu 🛏 KM 530 Several in Okinohama 🛏 Henro House River Mountain, Route 21 (Route B in the Route Guide)

There are different options to get from T38 to T39. The most common ones return from T38 either up the east coast or up the west coast across Nakanohama (John Manjiro's birthplace), Tosa-Shimizu, across Okinohama and to the bridge of Shimonokae River, just like we came.

A popular route (Route B in the Route Guide) is to turn left at the river and not pass the bridge (unless we want to visit the convenience store on the other side, there will be no food for the next 17 km) and to follow Route 21 along Shimonokae and Ichino River all the way until Hirata Station, which is just 2 km from T39. This is a beautiful walk across the forest and rivers. We reach Hirata Station and Highway 56. We follow the highway to the left for 1 km until we see the road sign leading us to T39. When reaching T39 Enko-Ji, we have also completed the first half of the official pilgrimage route.

There are other routes, e. g. along the west coast to Sukomo and then to T39 along Route 321, or going through the hills of the peninsula along Route 28:

- Route A in the Route Guide splits at the bridge at KM 538, and follows Routes 321, 346 and 46 until Mihara.
- A longer but very beautiful walk is to follow the cape along the west side all the way to Sukumo on Route 321, it add another 17 km to the distance

Temple No.39 – Enko-ji 延光寺

Fascination	*
Translation	Temple of the Beam of Light
Main deity	Yakushi Nyorai
Founded in	Jinki 1 (724)
Location	KM 565
Distance from last temple	53 km
Distance to next temple	27 km
Difficulty	Easy
Points of interest	Turtle with bell, Eye-curing well, Stone Monument from 1680

The last temple of Kochi (Tosa) prefecture surrounded by numerous Jizo, Nyorai and Bosatsu statues. According to legend, the temple's bell was brought by a turtle from the sea, as shown by the statue. The original bell is a national treasure and kept in a Tokyo museum.

The little well on the right of the main hall is said to cure eye-diseases.

The temple was founded by Gyoki but expanded to its arrangement with seven buildings later by Kukai. The main gate is also impressive. The present structure was built in 1891.

The turtles play an important role here, as the temple's sacred mountain is named Sekki-zan, "red turtle mountain". As the legend goes, a turtle came from the sea carrying the temple bell on its back.

Fascination	*
Walking distance	27 km
Elevation gain	300 m
Difficulty	Medium, 300 m altitude gain at Matsuo-Toge pass
Public transportation	🚂 from Hirata Station to Sukumo and 🚌 from Sukumo to Hirajo-Fudasho-Mae Station
Points of interest	KM 570 🛒 KM 571 🚻 KM 574 Sukumo Town, choice of pass or road 🚻 rest hut, Take Daishi KM 580 △ 300 m Matsuo-Toge pass Prefectural border to Ehime KM 585 Matsuo Daishi, 🛒 KM 589 ⛩ 🚻 Shinto-Shrine KM 592 Sozu River KM 593 Butsuganin (Bangai) 🚻
Where to stay	🛏 Several options in Sukumo 🛏 Several options in Ainan,

This is the beginning of the second half of the pilgrimage, and we also enter the third of the four prefectures, Ehime Prefecture.

The first 6 km from T39 take us along route 56 into Sukumo, a port town on the wonderful, rocky west coast of Shikoku.

We might continue along Route 56 (for instance if we travel by bike) and across the road tunnel but the main walking route takes us over Matsuo-Toge pass (300 m altitude), the hill north of the port, where we will enter Ehime prefecture.

It is also possible to continue along the coast from Sukumo on Route 7, which is about 30 minutes and 2 km longer, but maybe nicer to walk and easier to find.

Temple No.40 – Kanjizai-ji 観自在寺

Fascination	**
Translation	Kannon Temple
Main deity	Yakushi Nyorai
Founded in	Daido 2 (807)
Location	KM 593
Distance from last temple	27 km
Distance to next temple	51 km
Difficulty	Easy
Points of interest	Wall with Buddha statues Octagonal Hojuden Pavillon
Okunoin	Sasayama Jinja (Kanzeonji ruins) Mameki-Daishi KM 633 B6 Ryukoin at KM 635 Kujira Daishi on Kushima Island

This is the furthest temple from T1 during our pilgrimage. Kukai built this temple as a prayer temple for Emperor Heizei who ruled from 803 to 806. It has a glorious past: The temple was strongly supported by several emperors and also became the family temple of the lords of Uwajima. At one time it was considerably larger than today.

The main hall burned down in the Edo-era and again in 1959, it was rebuilt in 1964, made of concrete and iron. It is especially beautiful and includes a number of additional buildings as well as a garden. The temple runs a guest house.

T40 has four okunoin, all of them are far away.

1. Kanzonji is a ruin located about 30 km north at the peak of Sasayama at an altitude of 1065 m. To get there we need to take a different direction from Sukumo at KM 575, along Routes 56 and 332 northbound. Consult the route guide and make sure you have taken enough food. The detour, called Sasayama-michi, has long been considered a place of ascetic training. It ends at KM 620 where it merges with the main route in the town of Tsushima. The place is just 50 m from Sasayama shrine which symbolizes the mountain peak.

2. Mameki-Daishi is 40 km further along the main route, in the outskirts of Uwajima City at Km 632.
3. Ryuko-In, just 2 km further, is also classified as Temple B6
4. Kujira-Daishi on Kushima Island, 2 km west of Uwajima City.

Temple No. B6 – Ryukoin 龍光院

Fascination	*
Translation	Sanctuary of the Dragon Beam
Main deity	Juichimen Kannon Bosatsu
Location	KM 635
Detour	Located only 300 m from the pilgrimage route
Difficulty	Easy

Not much is known about Ryukoin, located on a hill next to Uwajima station. It is counted double, as a Bekkaku Temple but it is also an inner sanctuary of T40. The temple shares its space with several Shinto shrines. On the temple grounds, there is a stone engraved with a poem by Basho.

Founded as late as 1618, it was the prayer temple of the noble Date family of Uwajima Castle., which is just 500 m away.

It was destroyed twice in the 20th century: Once by a fire and once bombed by American B29 planes in WWII.

From the temple we will have a great view over a huge cemetary and over the city.

From T40 to T41 – KM 593 to KM 644

Fascination	**
Walking Distance: 50 km	Part 1: 11 km to Ainan-town KM 593-604 Part 2: 16 km to Tsushima KM 604-620 Part 3: 13 km to Uwajima KM 620-634 Part 4: 10 km to T41 KM 634-644
Elevation gain	1,300 m with 2 climbs
Difficulty	Steep
Public transportation	Part 1 [bus], Part 2 [bus], Part 3 [bus] Part 4 [train] from Uwajima to Muden
Points of interest	**Part 1 – 11 km** KM 595 [shop] [restaurant] KM 604 Ainan Town, trail leaves Route 56 **Part 2 – 15 km** KM 605 ↗↗ Steep forest part (4 km/12%) △ 500 m KM 606 Yanaginomizu-Daishi [toilet] KM 608 Shimizu Daishi [toilet] KM 614 Trail reaches Route 56 again KM 620 Tsushima Town [shop] [restaurant] [toilet] **Part 3 – 15 km** KM 622 Matsuo tunnel, bakery [toilet] hut KM 624 [shop] [restaurant] KM 625 [toilet] KM 627 [shop] [toilet] KM 631 [toilet] [shop] KM 632 [toilet] [shop] KM 633 O40 Mameki Daishi KM 635 [train] Uwajima, B6/O40 Ryukoin **Part 4 – 10 km** KM 636 [train] Kita-Uwajima Station KM 637 [toilet] KM 642 [train] Muden Station, [shop]
Where to stay	[bed] KM 620 Tsushima (several options) [bed] KM 635 Uwajima (several options)

This is a 2-day stage, divided into four parts for better planning. There are some alternate routes from T40 to T41 across the mountains, These are more difficult to walk and with less infrastructure. We will focus on Nada-Michi Route

Part 1: Nada-Michi Route is 50.1 km long and follows mostly Highway 56 for 10 km until we reach Ainan. In Ainan, look for the post office and its red mailbox at a pedestrian crossing where you leave route 56. But if you are cycling, or prefer flat terrain, for part 2, you can continue along the coast on Highway 56 for the next 10 km. This part is particularly beautiful due to its coastal panorama.

Part 2: For the main route, (this part is called Kashiwazaka Trail), turn right at the post office and continue along the canal (Kashiwa River) on our right to the end of the river outside the village. The path leads us across the forest and uphill for about 3 km until we reach the little Daishi Shrine where we are now at 300 m altitude. This is followed by a last, steep kilometer until we reach the peak at 500 m altitude and head down to Shimizu Daishi. After 6 km downhill through the forest, the trail reaches Highway 56 again at KM 614. Here, the landscape suddenly changes and the pilgrimage route follows Highway 56 or smaller parallel roads along the Howara river for about. 10 km until it reaches the town of Tsushima, where we find several places to sleep and to eat.

Part 3: 2 km outside Tsushima, Highway 56 passes through Matsuo tunnel, the longest tunnel on the trail, which is 1,710 m (or about 25 minutes of noise). Avoid it by following the stairs leading uphill on the left. The detour will add 130 m of climb and about 700 m of extra distance, and we will pass several huts. From the tunnel it is another 10 km to Uwajima. The city of Uwajima is another good place to stay and to pay visits to B6 Ryukiin near the station and to the amazing Warei-Jina shrine.

Part 4: At Kita-Uwajima, we follow the smaller route 57 which runs parallel to the train line. The noise of the city disappears quickly and we find ourselves back in the quietude of the countryside. T41 is 1.7 km north of Muden train station.

Temple No. 41 – Ryuko-ji 龍光寺

Fascination	**
Translation	Temple of the Dragon's Ray
Main deity	Juichimen Kanzen Bosatsu
Location	KM 644
Distance from last temple	50.1 km from T40
Distance to next temple	2.9 km
Difficulty	Easy
Points of interest	View over the town across the bell tower
Okunoin	Inari Jinja (on the grounds)

Ryuko-ji is another interesting example of temple separation. We are approaching it on a straight, symmetrical Sando. The buildings are on two levels: The Budddhist temple is on the lower level, while the Shinto shrine, Inari-jinja is on the upper level. Today, the shrine is the okunoin of the temple, and it used to be its former main hall until the separation in 1872, when a new Hondo was built at the lower level.

This explains the Shinto/Buddhist combination of gates: First a Buddhist gate on street level, then some Shinto Torii gates and a Buddhist-shaped gate at the top but instead of the muscular guardians we will find 2 guardian dogs as the gate now belongs to the Shinto shrine.

An Inari is actually a Shinto deity worshipped for fertility, good harvests and prosperous business. It often appears as a fox.

At this temple people used to pray for a good harvest and do so today more for a prosperous business.

Temple No.42 – Butsumoku-ji 仏木寺

Fascination	*
Translation	Temple of the Buddha Tree
Main deity	Dainichi Nyorai
Founded in	Daido 2 (807)
Location	KM 646
Distance from last temple	2.9 km
Distance to next temple	10.8 km
Difficulty	Easy
Points of interest	Statues of 7 happy deities Straw-thatched roof of the bell tower
Okunoin	Miokuri Daishi (KM 649)

T42 is just 2.9 km down the country road from T41.

While at T41, peasants pray for good harvests, at this temple, peasants pray for the health of their animals (especially cows) and for their lost pets.

Two unusual things about this temple: It has a Tsuyomon, a second entrance gate, and its beautiful belltower is the only one in Japan which has a thatched roof instead of wood or copper. It was built around 1700.

The belltower of T42

Fascination	**
Distance	10.8 km
Elevation gain	280 m (via tunnel) or 380 m (via pass)
Difficulty	Medium: 10 km with one hard climb
Public transportation	🚌 back to Muden and then by train to Unomachi
Points of interest	KM 647 Turn left at the dam, ↗↗ 13% △ 500 m KM 650 O42 Miokuri Daishi, Hanaga-Toge Pass △ 538 m or tunnel KM 651 Hanaga Jizo Hut KM 654 Minamori Daishi Hut KM 655 🛒 🍽 KM 657 O43 Hakuo-Gongen and T43.
Where to stay	🛏 KM 657 Several options in Unomachi

This is a quiet 3-4 hour walk with a steep climb in the beginning. After one km along Route 31, we will spot a lonely red vending machine on the roadside and a ramp further on to our left. We turn left and follow the ramp, up to the dam of a little lake. As we follow the road, getting higher closer to the freeway, it becomes a path which reaches Route 31 again. Following the road, we reach Hanaga Tunnel which is at 420 m. Again, it's either the noisy tunnel or another 100 m climb over the highest point of this stage. Hanaga-Toge pass, and the ones avoiding the tunnel will be rewarded with a little Daishi at the pass, Miokuri Daishi, which is the okunoin of T42.

From here, we walk 1.9 km downhill with a 10% descent, over the Hiji-Kawa-river, over the bridge, and we take a left turn following Route 29. After 4 km, we reach the outskirts of Unomachi, and after another 3 km uphill we finally get to O43 Hakuo Gongen, a deserted Okunoin, with its cedar trees and a sacred rock, and to T43.

Unomachi is a good place to stay. Kaimei School (the oldest wooden school building in western Japan, and the Museum of Ehime History with its modern architecture are also worth visiting if you are interested in ancient and pre-war Japan.

Temple No.43 – Meiseki-ji 明石寺

Fascination	**
Translation	Temple of the Shining Rock
Main deity	Senji Kannon Bosatsu
Founded in	6th century
Location	KM 657
Distance from last temple	10.8 km
Distance to next temple	70.5 km
Difficulty	Temple located 70 m above the city
Points of interest	O43 Hakuo Gongen, its cedar trees and painted ceiling
Okunoin	O43 Hakuo Gongen

Since early days, the hill has been a sacred place for graves and worshipping, and this temple is considered a central place for Shugendo, ascetic mountain monks. The temple's name can also be read as "temple of the sunrise rock", probably referring to the legend of a woman carrying a heavy stone at night and turning into a Boddhisatva when the sun rose. The rock can be visited at the okunoin. In the middle of the 6th century, an ascetic named Enshuin Socho founded a temple in this location to worship a Senju Kannon statue from China.

The temple was expanded in 734. But when Kukai visited the place in 822, he found it in desolate condition and it was renovated. In the Kamakura period (1185-1333) the temple again fallen into disuse and was renovated by Minamoto no Yoritomo. In the following centuries, it became the family temple of several samurai clans (Minamoto, Saionji, Date)

Today's buildings are from 1674, the main hall was built in 1874. The temple buildings have some beautiful woodwork.

Unomachi, where the temple is located, is a city of history with several landmarks, a museum, and ancient streets to be visited.

Fascination	***
Distance	Route A: 70.5 km or Route B: 73 km
Elevation gain	Route A: about 800 m, Route B about 500 m
Difficulty	Long stage with hard climb, not much food
Public transportation	This stage can be done by public transportation only up to KM 707. Kuma-Kogen can also be reached by 🚌 from Matsuyama Station (near T51).

Points of interest

Part 1:

KM 660 🛒🍴🚂 Kami-Uwa Station

KM 662 🛒🚻

KM 667 Huts 🚻

KM 674 Hut 🚻

KM 676 Beginning of detour to B7

KM 678 Onsen 🚻

KM 679 🛏️🚂 Ozu, Bridge

Part 2:

KM 682 B8 Toyogahashi 🚻🍴🛒

KM 690 🛏️🚂 Uchiko Station

Part 3:

KM 699 - 705 Several huts

KM 707 Tsukiawase 🚌 (130 m) ↗

KM 710 🍴 Udon ↗

KM 712 🚻 Hut ↗

KM 713 Ochiai Tunnel, Daishido, path to O51 Ishizuchiji

KM 717 ⛩️ Mishima Jinja 🚻 (348 m) ↗

KM 721 ⛩️ Katsuragi Jinja (527 m) ↗↗ trail 3 km/260 m

KM 724 △ 790 m Hiwada pass

Where to stay	
	🛏️ KM 679 Several options in Ozu
	🛏️ KM 690 Several options in Uchiko
	🛏️ KM 705 Ikadaya
	🛏️ KM 712 Tado Village
	🛏️ KM 726 Several options in Kuma-kogen

This 70 km stage is the third-longest stage on the pilgrimage. It takes us across some interesting places along the west coast and finally into the mountains to Kuma-Kogen, not at all monotonous, but with plenty of things to see on the way. Assuming we have stayed in Unomachi, we can divide this stage into three parts/days:
1. 21 km to Ozu,
2. 12 km to Uchiko and
3. 37 km to Uchiko to Kuma-Kogen and T44.

Part 1, T43 to Ozu (KM 659 to 680: 21 km): is an easy walk mostly along the Hiji-Kawa river and Route 56 to Ozu.

Part 2, Ozu to Uchiko (KM 680 to 692: 12 km) is just a 3-hour walk, and a day to rest our legs before we go on the strenuous 3rd part, doing some sightseeing in Ozu, visiting the Castle, Garyu Sanso (a Samurai's house), the little museum with early 20th century objects and Garyu-no-yu hot spring. All of this is situated on a pittoresque river-bend.But once we leave this beautiful place, we have to walk across a commercial area for over an hour until we are out of the city.

There are not many places to sleep on the 37 km of the 3rd part and it is not only long but it also includes a 500 m climb. The solution is to stay half a day in Ozu and to finish the 2nd day with the 3-hour walk to Unomachi and visit B8 on the roadside. (Depending on time and ambition, B7 can be included which would require another full day in Ozu). After a relaxing day in Ozu, it will be easier to tackle the exhausting 37 km until Kuma-Kogen.

Part 3, Uchiko to T44/Kuma-Kogen (37 km/800 m): Uchiko is the **last place to shop for food for the next 38 km** until we get to Kuma-Kogen. Uchiko is an old town which is partially well-preserved and worth visiting: After crossing the railway line, the pilgrimage route passes an old Kabuki theatre, a series of old merchant houses and movie house turned into a museum, an ancient wax factory. And if you are craving for some different food, there is even a beer pub under German management called

Zum Schwarzen Keiler on the alternative route, 500 m north of the river.

From here we will leave the sea level and enter the mountains, finishing 500 m higher than we started. The distance and climb are almost too much for one day. There is a possibility to shorten the difficult part 3: Take the Uchiko Town Community bus from Uchiko train station at 7:35 a.m. (or 9:05 during weekdays) to Tsukiawase (KM 708). The ride is 500 yen and it reduces the walking part to 20 km, still including a 650 m climb, which is still ambitious enough (See Route A in the Route Guide). There is an okunoin of T51 with a waterfall which might be worth visiting, it would be a detour of about 5 km.

Route B is a slightly longer but less tough climb and it is entirely paved. This is the better one to go for, in case you cycle, in case it rains or in case we want to avoid arriving in the dark. (Do not try Route A during the sunset, you might end up in the dark in the middle of the forest).

If all of these solutions sound too difficult or challenging, you can also take the train from Uchiko to Matsuyama and get to Kuma-Kogen by bus from Matsuyama, "backwards" from the north.

Kuma-Kogen is a town in a valley, built along the Kuma-river and Route 33. T44 is located in Kuma, T45 is about 9 km east, but the pilgrimage route returns to Kuma as it continues to T46, so it makes sense to stay in Kuma for two nights and visit T45 without heavy luggage.

One of the difficulties on this stage is finding a place to sleep. There are some, but not many.

There are several other places to stay in Kuma but they will be slightly pricier than usual backpacker hostels.

Temple No. B7 – Shusseki-ji 出石寺

Fascination	***
Translation	Temple of the Emerging Rock
Main deity	Senju Kannon Bosatsu
Founded in	718
Detour	16 km from KM 677
Difficulty	Hard: 750 m climb over 8 km

This remote temple offers fabulous views on the way up. It is dedicated to hunting and animals. Visiting it on foot takes about 7 hours up and down, so you need to plan a whole day. There are no shops after passing Iyo-Hirano train station, so to make sure you carry enough food and drink. The temple runs a guesthouse, but you must bring your own food.

Temple No. B8 – (Toyogahashi 十夜ヶ橋)

Fascination	**
Translation	Ten Nights' Bridge
Main deity	Miroku Bosatsu
Location	KM 683
Detour	none
Difficulty	Easy

Rather known by its nickname "ten nights' bridge", Eitoku-ji, this little Bekkaku temple is located on the left roadside on Highway 56, stuck between highway ramps and railroad tracks.

Some of the Bekkaku temples have popular nicknames, like B5, the mackerel temple. According to legend, Kukai had to sleep under the bridge here, cold and hungry, because there was no better place. Later he said that this night had felt like ten nights. The temple itself is modest, but the actual place to visit is under the bridge on the other side of the river (on your right if you look at the Daishido). You will see a statue of Kukai sleeping, covered with real blankets to keep him warm. The main temple was destroyed in the floods of 2018 and the Hondo is being rebuilt since 2020 further away from the road, its former place has been turned into the parking lot.

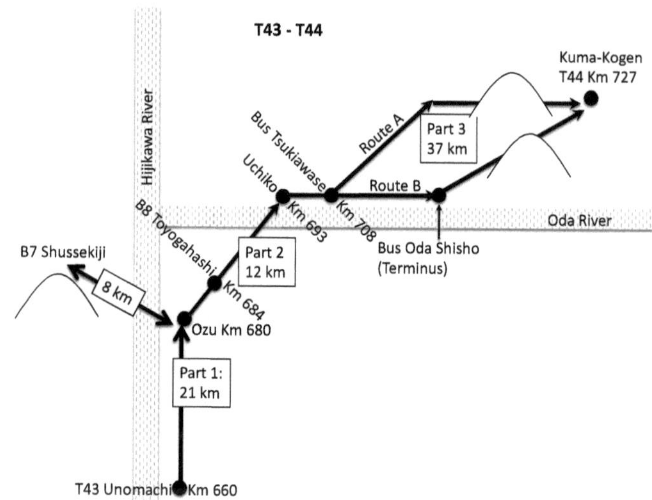

Temple No.44 – Taiho-ji or Daiho-ji 大寶寺

Fascination	*
Translation	Temple of the Big Treasure, or Temple of the Daiho era
Main deity	Juichimen Kanon Bosatsu
Founded in	Taiho 1 (701)
Location	KM 727
Distance from last temple	70.5 km
Distance to next temple	9.3 km
Difficulty approaching	100 m climb
Points of interest	Big straw sandals, two bells

T44 was built upon the request of Emperor Monmu, who had it named after his era, Taiho or Daiho era. It is located on the other side of the river in the forest about 100 m above the town, so there are some ramps and stairs to climb before we get there. The main gate is impressive and holds a pair of huge straw sandals integrated, which are replaced every century.

The temple burned down three times in its history: In 1152, during the Tensho era (1573-1592) destroyed by Motochika and in 1874.

From T44 to T45 and back to Kuma-Kogen

KM 728 to KM 749

Fascination	***
Distance	21 km from T44 to T45 and back to Kuma
Elevation gain	About 600 m
Difficulty	Difficult, steep climbs, no food
Public transportation	🚌 from Kuma-Eigyosho to Iwayaji-Mae (550 yen, see Route Guide for schedule)
Points of interest	KM 728 ↗↗ Tonomido Pass △731 m, ↘↘ KM 729 Route 12 (606 m alt.) KM 731 Hut 🚻 ⛩Sumiyoshi-Shrine KM 732 Hut KM 734 Beginning of loop: Route A, ↗↗ Turn right, uphill for 700 m with 20%, named "Hacchosaka, the slope 8 cho" KM 736 △ 785 m, ↘↘ to T45 (1 km at 18% descent) O45 Seriwari-Senjo **KM 737 T45**, hut, parking, end of Route B KM 741 Furuiwayaso, hot spring, hut, temple KM 741=KM 735 end of loop KM 746 ↗↗ △ 740 m Sembon Pass ↘↘ KM 749 Route 33 ⛩ Kodono-Shrine
Where to stay	Several guesthouses in Kuma-Kogen and between T44 and T45

This part describes the walk to T45 **and back to Kuma-Kogen** which it is a loop. With many ups and downs, this is not an easy stage and there are no shops or restaurants. T45 is a beautiful 3 hour walk from Kuma-Kogen, and the route continuing to T46 brings us back to Kuma-Kogen, so it is advisable to stay in the same place for two nights and to visit T45 as a day trip.

T45 is a mountain temple which can be reached from the top (Route A in the Route Guide) or from the bottom (Route B). Route A leads over some hills with a few short but steep climbs, and it reaches T45 coming from the top passing the okunoin Seriwari-Senjo. On your way back, or if you do not feel like walking a hilly mountain path, you can also take Route B across the valley or even walk the entire distance to T45 and back along Route 12 and leave or approach the temple from below.

The walking stage from T44 to T45 goes east from T44, over Tonomido Pass at 730 m. the pass can be avoided if instead you return from the temple the way you came and walk Route 12 across Tonomido tunnel. The approach to T45 from the top involves a heavy climb at

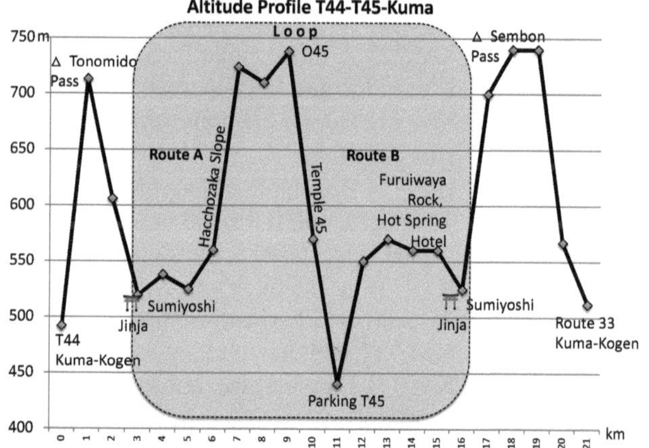

Hacchozaka Slope, passing the Okunoin Seriwari Zenjo and a very steep downhill part to T45. The approach via Route B is much easier to walk and passes the beautiful Furuiwaya valley.

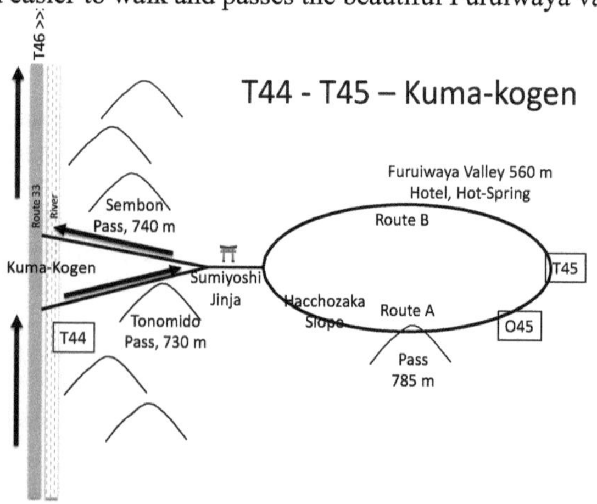

Temple No.45 – Iwaya-ji 岩屋寺

Fascination	***
Translation	Temple of the Rock Caves
Main deity	Fudo Myoo
Founded in	Konin 6 (815)
Location	KM 737
Distance from last temple	About 10 km
Distance to next temple	25.9 km
Difficulty	Difficult
Points of interest	Seriwari Zenjo 36 Statues of immortal youth Ladders and caves
Okunoin	O45 Seriwai Zenjo

This is certainly one of the most impressive temples and locations of the pilgrimage, and a temple that cannot be visited in just half an hour, so take your time. Like T27, it is situated on a steep mountain rock, and a Nansho, a difficult place to approach. It may well have been founded to support pilgrims seeking isolation in one of the many caves in the porous rock. T45 used to be an okunoin of T44 but received the status of an independent temple in 1874. The temple, including its archives, was destroyed in a fire 1889 and rebuilt in several stages from 1920 to 1978.

It can be approached from the top over the mountain, climbing down at the end, entering the temple grounds through the little wooden gate, or from the valley below, approaching from the parking lot. The second option takes about 15-20 minutes, first passing a number of booths selling souvenirs, later climbing several hundreds of steps.

Apart from the temple, some of the many caves are open for visiting. One of the gaps in the rocks is accessible via a long permanent ladder above the temple grounds. Traditionally, pilgrims put some coins into the moss covering the rocks.

There are Toilets near the parking lot and near the pilgrim's rest stop.

From Kuma-kogen to T46 – KM 749 to 763

Fascination	**
Distance	14 to 15 km (4 hours walking and visits to 2 temples = total time appr. 5 h)
Elevation gain	190 m
Difficulty	Medium: a short climb and a long descent, quiet country roads, 2.5 km unpaved
Public transportation	🚌 Kuma to Shiogamori, about 2 km walking to T46
Points of interest	KM 750 Public toilet KM 751 Kayo-chan Rest House KM 752 Hut 🚻, altitude 600 m KM 753 ↗ Continue on Route 44 (straight) KM 755 △ 702 m Misaka Pass turn right, beginning of trail KM 756 ↘↘ Sakura Rest House KM 757 ↘ Sakamotoya Hut 🚻 end of trail KM 759 ↘ Amikake-ishi temple KM 760 ↘ 🚻 Continue left over the bridge KM 763 T46
Where to stay	🛏 Kuma-Kogen, 🛏 KM 763 Chochin-ya (opposite T46) 🛏 Several options in Matsuyama

During this stage, we will leave the mountains for the plains. T46 is the first temple of a group of temples that ends with T51 in the city of Matsuyama.

For those of us who have stayed in Kuma-Kogen, this is a relatively easy walk (14 km) down to T46 which has a pilgrim hostel with a gear shop just opposite. We can even include T47 in that walk since it is just 1 km down the road and the entire stage is not too long. The shops in Kuma are the last chance to pick up some food for the day. The next store will be a bit further, at KM 768, 18 km from the start.

Kayo-chan House and Sakamotoya hut are very nice privately run rest places for pilgrims.

Matsuyama City begins after the bridge at KM 770 and the center is at KM 777, so considering just the distance, it might be possible to walk the 27 km from Kuma to Matsuyama in one day, but there would not be enough time for all the seven temples (T46-T51 and B9). So we should keep the remaining five temples and 12 km for the next day. There will be plenty to see.

The first 6 km take us out of Kuma-kogen along Route 33, during which we will climb 190 m. This will be the last climb for 3 or 4 days (until KM 839/T58). After 3.5 km, most of the cars will turn left and follow Route 33 into the tunnel, which is NOT open to pedestrians and bicycles. Our route, Route 440 from here, continues to the right uphill along the highway until we reach Misaka-Toge Pass after about 1.5 km. At the pass, there are some houses and a shop offering organic food. About 100 m BEFORE the pass, slightly before the route veers left, and passing the vending machines on the right, there is an unpaved road, marked with a grey signpost. This road becomes a path for 2.5 km downhill through the forest, where we will walk softly on fallen cedar leaves. The trail later becomes Route 207. It takes us close to T46 but we will end up on the wrong side of the river bed, so after about 3 km we cross the little bridge on the left. After about 2.5 km and passing two little temples (Amikake-Ishi and Empukuji), T46 will be on our left.

T47 is just 1 km further in the same direction. At this point we can choose to take the bus into Matsuyama and get back the next morning to continue the pilgrimage without luggage to T51.

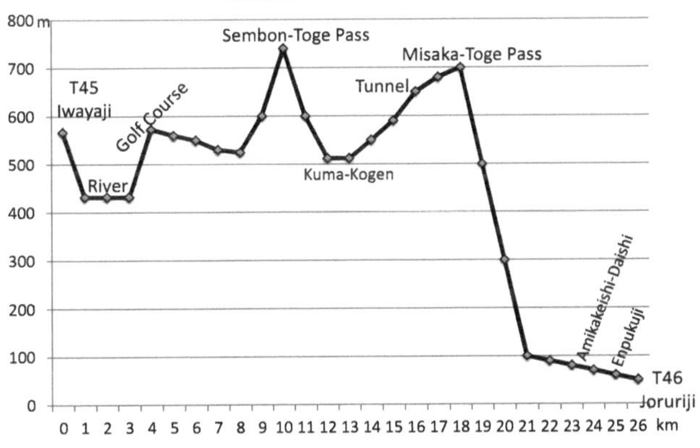

Temple No.46 – Joruri-ji 浄瑠璃寺

Fascination	**
Translation	Temple of the Pure Emerald
Main deity	Yakushi Nyorai
Founded in	Wado 1 (708)
Location	KM 763
Distance from last temple	25.9 km
Distance to next temple	1 km
Difficulty	Easy
Points of interest	1000-year-old juniper tree Buddha hands and feet, lotus flowers

T46 is the first of the eight temples of greater Matsuyama. A smaller but interesting temple, almost disappearing under its plants and trees, making it a shady, mossy and somewhat romantic place that feels like a garden.

The temple was built by Gyoki in 708, and restored by Kukai a hundred years later. It was later destroyed several times by warlords and by a wildfire in 1715. The buildings as we see them today are from 1784, financed by donations organized by a gentleman named Gyoon, a former village official who later became the had priest.

Behind the temple, there is a little park. The hexagonal monument with the metal plates commemorates the soldiers who lost their lives in the Pacific War during WWII.

The garden has a 20-m juniper tree said to be over 1000 years old.

Temple No.47 – Yasaka-ji 八坂寺

Fascination	**
Translation	Temple of Eight Slopes
Main deity	Amida Nyorai
Founded in	Taiho 1 (701)
Location	KM 764
Distance from last temple	1 km
Distance to next temple	4.4 km
Difficulty	Easy
Points of interest	Enma-do Pavilion The 10th step 8000 Amida Statues

Yasakaji is just 1 km down the road. It was recently renovated and now has a more representative appearance. It is surrounded by a large cemetery and was built in 701 by the founder of Shugendo, En-no-Gyoja Shokaku, on behalf of emperor Shomu, at a location where eight paths from hills of different directions came together, hence the name Ya Saka 八坂 (eight slopes).

After several destructions, the buildings we see were rebuilt in 1887 and 1892, shortly after the temple-destructions during the Meiji era.

The statue of its central deity was carved roughly 1000 years ago, and it is on display only every 50 years, the next time in 2034. It is ranked as a prefectural heritage. One of its particularities is the *Enmado*, the little temple between the Hondo and the Daishido. In Japanese mythology, Enma is a figure which decides on whether we end up in heaven or hell, represented here by its two little tunnels. On the stairs to the main hall, on the left side of the 10th step there is the "hand of salvation", a hand engraved that can be touched for good health.

Below the main hall, you can visit a cave with 8000 Amida-statues donated from several parts of Japan.

From the Daishido there is a beautiful panorama over Matsuyama.

From T47 to T51– KM 764 to 776

Fascination	***
Distance	12 km
Elevation gain	No major climbs
Difficulty	Easy and short
Public transportation	🚌 train line connecting Matsuyama with T49 at Kume Station.
Points of interest	**KM 764 B9 Monjuin** KM 765 Grave mounds, Ebara Castle grounds KM 766 Fudahajime Daishido 🛒 KM 767 Bridge over Shogenobu river KM 770 🍽 Turn left at the traffic light for O48, **KM 768 T48 Sairinji** **KM 770 🛒 T49 Jodoji** **KM 773 T50 Hantaji 🛒** KM 774 🛒 bridge
Where to stay	🛏 KM 776 Several options in Matsuyama

This is an exciting stage because for the first time since Kochi, after 400 km, we will return to a big city, with temples and okunoins every few kilometers. It is a shorter stage, with time to enjoy a hot bath at Dogo-onsen or one of the other bathhouses later.

This part of the city, south of the river, has a lot to offer. And the closer you look, the more you will find. Just one kilometer after leaving T47, we already pass B9 Monjuin and eight grave mounds, attributed to Emon Saburo's sons.Other sources claim they are much older, from the 5th century.

When I scrolled over the area on Google maps, I found 20-30 shrines and temples scattered over an area of one square kilometer. We will pass former Ebara Castle grounds (just 300 m northeast of B9) and a Bekkaku/Shinto ground named Fudahajime-Daishido, which is said to be the first temple where Emon Saburo tried to find Kukai and left a note.

This area has plenty of traces of an important past. Teiregi-no-yu, the modern onsen near the riverside, is a place where we can take a rest and spoil our tired legs from the last days. We have enough time.3 kilometers later, we cross the 500 m-wide bed of Shigenobu-river, entering Matsuyama, immediately reaching T48 on our right, another place with an accumulation of sacred places: its okunoin Jonofuji and a Bekkaku named Chozenji all in the same area.

T49 is only 3.3 km further across some urban areas, followed by T50 after only 2 kilometers and finally, at T51, we have reached the center of Matsuyama, or rather its Dogo Onsen neighborhood, which is famous for its hot springs, one of the oldest and most famous bath houses of Japan.

Matsuyama 松山 and Dogo-Onsen 道後温泉

Matsuyama, Shikoku's largest city, is the capital of Ehime prefecture and has appr. 500,000 inhabitants. Dogo-onsen, which only belongs to Takamatsu since the 19th century, is famous for its hot springs, it is considered to be Japan's oldest onsen, which already existed in 596.

Actually, Dogo Onsen, as famous as it may be, looks nicer from the outside than from the inside, and the other more modern onsens nearby (Asukanoyu and Tsubakinoyu) are considered the better choices by many. But the nightly view of the recently renovated Dogo Onsen, with its many roofs and lighting, is a wonderful place for a relaxed evening walk, maybe wearing a Yukata bathrobe while our walking clothes are in the washer. There are many other nice things to do in Matsuyama:
- taking the steam tram to the central part of town,
- going for a sake tasting at Yokota-Sake 150 m from Katsuyama-cho Station, or
- taking the ropeway up to the castle.

T51 Ishiteji is a place where you might easily spend 2 hours, and if you are not forcing yourself to walk the entire route "by the book", you could visit T52 and T52 the following day and spend another night in Matsuyama before heading toward the northern peninsula and Imabari.

Temple No. B9 – Monju-in 文殊院

Fascination	*
Translation	House of Monju (Bosatsu)
Main deity	Monju Bosatsu
Founded in	Unknown
Location	KM 764
Detour	None
Difficulty	Easy

This modest Bekkaku temple is at the place where Emon Saburo's house used to be (see T12 for the whole story).

Monjuin is one of the few remainders of the complex of temples once belonging to T47, which at its peak included as many as 84 buildings.

Emon Saburo receiving Kukai's blessing at O12 Joshin-an

Temple No.48 – Sairin-ji 西林寺

Fascination	**
Translation	Temple of the Western Forest
Main deity	Juichimen Kanzeon Bosatsu
Founded in	Tenpyo 13 (741)
Location	KM 768
Distance from last temple	4.4 km
Distance to next temple	3.3 km
Difficulty	Easy
Points of interest	Jonofuchi, Bamboo
Okunoin	Jonofuchi

Once again, we discover a temple with an entirely different atmosphere, and again we may wonder whether the okunoin (the well/pond located on the other side of the main road) might have been the original sacred site, even more so as the main temple looks quite new. In fact, the daishido was built in 2008, while the rest of the site was renovated between 1700 and 1842, after being in disuse from 1642.

Originally, the temple had been founded by Gyoki Bosatsu in a different location, built as a provincial temple, to go with the provincial shrine (Ichinomiya) and moved to this place by Kukai in 807 (The Ichinomiya is 5 km west along Route 33, and it actually shares its grounds with another Buddhist temple, Chotokuji)

All the buildings are tightly packed inside a square of walls, bordered by the highway to the west and a little canal to the south. There are some more buildings than usual. Entering from the main gate on the south side (the parking lot) starting from the left, we have

- The temple office
- The bell-tower
- A little Jizo temple and statue
- The main hall (looking straight)
- The Daishi-hall
- An Enma temple
- The Bamboo, where people pray for family harmony
- A tea-house

The okunoin Jonofuji with its pond has a legend of Kukai creating a well with good water-quality, ranked as one of Japan's 100 most important wells. (Yes, they have such a ranking)

Temple No.49 – Jodo-ji 浄土寺

Fascination	**
Translation	Temple of the Pure Land
Main deity	Shaka Nyorai
Founded in	Tempyo era (729-749)
Location	KM 771
Distance from last temple	3.3 km
Distance to next temple	1.8 km
Difficulty	Easy
Points of interest	O49 Ushinomine
Okunoin	Ushinomine

This temple, the imperial temple of Emperor Koken, who reigned from 749 to 758, has some Chinese elements from the Tang dynasty. It has several references to Kuya Shonin (902-973), a spiritual teacher and wandering monk who lived about 100 years after Kobo-Daishi and spent several years at this location. At one point in history, the temple grounds were close to one square kilometer in size and included 66 buildings, which possibly included some of the shrines nearby (I counted six). The 16th-century building was dismantled and rebuilt in 1965.

In addition to the buildings found in most temples, there are three additional halls to the left of the main hall dedicated to Amida-do, Kannon-do and Sa-do. The main hall is a national cultural heritage

It is an easy 10-minute walk up the hill, across the cemetery to the okunoin Ushinomie at the top of the hill.

Temple No.50 – Hanta-ji or Banta-ji 繁多寺

Fascination	**
Translation	Temple of Great Success
Main deity	Yakushi Nyorai
Founded in	Shoho era (749-756)
Location	KM 773
Distance from last temple	1.8 km
Distance to next temple	2.7 km
Difficulty	Easy, 40 m-climb upon arrival
Points of interest	Garden Belltower Ceiling Paintings

When walking to T50, do not follow Route 40 all the way but go right after 1 km when you see the old big stone lantern and pass across the graveyard. After passing some ponds, or rather water reservoirs, we reach T50, which allows a good view over Matsuyama City and the Seto inland sea.

Like T49, this temple also used to cover a very large space incorporating as many as 35 buildings.

The temple was founded by Gyoki, built on request by Emperor Koken (708-770). Kukai stayed here, but later the temple fell into disuse for about 300 years until it was restored under Minamoto no Yorimichi (988-1075).

The bell tower dates back to 1696 and has 24 beautiful paintings on its ceiling.

At this temple, people pray for success in exams and business.

The temple has many cherry blossom trees which make the visit particularly beautiful during Sakura season in march/April.

Temple No.51 – Ishite-ji 石手寺

Fascination	***
Translation	Temple of the Stone Hand
Main deity	Yakushi Nyorai
Founded in	Tempyo 1 (729) or in 670
Location	KM 776
Distance from last temple	2.7 km
Distance to next temple	11.1 km
Difficulty	Easy
Points of interest	Caves, stupa, museum
Okunoin	Ishizuchiji near KM 717 (between T43 and T44)

Finally, we have made it to the part of Matsuyama named Dogo Onsen, after the famous hot spring. Ishiteji is the next highlight on our pilgrimage. The second-largest temple area after T75 has everything it needs to be an attraction: It is near the city, it has a legend, it has a fascinating landscape, and it has plenty of places to explore.

The name takes us back once-again to the legend of Emon-Saburo (see T12 and B9). At this location, Emon Saburo is said to have been reborn as a child with a cramped, crippled hand. The hand one day opened and it held a stone which said "Emon Saburo reborn". The stone reappears as an element in many parts of the temple. But a sacred place was probably there much earlier, and if we look only at its natural environment, it occupies the space between the Ishite river and the hill behind it, with its caves which might have made it a perfect place for ascetic training.

In Sakuradani-cho, the area in which the hill is located, there are about 12 temples and shrines. Ishite-ji has had its name only since 813 or 892, having been founded in 728 or 729 or maybe even earlier, first named Annyo-ji. A leaflet, distributed in the temple, even dates its beginnings to 670 A.D. as some tiles from that period were discovered in an excavation.

The temple is a national treasure, the buildings we see today were mostly built about 700 years ago. It includes the following buildings and landmarks

- The main gate from 1318, which we reach after passing the tunnel with numerous souvenir shops.
- The main hall, across from the main gate, from the same period, which is considered a national treasure.
- The daishido is a little bit hidden to the right of the main hall, slightly back.
- The three-story-pagoda, in the center of the area, with a height of 24 m.
- The bell-tower with its bell, built in 1251.
- The caves behind the temples, which can be visited. One cave even opens to the back side of the rock where other temples containing 88 Jizo-statures can be visited as the path goes up the hill.
- The treasure museum on the east-side (the right side) of the area.
- Amida hall on the western side of the grounds.
- A smaller 5-story pagoda near the road.

If you decide to explore the hills, you may find

- A huge statue of Kobo-Daishi on top of a hill, reaching an altitude of 160 m
- A Burmese-style stupa, a landmark commemorating the victims of World War II

There is so much to see in this area that we should plan one to two hours for a visit. The grilled rice dumplings (omochi), the temple's signature food from the temple, used to be handed to the pilgrims for free.

You might consider to stay in Matsuyama for two, or maybe even three nights.

T51 – Ishiteji

石手寺

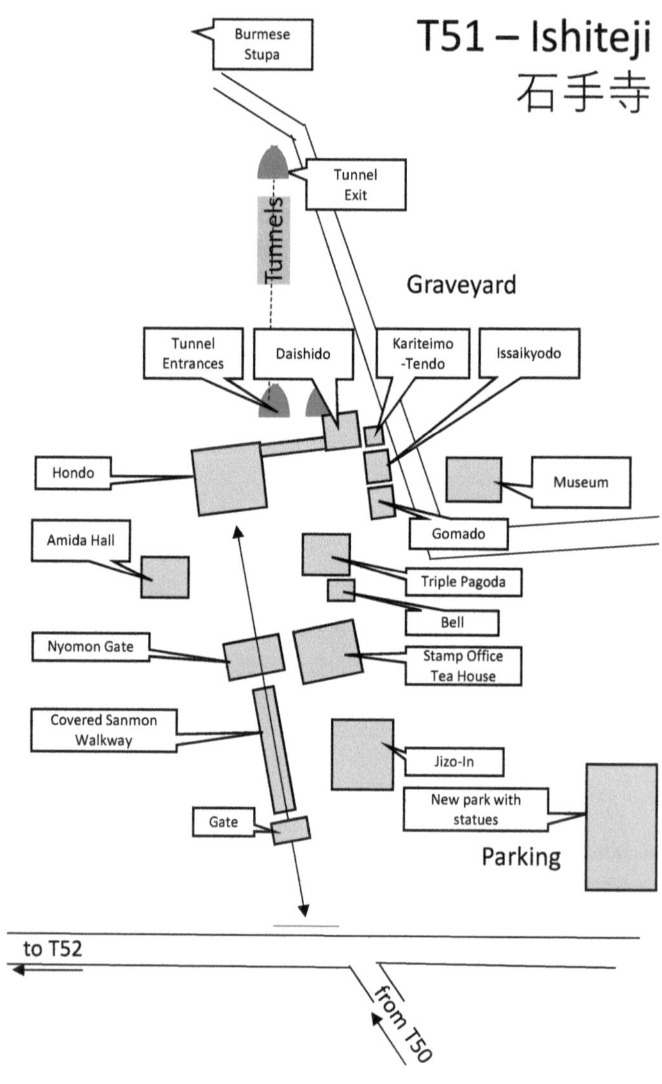

From T51 to T52 and T53 – KM 776 to 790

Fascination	**
Distance	14 km
Difficulty	Easy, mostly city walk
Public transportation	T51 is 1 km from the Matsuyama Streetcar line T52 is 2.2 km from Iyo-Wake train station Stopover in Matsuyama, T53 is near Iyo-Wake Station
Points of interest	KM 777 Gianji, Dogo Park **KM 787 T52** KM 789 **KM 790 T53**
Where to stay	Several options in Matsuyama

Historically, Matsuyama was a place where the pilgrims took a break to rest their tired bodies in the soothing waters of Dogo Onsen hot spring. The city also used to have some red-light areas, and there is a good reason why the pilgrims had the choice between staying in the city and avoiding its temptations by using the alternate route.

It is a short distance to T52 and T53, so we could continue for another 11 km to the village of Iyo-Hojo (KM 802), turning it into a day's hike, and enjoy the view on Kashima Island near the coast, a protected wildlife area.

As we leave from Ishite-ji and approach Dogo-Park, we pass a smaller temple with a cemetery on the roadside after 1 km. This one is called Gian-ji. In 1585, after losing a battle, the Kono-clan committed collective suicide at this temple by drinking poisoned water from the fountain, refusing to live under the new rulers. This is an important Bangai temple for pilgrims along the way. The fountain can still be visited.

The main pilgrimage route leaves Matsuyama along Highway 196. The route is mostly flat and almost leads us through the city at sea-level, but T52 is at 70 m altitude.

Temple No. 52 – Taisan-ji 太山寺

Fascination	***
Translation	Temple of the Big Hill
Main deity	Juichimen Kannon Bosatsu
Founded in	Yomei 2 (587)
Location	KM 787
Distance from last temple	11 km
Distance to next temple	2.7 km
Difficulty	About 0.8 km of climb at 9%
Points of interest	The 160kunoin Gate No. 2 The main hall
Okunoin	Kyogamori, top of the hill

According to legend, Taisanji was founded by a rich coal merchant named Mano Kogoro after he was saved in a storm. Having prayed to Kanon Bosatsu to save his life, he had this temple built to show his gratitude for surviving.

It may not seem so when we pass the first gate, but we have not arrived yet. From the first gate, in the village and at the foot of the hill, it is still 0.8 km up the hill. Gate 2, more impressive than the first one, follows after 200 m. The gate points in two directions and has guardians on both sides.

The main buildings are at an altitude of almost 70 m. The okunoin is 130 m higher on top of the hill, which means our way to the peak is another 500 m with a 26% climb. The peak displays a huge statue of Konzeon Bosatsu. The main hall is considered a national cultural property.

The temple once had 66 monk's cells. This is one of the oldest preserved temples buildings on the island, the main hall that we see today dates back to 1305. Women come here to pray to avoid conception.

Temple No. 53 – Enmyo-ji 圓明寺

Fascination	*
Translation	Temple of the Round Enlightenment
Main deity	Amida Nyorai
Founded in	Tempyo 1 (729)
Location	KM 790
Distance from last temple	2.7 km
Distance to next temple	34 km
Difficulty	Very easy
Points of interest	Virgin Mary statue Carved dragon at the upper right side of the hondo
Okunoin	Enmyoji (2 km northwest)

This temple is easy to reach, either by a flat, 40-minute walk from T52 or by train directly from Matsuyama to Iyo-Wake Station.

Coming from T52, its okunoin near the shore, bearing the same name, can be included in the walk. It is just a small detour of about 1 km. There is a reason why T53 and its okunoin have the same name, and why today T53 is in an unspectacular location: The okunoin near the beach was the original site of the main temple, but it moved to its current location in the 17th century. Before that, the temple served as official prayer temple for Emperor Shomu and Emperor Godaigo (The 96th Tenno, who lived from 1288-1339).

During the Edo period, when Christianism was prohibited, there were still many Christians in the area north of Matsuyama, as Christianism reached Japan from the west. Some of them secretly worshipped a statue located left of the Daishido depicting a Virgin Mary with her child.

From T53 to T54 – KM 790 to 824

Fascination	**
Distance	34 km
Elevation gain	100 m at Konosaka-slope, can be avoided
Difficulty	Long but easy walk along the coast
Public transportation	Train from Iyo-Wake to Onishi
Points of interest	KM 792 KM 793 Horie Station KM 795 Koyodai Station KM 800 Iyo-Hojo Station KM 801 Kashima Island, Yogo-In KM 804 Hut, Kama-Daishi KM 805 Asanami Station KM 812 Kikuma Station KM 814 Aoki Jizo, hut KM 815 Iyo-Kameoka Station, Enfukuji KM 818 KM 820 Onishi Stn., follow Route 196 KM 821 KM 823
Where to stay	KM 830 Several options in Imabari , e. g. Cyclo-no-ie near the station

This is a longer stage but with good infrastructure and some distraction. The first 10 km takes us along the coastal Route 347 until we get to Hojo, where we can explore Kashima Island, a nature resort just 200 m off the coast. The ferry runs several times a day. The island is just 300 x 400 m in size and has a camping ground.

Yogo-In, the Bangai Temple at KM 802, is said to keep Kukai's staff, sandals, and prayer beads.

In Hojo, we can choose whether we want to continue walking along the coast for 5 km or walk straight over the Konosaka slope (100 m altitude) which is the main route. It will be 1 km less but includes a short climb. Near the pass, we will pass another Bangai: Kama Daishi with Henro Goya Hut #27, which is a popular place for pilgrims to take a break.

At Asanami, the route touches the coastline again. Aoki-Jizo is a Bangai administered by Enfukuji or Enpukuji, located 1 km down the road.

The chemical installation dominating the landscape is a submerged natural gas tank and port. 7 km onwards, at Onishi, the route leaves the coast and takes a shortcut to the other side of the cape, to T54 and to Imabari. The detour via the cape would be about 15 km longer and the shortcut involves no major climb.

Among pilgrims, the northern capes of Shikoku are rarely discussed. While the southern capes, Cape Muroto and Cape Ashizuri, are mythical points along the pilgrimage due to their remoteness, reaching the northwestern cape of Shikoku is rarely reported or even mentioned and it does not even have a name. The pilgrimage route does not cover it but takes the shortcut, Google maps states no name for the cape, just for the beach. *Osumikaihin,* meaning the "beach of the big sea angle or corner". One would expect at least a Shinto shrine in a remote place like this, but that is not the case.

There are no shrines on the cape, but a series of temples coming up in Imabari: 6 temples over a distance of only 20 km. They can all be visited all in one day, but it would be too much of a distance including the climbs and the access to and from the hostel.

Imabari itself has about 150.000 inhabitants. This is thanks to its location next to one of the three huge bridges connecting Shikoku to the mainland, its port and fishing industry, and its production of premium towels dating back to the 19th century, when it was a place where high-quality cotton was grown here. Imabari is also a hub for cyclists heading for Shimanami Kaido, a cycling route connecting Shikoku with Honshu via several bridges and tiny islands. Imabari has a nice modern Onsen near the station named Kisuke-no-yado.

Temple No.54 – Enmei-ji 延命寺

Fascination	*
Translation	Temple of Long Life
Main deity	Fudo Myoo
Founded in	Yoro 4 (720)
Location	KM 824
Distance from last temple	34 km
Distance to next temple	3.7 km
Difficulty	Easy
Points of interest	Gate, bell, signpost from the 16th century
Okunoin	Chikami-yama (Chikamisan)

The original location of this temple was on the peak of Chikami-yama, roughly 2 km north of its current location. It was founded by Gyoki Bosatsu in the 8th century, fell into disuse shortly thereafter, and was revived by Kukai about 100 years later. Today, the mountain peak is merely a parking lot with a scenic point near the radio antenna and formally the location of its okunoin, as the temple was relocated to its present location in 1727.

Walking up the 2 km at 10% to the okunoin is worthwhile. We can look over the whole peninsula, the Shimanami-Kaido bridges, and the entire city of Imabari.

The temple gate, formerly an original gate from Imabari castle from the time before it was destroyed in the early Meiji era (19th century), is made entirely of zelkova-wood. The former temple must have been huge, with over 100 sanctuaries in the valleys and seven buildings at the main temple on the mountain peak. Today there are still 10-20 Shinto shrines, spread over the mountain on an area of 2-3 square km, that might have been part of this complex.

From T54 it is just a 3 km walk into the center of Imabari.

Temple No. 55 – Nankobo 南光坊

Fascination	**
Translation	Hall of the Southern Lights
Main deity	Daitsu-Chisho-Nyorai
Founded in	594 in Omishima Island
Location	KM 828
Distance from last temple	3.7 km
Distance to next temple	3.1 km
Difficulty	Easy
Okunoin	Oyamazumi Jinja

Initially a Shinto shrine, Nankobo does not have a -Ji at the end of its name, its main deity being a rare one (Daitsu-Chisho-Nyorai).

Its 165kunoin is also a Shinto shrine. It is not on a hill but in the middle of the city, and Koya-san has a branch office at the temple.

But there actually is a -ji, as the temple's full name is "Kōmyōji Kongō-in Nankō-bō". The temple also has a slightly confusing history. It was founded on Omishima Island, which is about 10 km north of Imabari, where it was a part of a group of about 20 temples, all ending in -bo, which refers to the hall of a monk's house. Later the temple was moved to its present location, destroyed and re-built several times. It still remains closely connected to Oyazumi shrine on Omishima Island.

The last destruction of the temple was caused by American air raids in 1945 at the end of WWII, aiming for the port (the bridge did not exist yet).

The buildings we see today were built between 1981 and 1991. So, in a way, this is at the same time one of the oldest and newest temples of Shikoku.

.

Temple No.56 – Taisan-ji 泰山寺

Fascination	*
Translation	Temple of the Sacred Mountain
Main deity	Jizo Bosatsu
Founded in	Konin 6 (815)
Location	KM 831
Distance from last temple	3.1 km
Distance to next temple	3.1 km
Difficulty	Easy
Points of interest	Tree of remembrance "Furo Matsu" Pine, planted by Kukai
Okunoin	Ryusenji

This modest temple is not even an hour's walk straight up the hill from Imabari. The name is derived from a temple of the same name in Shandong Province.

The temple area itself is rather small, but it is located in an area with other temples and shrines at the southwestern part of the hill, suggesting that this once used to be a larger array. Ryusenji, the Okunoin, is one of them, but if you take a closer look, there is also Okuma-ji, Midahachimangu, Ara-jinja, Mihoko-jinja and Mishima-jinja on top of the hill, where the long straight stairs lead to. Seven sacred places in a location of only 200 x 200 m.

When Kukai visited the area, the population was suffering from the effects of severe flooding of the Sojo river every rainy season. Kukai prayed here and memorialized the victims of the floods by planting a pine-tree dedicated to the deceased, and by building a prayer hall. Experienced in civil engineering, he also instructed the locals on building a levee to control the floods.

The temple Itself used to be the residence of Emperor Junna who reigned from 823 to 833, and the buildings were moved next to the sacred pine from the top of nearby Kinrinzan.

Women pray for relief from period pains at the nearby okunoin *Ryusen-ji*. T56 shares its area with four Shinto shrines.

Temple No. 57 – Eifuku-ji 栄福寺

Fascination	**
Translation	Temple of Fortune
Main deity	Amida Nyorai
Founded in	Konin era 810-824
Location	KM 834
Distance from last temple	3.1 km
Distance to next temple	2.5 km
Difficulty	Easy
Points of interest	The entire area including the Shinto Shrines
Okunoin	Iwashimizu Hachiman Jinja

It is just a 45-minute walk to T57, and on the way we pass the Henro Goya hut No. 41 at a place where a ferry used to cross the Soja river.

Eifukuji is yet another area where Buddhist temples and Shinto Shrines used to be united side by side, and a split was made during the Meiji era. In an area of about 300 x 300 m, we find Eifuku is situated between about a dozen of Shinto Shrines. The Shinto origin might be a reason why this temple does not have a gate.

Initially, this was a Shinto site called Iwashimizu Hachimangu with numerous temples and shrines. (Jojakuji, Ikanashi-Jinja, Iwashimizu Hachiman Jinja, Josabi, and others) The Shinto okunoin, today called Iwamizu Hachiman Jinja, offers a breathtaking view over the bay, which explains why this was a place where people prayed for safety at sea.

Temple No. 58 – Senyu-ji 仙遊寺

Fascination	**
Translation	Temple of the Mountain Ascetics
Main deity	Senju Kannon Bosatsu
Founded in	Around 680
Location	KM 836
Distance from last temple	2.5 km
Distance to next temple	6.2 km
Difficulty	2 km with a 10% climb at the end
Points of interest	Stupa View over Imabari and the sea
Okunoin	-

The next stage is one of the shortest. Short but steep. The path goes uphill, passing the Inuzuka reservoir, but the last 2 km are a painful 20% climb, if we follow the road uphill. If we take the shortcut across the first gate, it is shorter but even steeper. The temple is located 300 m from the peak of the mountain at 281 m altitude.

The temple was built over a timespan of 40 years by a hermit named Abo, who disappeared after its completion in 718. Kukai contributed the sacred well

The temple was destroyed and rebuilt in the Edo period and again, after a mountain fire, in the Meiji period by a monk named Yuren Shonin. A little stone stupa behind the hand wash basin, commemorates him. Yuren was the last person in Japan to pass away from "Sokushin Jubutsu", self-mummification[1], in 1871. Finally, the temple was rebuilt in 1947.

The temple itself is unspectacular but offers a beautiful view over Imabari and the Shimanami Kaido, and it has a guest house.

---

[1] Self-mummification is a process, where a person continues meditation under particular circumstances over several years, gradually eating and drinking less until death slowly sets in, but due to particular nutrition during that period, the body does not decompose after death

T58 Senyu-ji

Guesthouse
Path
400 m 25%
Sanmon
Gate
(alt. 180 m)
Toilet
Hondo
(alt. 280 m)
Daishido
Panorama
Bell
Mt
Sakurei
281 m

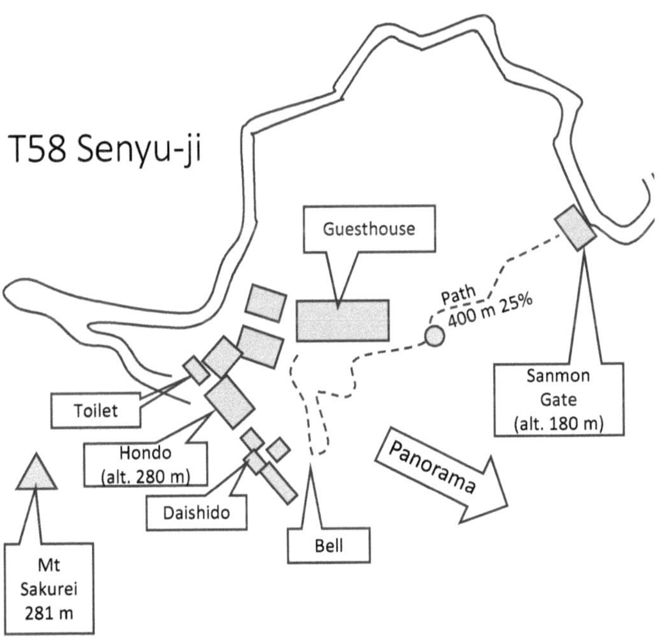

From T58 to T59 – KM 836 to KM 843

Fascination	*
Distance to	6.2 km
Elevation gain	Downhill and flat
Difficulty	Easy
Public transportation	Not available
Points of interest	KM 837 hut, choice of routes KM 840 Bakery 🛒 KM 841 🚂 Iyo Tomita Station KM 842 🛒
Where to stay	Guest House of T58 Imabari city (1 train stop or 5.3 km away)

Heading down to the coast again, it will take us only about 90 minutes to reach T59. After the first 500 m downhill, at the rest area that includes a hut, there is a wooden signpost where we have a choice between two routes of the same length:

- The main route that continues along the road and takes us straight downhill for another 2.5 km and then we turn right before the railroad tracks. There is a bakery and a Lawsons on the way, or …

- The alternative route that follows the wooden sign "国分寺 6.2 km" (Kokubunji 6.2 km) to the right. We head downhill into the forest. The forest path is 1.2 km, we then cross Route 155, which we follow to the right for another kilometer. This route offers an Udon restaurant and a Bangai: Chikurinji, founded by Gyoki Bosatsu in Tempyo 7 (755). For a visit, turn right when you get to the pedestrian crossing with the little bridge, it is 400 m away. If you turn left instead, and follow the river (which will flow on your right), you will pass a little Ramen restaurant after 800 m and reach the Udon restaurant after another 300 m.

Temple No.59 – (Iyo) Kokubun-ji 国分寺

Fascination	**
Translation	Iyo Provincial Temple
Main deity	Yakushi Nyorai
Founded in	Tempyo 13 (741)
Location	KM 843
Distance from last temple	6.2 km
Distance to next temple	27.9 km
Difficulty	Easy
Points of interest	Ruins, black vase

Iyo-Kokubunji is the last of the Imabari-temples and the official temple of Iyo (Ehime) Prefecture. It used to be much bigger, arranged as a Shichido-Garan (7-hall compound) when it was also the location of the Iyo government, and it was financially backed by several influential local families.

This temple too was founded by Gyoki Bosatsu upon request of Emperor Shomu. Its landmark was a 7-storied pagoda of an estimated 60 m height. After several destructions, it was rebuilt at its current locations in the 18th century. The impressive corner stones of the early buildings can still be seen on the former temple site 150 m to the east. Their size makes you wonder how such stones were handled during construction work 1,000 years ago.

The temple sadly burned down 4 times, but today's T59 still has something majestic. The oldest buildings seen today were built in 1789. The black vase next to Kukai statue can be touched when praying for relief from illness.

Fascination	***
Distance	27.9 km
Elevation gain	749 m
Difficulty	Difficult at the end (steep and long climb) Try to include a night in Nyugawa
Public transportation	For 7 km: 🚂 Iyo Sakurai Station to Iyo-Miyoshi Station (KM 854). T60 can also be reached easily by 🚌 from Iyo-Saijo Station (at KM 892, after T64) and shuttle bus.
Points of interest	KM 844 🛒 KM 845 🚂 Iyo-Sakurai Station KM 847 Yunoura Hot Spring 🍽 KM 849 ⛺ 🚻, follow Route 159 left under the expressway and over the rails KM 850 Bangai Sendanji 🚻 KM 854 🚂 Iyo-Miyoshi Station, Hut, 🚻 KM 855 2 km to Nuygawa. Higiri Daishi, KM 856 turn left 🛒 ⛩ Warei Jinja, detour to B10 KM 859 Detour to B11, 🛒 🚻 KM 862 🛒 O60 Myounji ⛩ KM 863 Komachi Onsen KM 865 Hut KM 869 Hut 🚻 end of paved section KM 870 Henro Korogashi (hard climb)
Where to stay	🛏 Henro House Oyado Sukeya 1 km from Nyugawa Station, several options in Nyugawa, 🛏 KM 881 Nojima House

This is one of the pilgrimage's most interesting stages. It takes us back into the mountains with some interesting things to see along the way: A major Bangai, B10, B11, an okunoin of T60, and one of the toughest climbs.

The stage itself could be done on one day, but with all the places to visit and the climb, we would end up in T60 at 750 m altitude in the late afternoon with no place to stay. It makes more sense to stay in Nyugawa, for one night. This would allow us to reach T60 after 16 km the next day around noon and to get off the mountain again in the afternoon to our accommodation for the night.

At any rate, the beginning of the stage is quite easy, basically following the railroad tracks and Route 196 for the first 6 km up to the blue road sign that points to the right for Miyoshi and Route 159. We follow Route 159, and after less than one km we reach a Bangai temple named Sendan-ji, sharing its ground with another temple called Seta Yakushi or Seta Kusushi. At the parking lot and the vending machine with the grey stone marker, we follow the little road that leads downhill to the left.

For the next 6 km, we should keep a close eye on our route guide to make sure we get to Warei Jinja situated at a crossing where we can choose to take the 4 km detour to B10, a beautiful mountain temple we should not miss. From here, it is about 10 km to go to T60. About 1.5 km after crossing the Nakayama-river on Route 147, we can pay a visit to Myoun-ji, the okunoin of T60, which shares its grounds with the four Shinto shrines on our right which come first.

We are now at KM 863 and the climb will get tougher with 9 km to go. We continue along Route 147 until the road suddenly ends 6 km later at a rest hut. From here, there is a marked path at the wooden sign post pointing to the left that says "No. 60 Yokomine-ji 2.2 km" in Japanese. 2.2 km is the good news, the bad news is that they include a 560 m climb, which means the average gain is 28%! The Route Guide recommends avoiding this part after rainfall as it might be slippery, so no wonder this is a "Henro Korogashi" place, a "place where the pilgrim collapses."

Evaluate your risks wisely, slipping and maybe breaking your ankle if you are the last person on this path at the end of the day, possibly alone, is not a nice situation to be in. Also the shortest way down from T60 is challenging and not recommended when wet. But reaching T60 at one of the highest points during the pilgrimage is an incredible experience.

Temple No. B10 – (Nishiyama-)Koryu-ji 興隆寺

Fascination	***
Translation	Temple of Prosperity
Main deity	Senju Kannon Bosatsu
Founded in	642
Location	4 km off KM 856
Detour	6 km
Difficulty	Easy but last 2 km have a 9% climb
Points of interest	Location, 3 storied pagoda

It would be a mistake not to visit T10. Like many Bekkaku temples, Koryuji is just as impressive as many of the 88 main temples.

As we approach it, passing a cemetery and enjoying an amazing panorama looking back, the last kilometer uphill has something magic, especially when we finally reach the red bridge to our left as the paved road ends. The temple is very quiet and surrounded by a beautiful aura, especially in autumn. The stamp office is in the administration building below the temple. This temple claims to keep a writing brush used by Kukai.

Temple No. B11 – Ikiki Jizo 生木地蔵

Fascination	*
Translation	Jizo of the Living Tree
Main deity	Ikki Jizo Bosatsu
Founded in	?
Location	1 km off KM 860
Detour	2 km
Difficulty	Easy
Points of interest	Camphor tree root

This temple became famous for a Jizo statue carved into a camphor tree root. After 1,000 years, the tree collapsed during a typhoon in 1939 and its root is now kept under a roof.

Temple No.60 – Yokomine-ji 横峰寺

Fascination	***
Translation	Temple of the Side Peak
Main deity	Dainichi Nyorai
Founded in	Hakuchi 3 (651)
Location	KM 871
Distance from last temple	27.9 km
Distance to next temple	9.8 km
Difficulty	Difficult, very steep
Points of interest	Rhododendron (from May)
Okunoin	Myounji (KM 862) Hoshigamori (above T60) Seirakuji (KM 881 near T62)

We are now approaching one of the highest areas of the pilgrimage: T60 is located at an altitude of 750 m at the foot of Mount Ishizuchi (1,921 m), the highest mountain of Shikoku and western Japan. The peak of Mt. Ishizuchi is only 6 km south of T60. We have only been higher up a few times so far: On our way to T12 (745 m), to T44 (790 m) and to T45 (785 m).

Due to its difficult approach, this temple is a Nansho Temple. The approach from Iyo-Saijo Station by bus is easier via the road, that was built only in 1984. Taking the public bus, we need to transfer to a smaller shuttle bus using the private road halfway up. The temple is not located on top of the mountain but slightly lower, protected in a steep valley, and approached from the top.

T60 used to be a sort of okunoin of Mount Ishizuchi, destroyed during the 19th century during the anti-Buddhist unrests and restored in 1909. On this occasion it was also granted its official status as temple No. 60 and given its name. This temple has a particular aura due to its location, position and the panoramic views. It is a combined temple and Shinto shrine, even with a Yamabushi tradition. Its okunoin Hoshigamori is another 300 m uphill on a mountain peak. From there, we can walk to O64 Okumaegamiji at Mt. Ishizuchi in about 5 hours, or even to the peak, which is spectacular, staying at its guest house.

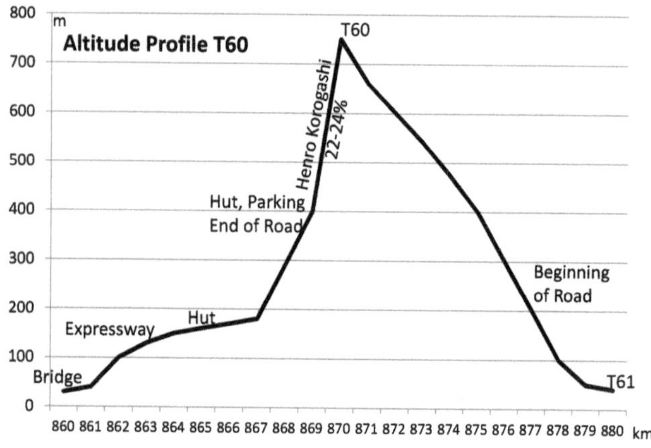

Altitude Profile T60
m
800
700
600
500
400
300
200
100
0
T60
Henro Korogashi
22-24%
Hut, Parking
End of Road
Beginning
of Road
Expressway
Hut
Bridge
T61
860 861 862 863 864 865 866 867 868 869 870 871 872 873 874 875 876 877 878 879 880 km

From T60 to T64 – KM 871 to 887

Fascination	***
Distance	16 km
Elevation gain	Descent and flat
Difficulty	First 7 km path downhill
Public transp.	🚌 from T60 to Iyo-Saijo, from there train to Iyo-Komatsu, 20 min. walking
Points of interest	KM 876 O61 Shirataki Waterfall meditation KM 879 Camping ground, rest hut **KM 880** ⛩ O61 Takagamo Jinja **T61 Koon-ji** KM 881🛒 O60 Seirakuji, 🛒 **KM 882 T62 Joju-ji,** 🚂 Iyo-Komatsu Stn. O62 ⛩ Ichinomiya Jinja 🛒 KM 883 🚂 Iyo-Himi Station 🛒 🚻 hut **KM 885 T63 Kichijo-ji** KM 885 O63 Shibanoi KM 886 O64 Ishizuchi-jinja **KM 887 T64 Maegami-ji** 🚂 Ishizuchiyama
Where to stay	🛏 KM 891 Several options in Iyo-Saijo

The direct path from T60 down to T61 is not recommended when it is wet. It is safer to walk along the toll road via Kurose dam and to T63.

After the challenge climbing up to T60, the next stage includes 10 km of downhill, the first 5 km leading on a path to O61 Shirataki, a place for waterfall meditation in a steep valley, and later on small roads. 2 km after O61 Shirataki, there is another rest hut at the edge of a water reservoir, and we walk another kilometer until we arrive at the grounds of T61 with its strange, 20th-century architecture. On the way, we pass a campground with a hot spring on the way, close to the expressway.

The following temples and okunoins are close. Between KM 880 and KM 887, we can visit four main temples and four okunoins over a distance of less than 7 km. Especially O64 Ishizuchijinja should not be missed. After T61, the infrastructure improves and there are several convenience stores. T62, T63 and T64 are located along the railroad and Route 11 within the next 6 km.

Temple No. 61 – Koon-ji 香園寺

Fascination	*
Translation	Temple of the Incense Garden
Main deity	Dainichi Nyorai
Founded in	6th Century
Location	KM 880
Distance from last temple	9.8 km
Distance to next temple	1.4 km
Difficulty	Easy
Okunoin	Takagamo Jinja (KM 880) Shirataki (KM 880)

Koonji was founded in the 6th century and is one of the oldest temples of the pilgrimage.

Most people are surprised and some are confused when they see T61 for the first time, facing a modern concrete hall with the dimension and shape of a suburban gymnasium. This hall is 16 m high and was completed in 1976, it functions as a Hondo and Daishido and can seat up to 620 people. Outside, to the right of the big hall, there are three smaller sanctuaries. The one on the left is dedicated to prince Shotoku, the founder of the temple.

This temple became very prosperous after it founded an association for safe child birth with 20,000 members. The entire infrastructure seems to be designed to manage large groups of visitors – its proximity to the highway and expressway, its large parking spaces for busses. This explains the big hall.

There used to be a booth at the parking lot, offering stamps for T62, since T62 is located in a cramped area without space for busses to park. Apparently, this was done without the consent of T62, because the stamp obtained at the T62 office is a different one. There was a conflict within the temple association about this for a while, but it was settled in 2019.

In 2024 the temples was building a new administration building with traditional architecture.

Temple No.62 – Hoju-ji 宝寿寺

Fascination	*
Translation	Temple of Wealth and Happiness
Main deity	Juichimen Kannon Bosatsu
Founded in	Between 729 and 749
Location	KM 883
Distance from last temple	1.4 km
Distance to next temple	1.5 km
Difficulty	Easy
Okunoin	Ichinomiya Jinja

After a 20-minute walk we get to T62, a small temple in a village, that for a while explicitly did not welcome bus pilgrims due to lack of space. On this walk we can visit to the okunoin of T60, Seirakuji.

T62 is another temple built on the request of Emperor Shomu. At first, this temple was located next to the Ichinomiya shrine of Iyo-prefecture, which means being the prime Shinto shrine of what is today Ehime prefecture, and its first location was 1 km north, near the Nakayama-river in a place called Shiratsubo. The temple was moved to its current — safer — location in 1145 as the old location turned out to be disastrous due to regular floodings of the river.

In 1679, the shrine was moved for the same reason, which explains the shrine's modest appearance in relation to its initial function. After several destructions across the centuries, Hojuji was finally rebuilt in 1887, but its entire grounds were moved by 100 m east when the railway was built in 1924, and later lost its southern part when the highway was built. While T61 prospered in the 20th century, T62 is now stuck between the highway and the railroad, a victim of modern times. Ichinomiya Jinja, now its okunoin, is located on the other side of the railroad and rarely visited. To cross the railroads, we can use an underpass east of the train station.

T62 was renovated in 2019 and it has vending machines for pilgrim souvenirs in the daishido.

Temple No.63 – Kichijo-ji 吉祥寺

Fascination	*
Translation	Temple of Lakshmi
Main deity	Bishamonten
Founded in	Between 810 and 824
Location	KM 883
Distance from last temple	1.5 km
Distance to next temple	3.4 km
Difficulty	Easy
Points of interest	Fulfillment stone Kiguri Kichijo (Statue Pass)
Okunoin	Shibanoi

Just like T62, also T63 is not at its original location. T63 was founded in the Konin era (810-824). Until 1585, this temple was located near Mount Sakamoto, roughly 3 km southeast of the current location, and it used to run a complex that included 21 buildings. Today, there are a number of Shinto shrines slightly north of Mt. Sakamoto, where the original temple might have been: About 1 km north of lake Kurose, about 3 km southeast of the current location. In 1585 the temple was destroyed and rebuilt in its present location in 1659, on the grounds of another temple called Sugiji.

This is the only temple devoted to Bishamon, one of the four heavenly kings. It is named after Kishijo-Ten, the Japanese name for Lakshmi, the Hindu goddess of wealth and fortune. Legend says that as early as 587, Bishamonten appeared to help prince Shotoku Taishi during a battle and saved him. Prince Shotoku Taishi, by the way, is pictured on the 10,000 yen bills. He said to be the founder of Japanese Buddhism, or, at least the earliest prominent supporter.

Like T53, T63 also has a Virgin Mary statue that was worshipped across the Edo period when Christianism was forbidden. This one was given to Chosokabe by a Spanish captain.

The okunoin, Shibanoi is on the other (south) side of the highway, only about 300 m from the main temple.

Temple No.64 – Maegami-ji 前神寺

Fascination	***
Translation	Front-God-Temple
Main deity	Amida Nyorai
Founded in	650-700
Location	KM 887
Distance from last temple	3.4 km
Distance to next temple	45 km
Difficulty	Easy
Points of interest	Torii gates when approaching, Gongendo (Shinto hall)
Okunoin	Ishizuchi Jinja, Okumaegamiji

The two huge Torii gates we pass 600 m and 300 m before reaching the sacred place already suggest that we are approaching a special location. But this is not the temple but Ishizuchi-jinja, an impressive shrine on the former temple area.

Mae-Gami-Ji literally means "Front-God(s)-Temple", a name carrying a very strong statement: Originally, this temple was located on the peak of its highest mountain, Mount Ishizuchi, which explains its Shugendo tradition. Later it was moved to the current shrine's location.

During the Meiji temple separation, that area was declared Shinto and the temple was relocated to T64's current location 500 m east, still symbolically very close to Mount Ishizuchi, about 6 km north of the sacred peak. The Shinto shrine on its former premises near the peak is now an okunoin of T64. Due to its status, this temple always had many supporters, starting with Emperor Ganmu who, after recovering from serious illness around the year 800, sponsored a massive temple expansion to a seven-hall complex (shichido garan). Subsequently, several other emperors used Maegamiji as a prayer temple.

This temple is also impressive due to its size. The entire area is about 300 m long. The complex includes the main hall (150 m behind the Daishido, so keep on walking), the wings of the main temple, a Yakushi hall, a Goma-hall and the Shinto Gongendo hall, slightly hidden on a little hill on the right side behind the main hall.

From T64 to T65 – KM 887 to 932

Fascination	**
Distance	45 km
Elevation gain	350 m, 250 m over 3 km at the end
Difficulty	Medium, long walk, easy climbs
Public transportation	🚂 JR Yosan from Ishizuchiyama to Iyo-Mishima, from there 6 km walk to T65 or 🚌 from Iyo-Mishima Stn. To Sankakuji-guchi, walk 2.2 km
Points of Interest:	KM 887 Lawson's 🛒 Yunotani Onsen KM 890 🛒 Bridge 🛒 🍽 KM 891 🚂🛏 Iyo-Saijo Stn., 🚌 to T60 and Mt. Ishizuchi KM 892 🛒 🍽 KM 893 hut KM 895 🛒 🍽 hut KM 900 🛒 🍽 KM 902 2 km to 🚂 Niihama Station 🛒 🍽 🚻 KM 903-906 🛒 🍽 on Route 11 KM 908 ↗ Shokaku-ji △ 160 m ↘ KM 914 B12 Enmeiji, hut KM 915 🚂 Iyo-Doi Station 🛒 KM 917 🛒 🚻 ⛩ KM 919 🛒 KM 922 🚂 Iyo-Sangawa Station 🛏 KM 927 🚂 Iyo-Mishima Station 🛒 🍽 🚻 🛏 Last store for 40 km KM 928 🛒 Supermarkets, beginning of climb ↗↗ KM 929 Togawa Park, hut 🚻 ↗↗ KM 932 △T65 351 m
Where to stay	🛏 KM 891 Several options in Iyo-Saijo 🛏 KM 922 Youth Hostel Shin Hasedera

On this last longer stage of the pilgrimage, we move from the north eastern to the north western part of Shikoku, more or less along the JR Yosan train line. There is plenty of infrastructure along the way, and near B12. But **pick up some food for the two days that will follow later!**

Temple No. B12 – Enmei-ji 延命寺

Fascination	*
Translation	Temple of Longevity
Main deity	Jizo Bosatsu
Founded in	Between 810 and 824
Location	KM 915
Detour	-
Points of interest	Pine trunk

The popular name of this Bekkaku is Izarimatsuji, "sit-pine-temple", referring to a legend that Kukai had planted a pine in this place. When he returned to this place, a handicapped man sat under the pine. Kukai was able to heal him by praying for him and handing him a piece of consecrated paper.

The huge trunk of the pine is still on the premises under a roof.

This is a tiny temple with just one building. The temple sends out consecrated paper to people who believe in its healing power.

Temple No.65 – Sankaku-ji 三角寺

Fascination	***
Translation	Triangle Temple
Main deity	Juichimen Kannon Bosatsu
Founded in	Tempyo era 729-749
Location	KM 932
Distance from last temple	45 km
Distance to next temple	19.3 km
Difficulty	3 km with a 10% climb
Points of interest	Old cedar trees, cherry blossoms, triangular pond
Okunoin	B13 Senryuji (3 km southwest)

As we have made it up the hill, out of breath after 3 km at 10%, we reach a temple area that has a truly majestic aura. The temple's name goes back to a triangular base for an altar, the *Bentendo* that can still be seen today in the little pond. The gate is a *Shoro-Mon*, a gate that includes a bell instead of having a separate bell-tower.

The temple's central object of worship is an eleven-faced Kanon-Bosatsu statue made of Hinoki wood during the Heian period, which is shown to the public only every 60 years. The last viewing was 1984, so the next time will be in 2044.

This is another temple that was destroyed by Chosokabe. The current main hall was built in 1849 and restored in 1971. Initially, this temple had 300 hectares (3 square km) of land. Like T64, the area is a shichido-garan, a 7-building complex, which in this case includes:
-	a special building to worship Yakushi (a healing Buddha),
-	the guesthouse
-	the Bentendo in the triangular pond
-	the residence of the local monks
-	the bell-gate
-	the Hondo and the Daishido

Temple No. B13 – Senryu-ji 仙龍寺

Fascination	**
Translation	Hermit Dragon Temple
Main deity	Kukai
Founded in	815
Detour	4.4 km from T65/KM 932 to B13 6 km from B13 to KM 936 The detour to B13 is 5 km longer than the direct route
Difficulty	Difficult
Points of interest	Cave

B13, which is at also an okunoin of T65, is one of the less visited temples. The 7 km the detour does not sound like a major effort, but if we take a look at the topography, well shown in the Shikoku 88 Route Guide, we can see that visiting B13 after T65 involves major climbs:

- The 4.4 km from T65 to B3 include 430 m of elevation gain, the Route Guide indicates this part will take 2h 10.
- The 5.1 km back from B3 to KM 936 on the main route have another 270 m of elevation gain

It means the entire detour of 9.5 km has about 600 m of elevation gains, the entire detour will take about 5 hours including the temple visit.

The reward is a most unusual, beautiful temple, a cave temple hidden deep in a valley, with Kukai himself as a main deity. The temple is a beautiful, ancient, carved wooden building hidden at the edge of a mountain. The main hall is a cave.

There is a Henro House (Mori-so) at KM 938, so T65 and B13 can be done on one day if leaving from Iyo-Mishima. That would be a 20 km hike with 800 m elevation gain, more than enough for one day. Another possibility would be to stay at the Henro House for 2 nights and visit B13 on the extra day.

There is a spot for waterfall meditation, Kyotaki, 200 m west of B13.

From T65 to T66 – KM 932 to 951

Fascination	**
Distance	19.3 km
Elevation gain	550 m
Difficulty	Partly difficult, no food
Public transp.	Not available
Points of interest	KM 932 T65 △alt. 351 m ↘ KM 937 crossing (see map), 2 huts KM 939 B14 Jofukuji alt. 225 m KM 941 Henro-goya hut no. 37 KM 942 🚌 Hichida Bus stop KM 943 Sakaime Tunnel △ alt. 314 m entering Kagawa Pref. KM 946 🚻 Route 8, alternative route KM 947 🚌 🍽 Unpenji-guchi alt. 282 m ↗↗ KM 949 alt. 680 m ↗↗ KM 950 alt. 800 m ↗↗ **KM 951 T 66** △ alt. 911 m
Where to stay	🛏 KM 938 Henro House Mori-so 🛏 KM 946 Minshuku Okada

This is another special stage: We are entering the last prefecture, Kagawa, after the first 10 km. And we will hit the highest point of the pilgrimage, T66, which is at 911 m. **Take enough food** with you since there is no shop on the way.

The first 7 km will lead us along a ridge with a smooth descent and occasional panoramic views over Shikoku-Chuo to our left. At KM 937, where we cross Route 5, we need to be sure to stay on the correct road, the road with the rest hut, public toilet and parking on the right. 750 m further, there is another good rest hut on our right called Yukikobo, run by a local company that produces Yakuniku barbecue tables. Just after visiting B14, we reach Route 192, which we will follow for 7 km to a blue sign showing "Kanonji Route 8 to the left".

The **main route** would take us across the village, underneath the expressway (KM 947) and then we would need to find the path going steep uphill until we reach the crest road. There is a ramen restaurant at Unpenji-guchi bus stop. It is difficult to find and very steep, but shorter (6 km from Route 8 crossing). The **easier, alternative route** is 10 km, paved and easy to find: At the traffic light of KM 946, we turn left, follow Route 8 for 5.4 km (the green road in the Shikoku 88 Route Guide Map No. 79, middle), through Manda tunnel. Right after the tunnel, we take the smaller road (the crest road) to the right for 11.6 km until we arrive at T66.

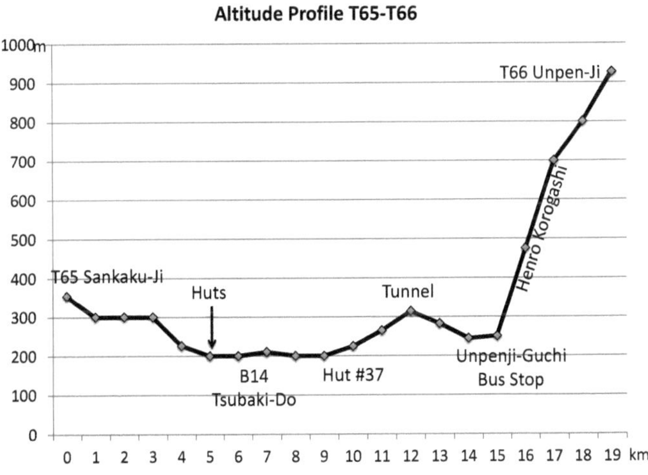

The Crossing at KM 937

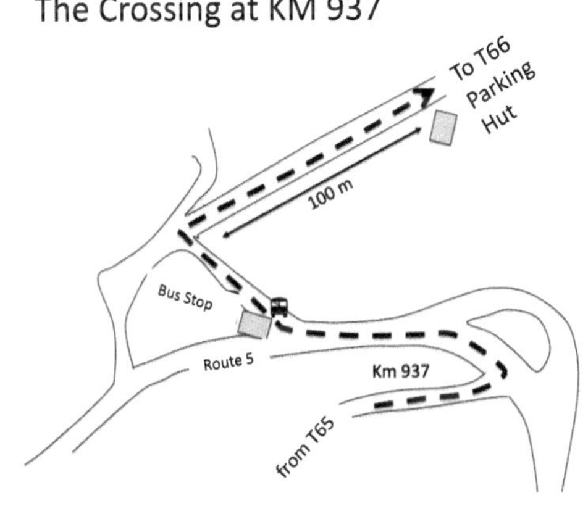

Temple No. B14 – (Tsubakido) Jofuku-ji 椿堂常福寺

Fascination	*
Translation	Camelia Sanctuary
Main deity	Enmei Jizo Bosatsu
Founded in	unknown
Detour	-
Difficulty	easy

This is a tiny temple situated along the main route on a slope above the highway. The temple is small, but the family who runs it is very kind to pilgrims.

Temple No. B15 – Hashikura-ji 箸蔵寺

Fascination	***
Translation	Chopstick Temple
Main deity	Kompira Dai Gongen
Founded in	828
Detour	29 km
Difficulty	1 km at 40% (400 m elevation gain), ropeway available
Points of interest	Stairway, Trees, Panorama

Hashikuraji is a beautiful temple with some elements of Shinto and Shugendo.

It can be reached by continuing along Route 192 at KM 947 across Awa-Ikeda and 4 km further along the north side of the river. The temple is situated 400 m above Hashikura Station.

There is a ropeway for those not wishing to climb the 1 km at 40%, it is 1,540 yen round trip. Visiting this temple on foot will add a one-day detour, and it is possible to get there by train from T75 (JR Dosan line to Hashikura Station). There are several places to stay in Awa-Ikeda.

Temple No.66 – Unpen-ji 雲辺寺

Fascination	**
Translation	Temple of Hovering Clouds
Main deity	Senju Kannon Bosatsu
Founded in	807
Location	KM 951
Distance from last temple	45 km
Distance to next temple	9.9 km
Difficulty	Very difficult
Points of interest	500 Rakan statues, panorama
Okunoin	B16 Hagiwaraji (6.5 km)

The temple is listed as a temple of Kagawa prefecture but, actually , it is located on the south side of the peak, which geographically is Tokushima prefecture. The crest trail, which we have walked for the last 2 km, marks the prefectural border.

We are now at the highest point of the pilgrimage: 912 m. Temple B20, by the way, is at almost the same altitude. Unpenji has suffered the same fate as many other temples along the pilgrimage. Enshrined by Kukai, destroyed by Chosokabe in the 16th century, fallen into disuse. The temple can also be accessed by Ropeway. In the 20th century, after the ropeway was built, the temple began to do very well thanks to the many visitors. It was renovated in the 1990s.

The temple grounds are decorated with 500 recently-built Rakan statues (followers of Buddha), some of them humorously shaped with funny faces. The temple is beautifully located with an amazing view, but, due to its young age, lacks patina.

If you intend to avoid the tough climb to T66, you can also take the ropeway. As an overseas visitor you will get 50% discount.

From T66 to T67 – KM 951 to 961

Fascination	**
Walking Distance	9.9 km, 13.9 km via B16, 6.3 km from the bottom ropeway station
Difficulty	Medium (downhill) but unpaved, no food
Public transportation	Not available
Points of interest	KM 952 Peak, Antenna, turn left ↘ KM 957 Taniguchi 🚌 🚻 KM 959 Iwanabe pond, hut, 🚻 ⛩ (1.5 km to 🛒)
Where to stay	🛏 KM 963 Minshuku Shikokuji

Now we are really entering Sanuki = Kagawa-prefecture. The route continues for one km on the mountain peak until we reach the antenna. Here, it splits and we can follow the path either to T67 via B16 Hagiwaraji or the direct route to T67. The detour via Hagiwaraji is 4 km or 90 minutes longer, which includes the temple visit:

-    T66 – 7.5 km – B16 – 6.4 km – T67, or
-    T66 – 9.9 km – T67

The entire section is downhill. On this stage, we enter Kagawa (Sanuki) prefecture, symbolically the prefecture of Nirvana.

Temple No. B16 – Hagiwaraji 萩原寺

Fascination	*
Translation	Bush Clover Plain Temple
Main deity	Jizo Bosatsu
Founded in	806-809
Detour	4 km
Difficulty	Easy
Points of interest	Bush clover products

Hagiwaraji shares its location with two other temples: Hagi-An and Jizo-In, the latter being the oldest site of the three. The temples are located between several ponds at the foot of the hills.

Products made from bush clover are sold in the shop, which also serves as a stamp office

Temple No.67 – Daiko-ji 大興寺

Fascination	**
Translation	Temple of Great Prosperity
Main deity	Yakushi Nyorai
Founded in	742
Location	KM 961
Distance from last temple	9.9 km
Distance to next temple	8.8 km
Difficulty	Easy
Points of interest	Nyomon Guardians

This majestic temple, located in a grove, was founded in 742, rebuilt by Kukai by imperial decree in 823, destroyed by Motochika, aroud 1596. The main hall was finally rebuilt after almost 150 years in 1741. The long stairway from the east (appr. 50 m) was completed in 1789. This temple has a history involving two sects simultaneously, Shingon and Tendai.

Formerly the temple had over 30 buildings. Some of its wooden statues are considered cultural heritage, especially a seated Yakushi Nyorai statue 84 cm tall, made of Hinoki wood, carved by Kukai himself. The two majestic Deva statues at the gates are the largest ones in Shikoku, measuring 314 cm in height. They were made in 1274 by the famous artist Unkei. This temple has two exceptional buildings: The Tendai-Daishido, on the right side of the Hondo is dedicated to Tendai-Buddhism and there are two Shinto shrines under a roof dedicated to the saints of Kumano.

From T67 to T68 and T69 – KM 961 to 970

Fascination	*
Distance	8.8 km
Difficulty	Easy
Public transportation	🚌 from Kanonji to Mukai Shinden, walk 1.5 km
Points of interest	KM 963 Udon 🍜 500 m east KM 970 Kanonji Station and city
Where to stay	🛏 KM 969 Several options in Kanonji

Easy 2.5-hour walk straight into Kanonji city.

Fascination	***
Translation	Temple of God's Mercy Temple of Kannon
Main deity	Amida Nyorai and Sho-Kannon Bosatsu
Founded in	Taiho 3 (703)
Location	KM 970
Distance from last temple	8.8 km
Distance to next temple	4.6 km
Difficulty approaching	Easy
Points of interest	2 temples, garden, coin, park
Okunoin	O68 Kotohiki Hachimangu

These two temples share a common area at the foot of Mount Kotobiki, which is situated at the mouth of the Saita river. Today, the south side of the hill is the Shinto area, while the north and the northeastern side became Buddhist. The entire hill is sacred ground as there are no less than 15 Shinto shrines in the area.

Kotohiki Hachimangu, the shrine on top of the hill, is the okunoin of T68 but it used to be the original temple location. In the Edo period, the temples were ranked differently: T69 was an official pilgrimage temple, while T68 was just an okunoin of Kotohiki Hachimangu. This was reversed in the temple separation of the Meiji-era in 1872 and both temples had to share common ground. T69 is historically the more important temple in the current spot and contributes more buildings to the ensemble. The current main hall of T69 was built in a traditional style in 1959, while T68 has a modern main hall built in 2003. It is said that Kukai himself was the 7th head priest of T69. A new office was built in 2022.

One hour should be included to visit the coastal park and the hill with the okunoin, which offers an amazing view of the "big coin": a sand sculpture named Zenigata Sunae, which, when viewed from higher above the hill, creates an illusion of being round while it is actually oval. The sculpture was made in the 16th century, its diameter is 80 to 120 m, and the area, blocked for the public, is regularly maintained and the coin re-carved.

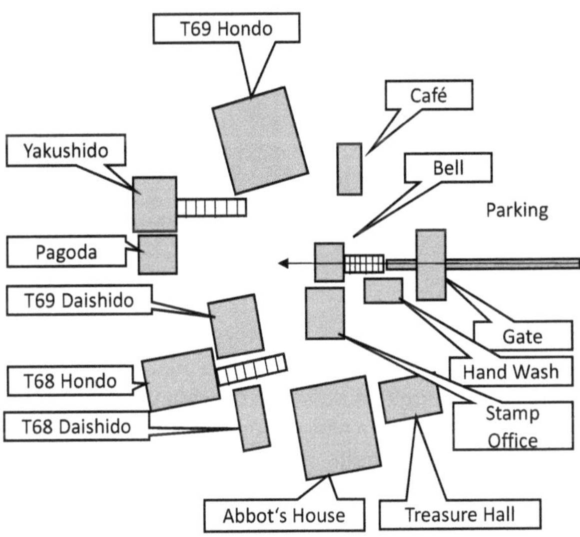

From T69 to T70 – KM 971 to KM 975

Fascination	*
Walking Distance	4.5 Km
Difficulty	Easy and short walk along a river
Public transportation	Possible, but would only save 2 km
Points of interest	KM 972 Udon
Where to stay	KM 969 Several options in Kanonji, e.g., Fujikawa Ryokan

From T60 to T70 it is just a one-hour walk along the Saita-river.

One possibility to organize this part of the pilgrimage is to stay in the town of Kanonji for two consecutive nights, visiting T69, T69, the coin, and Kotohiki park in the morning, walk to T70 in the afternoon, and return to the city by train to continue the next morning from Kannonji or T70 to T71.

Temple No. 70 – Motoyama-ji 本山寺

Fascination	**
Translation	Temple of the Main Mountain
Main deity	Bato (Horsehead) Kannon Bosatsu
Founded in	807
Location	KM 975
Distance from last temple	4.5 km
Distance to next temple	11.6 km
Difficulty approaching	Easy
Points of interest	5-story Pagoda
Okunoin	Myoonji (KM 976) Koryuji (3 km north)

Motoyama-ji's location is unspectacular, but the temple is impressive through its number of buildings. It was founded by Kukai. The Hondo is a national treasure built in 1300, one of the oldest surviving temple buildings in Shikoku. The 5-story pagoda was built with private funds from 1894 to 1913. In Shikoku, there are only four other temples with 5-storied pagodas: T31 Chikurinji, T86 Shidoji, T75 Zentsuji and Honen-ji near Takamatsu. During in 2019, there was a funding initiative to rebuild the pagoda, constructions were ongoing in 2023.

The main gate is not located opposite the main hall, which is unusual. There is a memorial hall dedicated to about 8000 Japanese citizens, who died in Manchurian war in the 1930's. The two large buildings on the north side, to the right after entering the main gate, are the abbey and the guesthouse. The little Chinju-do just left of the gate was built in 1547 and has a roof made of cypress bark.

This temple was not destroyed, but used by Chosokabe as a headquarter, unlike its okunoin *Myoonji,* just 1 km further along the route, which was destroyed in 1575 and was rebuilt only recently.

T70 has another okunoin, Koyuji, located 2.5 km north-east on the other side of the railway line (1 km west of Hijidai Station), a deserted place where ruins and old stone grave markers are still left and can be visited in the forest.

From T70 to T71 – KM 975 to KM 986

Fascination	*
Walking Distance	11.6 km (1/2 day)
Elevation gain	150 m climb at the end
Difficulty	Easy 3-hour walk
Public transportation	JR Yosan Line from Motoyama to Tsushimanomiya, 5 stations and a 3.3 km walk at the end
Points of interest	KM 976 Sushi, O70 Myoonji KM 977 Udon KM 981 Takase Station KM 985
Where to stay	KM 983 Shippo-ya KM 996 Several options in Zentsuji

An easy walk without much to see along Route 11, as we approach the next group of temples, but the last km includes a 12% climb.

Temple No. B18 – Kaigan-ji 海岸寺

Fascination	**
Translation	Seaside Temple
Main deity	Sho Kannon Bosatsu
Founded in	774
Detour	The total distance between T71 and T72 including B18 is 8.8 km
Difficulty	Easy
Points of interest	Kaiganji Daishido hill

Kaiganji is related to Kukai's childhood, as he grew up nearby. It is also considered an okunoin of T75. Formerly, this temple had 49 buildings. Kaiganji might have been worshipped as the sacred place where the Hirota river flows into the sea.

B18 is Bekkaku temple with an Okunoin: The pagoda on the little hill on the other side of the railroad named Kaiganji Daishido. Take a walk up the hill, the place has a certain magic.

The Mairi Path (T71-77), Kotohira, B17 and B18

With T71, we reach the next group of temples. We will visit seven temples spread over a distance of only 16 km around the city of Marugame. It is worthwhile to stay near Zentsuji or near T75 or 76 for at least two nights, visiting T71-T77 on one day and B18, Kotohira and maybe B17 on the next day. Also, plenty of time should be included for T75, Shikoku's largest temple.

This route from T71 to T77, is called the Mairi Path. Many people walk it in the other direction, from T77 to T71 to worship the dead.

Should you try to walk the entire Mairi Path in one day, be sure to be on your way at 7 a.m. visiting the last temple before 5 p.m. when the office closes. Assuming you have stayed in Marugame or Tentsuji and you start at T77, your day will be filled with a 16 km walk and seven temples. Here is an agenda which allows 30 minutes per temple, time for lunch, moderate speed, and reaching the last temple before 5 p.m.:

07:00	T77
07:30	Walk 4.1 km
08:30	T76
09:00	Walk 3.7 km
10:00	T75
11:00	Walk 1.8 km
11:30	T74
12:00	Udon lunch nearby
12:30	Walk 2 km
13:00	T73
13:30	Walk 1 km
14:00	T72
14:30	Walk 3.6 km
16:00	T71

Temple No. 71 – Iyadani-ji 弥谷寺

Fascination	***
Translation	Temple of Eight Valleys
Main deity	Senju Kannon Bosatsu
Founded in	Around 724
Location	KM 986
Distance from last temple	11.7 km
Distance to next temple	3.6 km
Difficulty approaching	Steep climb, followed by over 400 steps
Points of interest	Shishi no Iwaya (Cave) Rock engravings View over Sanuki plain

The old name of this temple was Yakuni-Dera, temple of eight countries, as eight provinces could be seen from the top of Mount Iyadani. Like T10, T27 and T45 (remember?), T71 is another temple of staircases, and a "vertical temple" built up a rock. The entire mountain is considered a sacred site and listed as one of the three largest sacred sites of Japan. Even the water flowing down from the mountain is considered sacred.

After reaching the gate, we need to climb another 400 steps until we reach the main part of the temple. At this temple, we are allowed to enter and cross the main hall in order to reach the sacred cave where Kukai meditated. This cave is a place with a particular ambience and should not be missed.

The other parts of the temple are reached by climbing the other staircases. There are more caves and numerous carvings in the rock, which, from a particular angle, has the shape of a lion. In addition to the regular temple buildings, this one also has a treasure pagoda, a tea house and a Juodo (Ten Kings' Hall). People come to this temple to be cured from walking disabilities and to pray for the dead.

When planning your day, make sure to reach the temple gate before 4 pm to enjoy visiting the premises with enough time.

Temple No.72 – Mandara-ji 曼荼羅寺

Fascination	**
Translation	Mandala Temple
Main deity	Dainichi Nyorai
Founded in	596
Location	KM 989
Distance from last temple	3.6 km
Distance to next temple	0.6 km
Difficulty approaching	Easy
Points of interest	Ceiling of the main hall

Getting to T72 barely takes an hour. On the way, near the pond on our left, we will pass a Bangai temple named Shichibutsu Yakushi, almost hidden, with the exception of a little stone statue under a metal roof. According to the legend, this statue was carved by Kukai.

At first glance, Mandaraji does not display anything unusual, especially not after the impressions we have carried along from T71, but this pretty little temple is the oldest of the 88 temples.

Mandaraji was the temple of Kukai's family, the Saeki-clan. Until 807, the temple's name was Yosakaji (temple of the four slopes), but upon his return from China, Kukai added new buildings and enshrined mandalas he had brought, and renamed the temple to its present name.

The temple used to have a huge pine-tree, planted by Kobi Daishi, which had a diameter of 17-18 m and a height of only 4 m. Due to its umbrella-like shape like two sedge-hats, it was called Kasamatsu ("umbrella pine"). The pine was eventually badly damaged by pine worms and cut down in 2002. A sitting Kukai statue was carved into the trunk, and the statue is now kept in the temple.

In the middle-ages, this temple had a much larger area, comparable to the size of T75.

Temple No.73 – Shusshaka-ji 出釈迦寺

Fascination	*
Translation	Shaka Nyorai Appearance Temple
Main deity	Shaka Nyorai
Founded in	Between 710 and 800
Location	KM 990
Distance from last temple	0.6 km
Distance to next temple	2.7 km
Difficulty approaching	Easy, but 500 m with a 10% climb at the end
Points of interest	O73 Shashingatake Zenjo
Okunoin	Shashingadake Zenjo

Apart from T68 and T69, which share the same area, the distance between T72 and T73 is the shortest distance between two temples on our pilgrimage. Shusshakaji is located at the foot of Mount Gahaishi.

From the temple, its okunoin Sashingadake Senjo, can be seen on the mountain over 300 m above. If you would like to have a closer look, the climb is very steep but short: 1.4 km at over 20%.

The okunoin clearly plays the more important role here, suggesting that T73 was mainly intended as a hub at the bottom of the hill to look at the okunoin. With its peak at 481 m altitude, Mount Gahaishi is the highest mountain near Kukai's home.

There is a legend that, as a boy, Kukai jumped from the cliff, ready to throw away his life unless he would be saved by Shaka Nyorai so that he would survive to save many other people.

A separate stamp is available at T73 for visiting the okunoin.

Temple No.74 – Koyama-ji 甲山寺

Fascination	**
Translation	Helmet-Mountain Temple
Main deity	Yakushi Nyorai
Founded in	Early Heian, about 800
Location	KM 993
Distance from last temple	2.7 km
Distance to next temple	1.8 km
Difficulty approaching	Easy
Points of interest	Bishamonten Cave

This small temple was founded by Kukai and financed using some of the funds available after Manno-Ike Reservoir had been repaired under Kukai's supervision. Apparently, he had known the cave since his childhood days and built the temple after encountering a hermit who promised to take care of the temple if it was built. To build the temple, Kukai used funds left from the budget he had received to build the Manno reservoir. (See B17)

The name of the temple refers to the helmet-shaped hill of the same name behind it. One third of the hill has already disappeared, converted into construction material by the nearby quarry, but T74 is a well-kept beautiful little location with palm trees and the Bishamondo built 12 m into the cave.

Although it is not old, not large and even located next to the quarry's concrete factory, this temple has its own particular beauty.

The little Udon shop, located nearby on the way to T75, is the perfect place for a lunch break. It is run by an elderly couple and decorated with pictures of sumo wrestlers.

Temple No.75 – Zentsu-ji 善通寺

Fascination	***
Translation	Temple of the Correct Way
Main deity	Yakushi Nyorai
Founded in	Daido 2 (807)
Location	KM 996
Distance from last temple	1.7 km
Distance to next temple	3.7 km
Difficulty approaching	Easy
Points of interest	Kaidan Meguri darkness walk, 5-story pagoda, camphor tree
Okunoin	B18 Kaiganji

Zentsu-ji, at 45,000 sqm, is clearly the largest and most important temple in Shikoku. Together with Kyoto's To-ji and Koya-san, the three temples are considered "the three major temples of Kobo". This temple deserves a longer stay. It is split into an eastern and a western part and is best visited from east to west, entering from the eastern gate. The two areas were considered separate temples during the Edo period and were combined only in the Meiji-era 1868.

To-in, the eastern sanctuary, also named Garan, used to be an area next to the Saeki (Kukai's family) residence. Upon his return from China in 807, Kukai built this temple on a piece of land given to him by his father, next to his family home, and named it after his father. This part includes:
- Three gates: the red gate on the east side, the main gate on the south side, built after the Russo-Japanese war, and the central gate on the west side, leading over to the western area.
- The main hall, built in 1699. The Yakushi-Nyorai statue inside is over 3 m tall
- The hexagonal sutra-store
- The bell-tower (built 1958)
- The 5-story pagoda (45 m tall, completed in 1902)
- Two camphor trees said to be over 1000 years old
- Several smaller temple buildings

- 3 stone stupas in the southeastern corner commemorating three important priests

Sai-in, the western part, is also named Tanjo-in (birth-sanctuary) although possibly Kukai may have been born near B18. The temple was built during the Kamakura period (13th century) on the grounds where the Saeki home used to stand.

We can enter it coming from the eastern part or from the parking lot with the souvenir store in the west.

The Miedo is the central temple in the area, built on the very location of the Saeki family home. Other points of interest on the west side include
- The Kaidan Meguri (a 1completely unlit tunnel, which can be visited)
- The treasure building
- The abbey and its guesthouse on the south side
- An assembly hall and several smaller sanctuaries on the north side
- A Burmese pagoda commemorating the victims of WWII in Burma

Finally, we can leave the area on the west side across a little bridge named Saisei-bashi, "bridge saving the world" which leads over the trench to the large parking lot.

Some recommended accomodations in Zentsu-ji near T75:
- KM 993 Henro House Tsurukichi (1.4 km from T74)
- KM 995 Iroha (guesthouse of T75)
- KM 997 Kaze-no-kuguro
- KM 997 Henro-House Olive (Women only)
- KM 999 Micasa Sucasa next to Konzoji Train Station
There are also some business hotels near Zentsuji Station

T75 – Zentsu-ji 善通寺
Western Part (Sai-in)

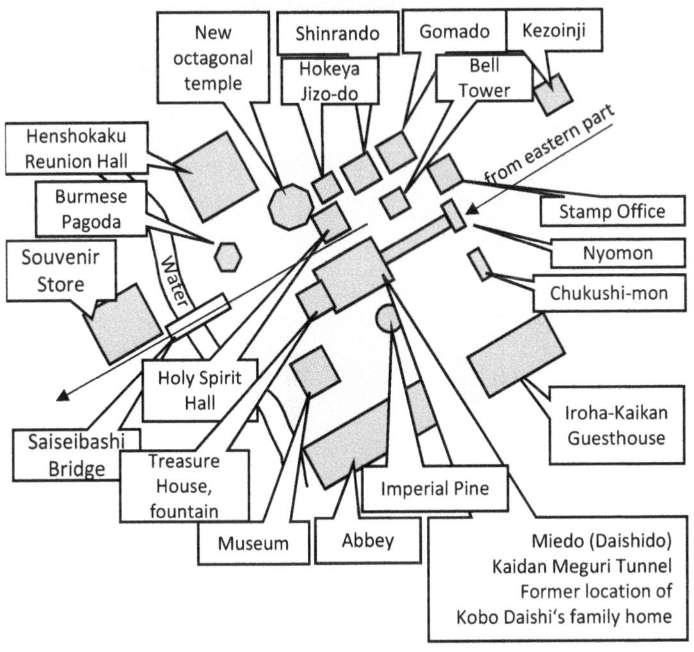

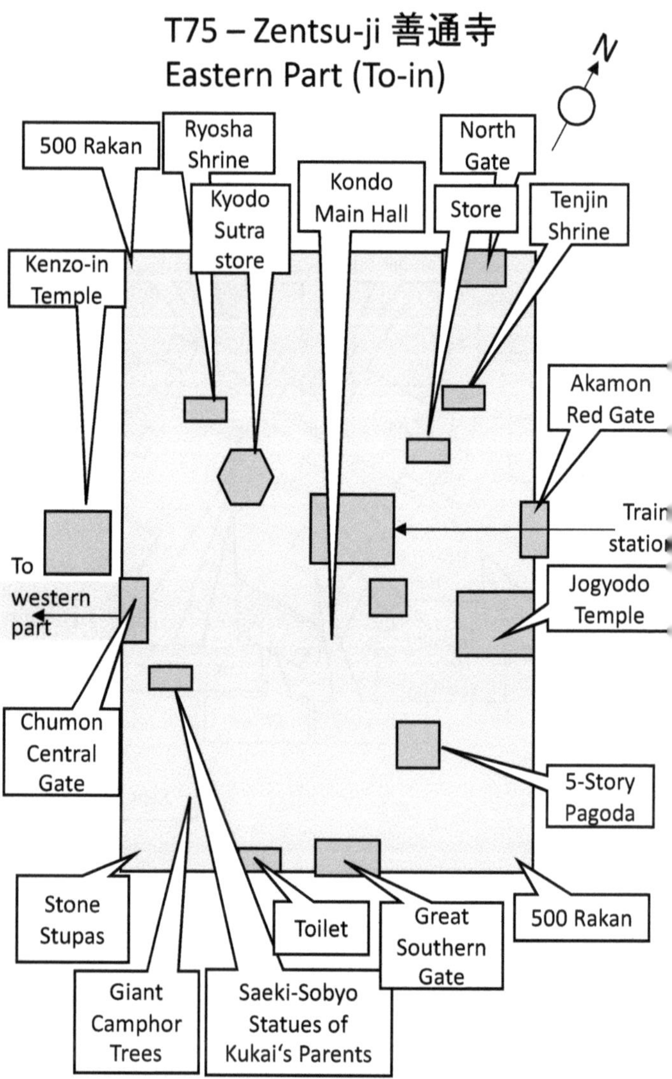

T75 – Zentsu-ji 善通寺
Eastern Part (To-in)
N
500 Rakan
Ryosha Shrine
Kyodo Sutra store
Kondo Main Hall
North Gate
Store
Tenjin Shrine
Kenzo-in Temple
Akamon Red Gate
Train station
Jogyodo Temple
To western part
Chumon Central Gate
5-Story Pagoda
Stone Stupas
Toilet
Great Southern Gate
500 Rakan
Giant Camphor Trees
Saeki-Sobyo Statues of Kukai's Parents

Kotohira 琴平

Kotohira is a city located 6 km south of T75. It is famous for *Kotohiragu*, a major Shinto shrine located on a mountain above the city. Here people pray for the safety at sea, which explains why the shrine is decorated with boats and boat parts of various sizes. The detour is strongly recommended.

For centuries, it was common practice by Henro to include a visit to Kotohiragu. Walking up the many stairsteps from the city to the shrine is a memorable experience, and there are several dozens of smaller shrines on the hill. The peak with the main shrine offers a fantastic view over the plains of Kagawa all the way to the Seto Inland Sea. The city is very popular with Japanese tourists. It can easily be reached by train from Zentsuji (one stop on the Dosan Line but trains run only a few times a day) or from Takamatsu (Kotoden Kotohira Line).

B17 Kannoji 神野寺 (Jinnoji)

Fascination	*
Translation	Temple of the Field of the Gods
Main deity	Yakushi Nyorai
Founded in	Konin 12 (821)
Detour	26 km
Approaching on foot	Relatively easy
Points of interest	Manno-Ike

From Kotohira, it is another 90-minute flat walk of 6 km to Manno-Ike and B17. However, doing the entire detour to Kotohiragu and B17 on foot in one day might be a bit too much. Kanno-ji is a tiny temple located at the shore of Manno-Ike, an ancient reservoir once rebuilt by Kukai providing the area and its rice fields with a reliable water quantity (see T74). It was once Japan's largest reservoir. Like T84, Kanno-ji was built by Kukai as a guardian temple for the lake, but it was burned down in 1582 and fell into disuse. Finally, in 1934 a private initiative called the "Manno Daishi Group" had it rebuilt.

B17 is a 30-minute walk from Shiori Station on the Dosan-line, which can also take us to B15 and Awa-Ikeda.

Temple No.76 – Konzoji 金倉寺

Fascination	**
Translation	Temple of the Golden Warehouse
Main deity	Yakushi Nyorai
Founded in	774
Location	KM 999
Distance from last temple	3.7 km
Distance to next temple	4.1 km
Difficulty approaching	Easy
Points of interest	Exhibition about General Nogi

As we continue our walk along the temples of the Mairi path, T76 is just a one-hour walk from T75. But we are moving from a popular, busy place to a rather quiet, medium-sized temple.

Konzoji is the birthplace of Kobo-Daishi's nephew Chisho Daishi, the founder of the Tendai sect.

In the 9th century, the temple grounds measured 32 square km and included over 100 buildings. Originally named Dozenji after its founder, the temple was renamed in 928.

This temple was the residence of General Nogi (1849-1912). Nogi had been governor of Taiwan and acted as an important mentor of young emperor Hirohito. He had led the occupation of Port Arthur (Dalian) during the Russo-Japanese war in 1904-05. Nogi had been successful in his military career, supporting the imperial troops during the uprise of samurai clans in the Satsuma rebellion, but was later blamed for some unfortunate decisions in the Russo-Japanese war, during which although successful, he had lost both of his sons. The battle of Port Arthur had caused almost 60.000 casualties in the Japanese army. Nogi spent the rest of his life in deep regret for the casualties on both sides. He and his wife eventually ended their lives by Seppuku when emperor Meiji passed away. General Nogi and his wife are worshipped in the temple.

There is a popular Udon restaurant just outside the temple.

Temple No.77 – Doryuji 道隆寺

Fascination	*
Translation	Temple of the Appearing Path
Main deity	Yakushi Nyorai
Founded in	Wado 5 (712) or 807
Location	KM 1003
Distance from last temple	4.1 km
Distance to next temple	7.4 km
Difficulty approaching	Easy

T77, the last (or — if visiting in reverse order — the first) of the Mairi temples is another example of a smaller temple with a greater past.

Located in an unspectacular location by the roadside, the temple is memorable for its 255 Kannon statues. Formerly, mulberry trees grew in this area and silk was produced. The temple became an imperial temple. This temple once had 23 buildings, but the complex was gradually destroyed by an earthquake in the Jigen-era (976-978) which led to a collapse of its pagoda, and by several fires, earthquakes and battles including a destruction by Chosokabe Motochika.

Apart from the regular buildings, there is also a 2-story treasure pagoda which was only finished in 1985 and a hall dedicated to an ophthalmologist named Kyogoku Samanosuke.

The red Torii gates lead to a small Shinto shrine where the spirit of the north star is worshipped.

There is a pilgrimage shop with a larger next to the temple gate.

From T77 to T79 – KM 1003 to KM 1016

Fascination	*
Walking Distance	13 km
Difficulty	Easy
Public transportation	Train from Tadotsu to Utazu (T78) and Yasoba (T79)
Points of interest	KM 1003 🛒 KM 1004 🍽 KM 1005 🛒 KM 1006 🚂 Marugame Station 🛒 🚻 Hut, Museum, Castle KM 1008 🍽 🛒 KM 1009 🛒 🚻 🍽 ⛩ Hut 🚂 Utazu Station **KM 1010 T78 Gosho-ji** KM 1011 🚻 🍽 Hut KM 1013 🚂 Sakaide Station 🛒 Kamada Museum 🚻 KM 1014 Hut KM 1015 Yasoba-no-mizu **KM 1016 T79 Tenno-ji** 🚂 Yasoba Station
Where to stay	🛏 KM 999 Micasa Sucasa 🛏 KM 1006 Several Options in Marugame

This is an almost straight walk along Route 33, across Tadotsu, Marugame Utazu and Sakaide, through suburban infrastructure with plenty of convenience shops and restaurants along the way.

Utazu is a connecting point to Japan's main island Honshu. The trains coming from Okayama have their first stop in Shikoku in Utazu and Sakaide Interchange is the first expressway exit on the island when coming over Seto bridge from the north.

At KM 1013 we will pass Kamada Museum which inspired novelist Haruki Murakami for his book "Kafka on the Shore". The building, a library in the book, is actually a museum of local history built by the neighboring Kamada Soy Sauce Company, one of the oldest in Japan.

Temple No.78 – Gosho-ji 郷照寺

Fascination	**
Translation	Temple of the Pure Land (Paradise)
Main deity	Amida Nyorai
Founded in	Jinki 2 (725)
Location	KM 1010
Distance from last temple	7.3 km
Distance to next temple	6.1 km
Difficulty approaching	Easy
Points of interest	30,000 Kannon statues Painted ceilings, panorama over Seto Inland Sea

The temple, built in Utazu on the foot of Mount Aonoyama, offers a splendid view over the city of Sakaide and Seto Bridge.

It is built on a series of plateaus connected by stairways. In Utazu, on the flatland between Mt. Aonoyama and the Daisoku river, there are about 20 sacred places in an area of only one square km.

This temple was founded by Gyoki Bosatsu and turned into an important location for the founding of other Buddhist sects: Jishu Buddhism was founded here by Ippen Shonin in 1288 and this is the only temple among the 88 that is run by the Jishu Sect.

At first called Dojoji, the temple was also destroyed in the 16th century but soon rebuilt, completed in 1664 and renamed to Goshoji.

Next to the Daishido a tunnel displaying 10.000 miniature Honzon figures made of bronze can be visited, they were donated by different parts of Japan.

The Koshin-hall displays a statue of blue-faced 6-armed Shomen-Kongo, which stands for good health.

Temple No.79- Tenno-ji 天皇寺

Fascination	***
Translation	Emperor Temple
Main deity	Juichimen Kannon Bosatsu
Founded in	between 757 and 767
Location	KM 1016
Distance from last temple	6.1 km
Distance to next temple	6.8 km
Difficulty approaching	Easy
Points of interest	Shiraminegi Shinto Shrine Triple Torii Gate Yasoba no Mizu (KM 1015)
Okunoin	Shiraminegu next to T79 Rurikoji on the hill Fudonotaki Manishoin 1 km

The 6 km walk to T79 along the Yosan railway line through the city of Sakaide is easily done in 1.5 hours. Where Highway 33 meets the railway line, we need to cross the railway towards the hill. After another 500 m, we reach a most unusual sacred place: Over a stretch of about 200 m, we are passing a complex of T79 with two of its okunoins (Shiramine-gu and Ruriko-ji) and a Bangai (Yasoba-no-mizu) to discover. Just like T78, this temple was founded by Gyoki Bosatsu under the name of Manishuin, it later it fell into disuse and was renovated by Kukai in the 9th century.

The name "Emperor Temple" refers to the story of Emperor Sutoku, who had fled from Kyoto after a struggle to maintain his power against other elements of the imperial family during the Hogen-rebellion. He arrived in 1156, using Tenno-ji as his residence in exile, but died in 1164. His body was preserved in the nearby pond (Yasoba no mizu, the pond with the little tea house we have passed as we approached the temple.) until orders came from Kyoto on how to deal with his corpse. He was finally buried 6 km east, on the mountain near T81at KM 1029.

The area is a beautiful combination of Shinto shrine and Buddhist temple. Visit the entire area, and have some tea and traditional sweets in the pavillon at the little pond.

Takamatsu 高松

It is time to plan our last week, the days during which we will visit the last 9 temples - T80 to T88 and maybe B19 or even B20. B19 is conveniently located in the western part of Takamatsu, but B20 is very remote, way up in the mountains at 910 m altitude, the same as T66.

The purist approach, of course, would be to walk, stay on the route, walk, etc. A different option would be to stay in the same place in Takamatsu for several days and walk to several temples every day, carrying only lighter luggage for the day and to return to our accommodation at night using public transportation.

Takamatsu is a modern city of 419.000 inhabitants. It has always been an important hub to mainland Japan and to the smaller islands in the Seto Inland Sea. On July 3rd, 1945, the city was burned down by the U.S. Air Force, which dropped 800 tons of incendiary bombs destroying nearly 80% of the city.

Today, Takamatsu is an interesting city with some nice backpacker accommodations. A plan to complete our pilgrimage, with four or five nights in Takamatsu, might look like this:
Day 1: T80-T81-T82 and B19, continue to Takamatsu by bus
Day 2: T83 - T84 - T85, return to Takamatsu by train
Day 3: T86-T87-T88, return to Takamatsu by bus and train
Day 4: Ritsurin Gardens, city stroll
Day 5: Return to T1 and Tokushima

Takamatsu also has some other interesting places to visit: Ritsurin Gardens, 6 km north of T83, is one of Japan's most beautiful gardens, Shikoku Mura, near T84, is a nice open-air museum and Takamatsu also offers a connection by ship to the islands of Naoshima and Shodoshima: Naoshima is famous for its Ando architecture museum, while Shodoshima has an amazing 88-temple pilgrimage of its own which takes about 2 weeks.

Altitude Profile T80 - T82

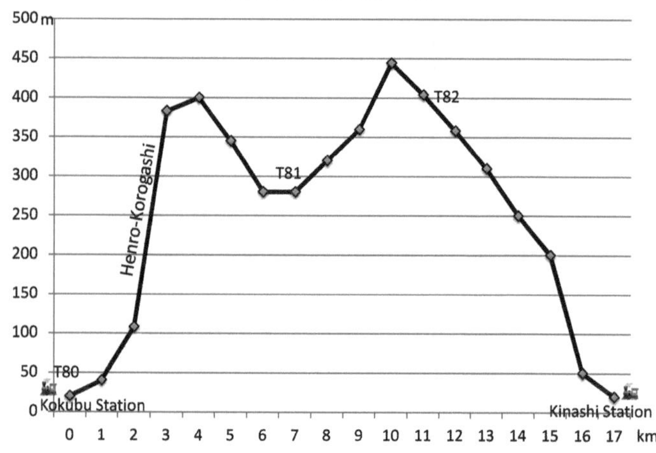

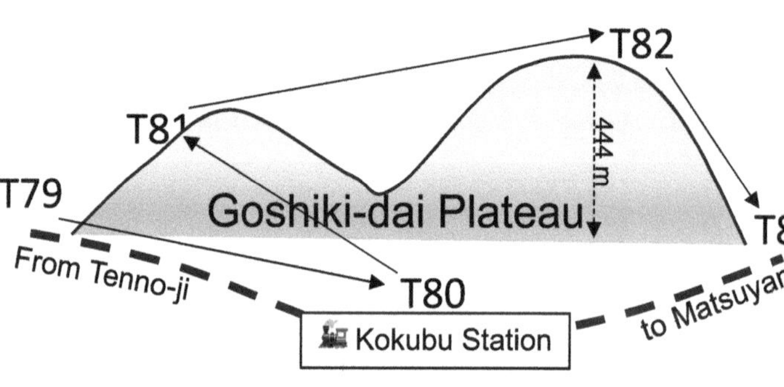

From T79 to T80 – KM 1016 to KM 1023

Fascination	**
Walking Distance	6.7 km
Difficulty	Easy
Public transportation	🚂 from Yasoba to Kokubu on Yosan line (2 stops)
Points of interest	KM 1016 🚂 Yasoba Station KM 1017 🛒 🚻 KM 1019 🛒 🚂 Kamogawa Station KM 1020 🍜 Udon KM 1023 🍜 🚂 Kokubu Station
Where to stay	🛏 KM 1016 Henro House Yasoba 🛏 KM 1024 Azusa

The route of this stage connects T79 Tennoji with the first temple on foot of the colorful Goshikidai Plateau. T80 is at the bottom, 300 m lower near the Kokubu train station. The common route is a simple, flat walk of about 2 hours to T80 Kokubunji.

We can visit the temples in their numerical order, but remembering emperor Sutoku (see T79), we can also follow an alternate route which first takes us from T79 directly to Emperor Sutoku's grave close to T81, then we can continue to T82 and return to T80 at the foot of the mountain. The distance from T79 to the emperor's grave is 6.3 km.

Temple No.80 – Kokubun-ji 國分寺

Fascination	**
Translation	(Sanuki) Prefectural Temple
Main deity	Juichimen Senju Kanon Bosatsu
Founded in	741
Location	KM 1023
Distance from last temple	6.8 km
Distance to next temple	6.7 km
Difficulty approaching	Easy
Points of interest	Kondo Ruins, 88 Nyorai statues along the path, bell, miniature model

Founded by Gyoki Bosatsu, T80 is the prefectural temple of Sanuki prefecture (Today Kagawa). This is the only temple in Shikoku where the entire area is considered a national historic treasure. If we enter from the south side, we walk 140 m across the temple grounds along the sando towards the main hall passing a number of smaller temple elements, which is impressive.

This temple also has Shikoku's oldest temple bell, which — together with the main hall— is classified as a cultural treasure. The main hall was built in the Kamakura period (1185-1333). The statue of the main deity is only on display every 60 years, the next time will be in 2040.

The Daishido also functions as a temple office and souvenir and equipment shop.

The actual temple space is large, appr. 200 x 200 m. Behind the temple there is a large open space with a scale model of the former buildings. We can visit ruins on the temple grounds, which highlight the temple's former importance, including the cornerstones and foundation of a 7-story pagoda that was higher than the pagoda of Toji-Temple in Kyoto.

Take the time to visit the entire premises.

From T80 to T81 – KM 1023 to KM 1029

Fascination	***
Walking Distance	6.6 km (about 2.5 hours)
Elevation gain	330 m
Difficulty	Steep, 1 km with 20%, climb, no food
Public transportation	Not available
Points of interest	KM 1025 ↗↗ Hut 🛖 Henro Korogashi KM 1026 ↗↗ Route 180, turn left KM 1028 turn right onto trail, then left KM 1029 O81 Bishamon-kutsu, cemetery
Where to stay	🛏 KM 1023 3 hostels near T80, Takamatsu (by train)

This beautiful and exciting stage takes us up onto *Goshikidai*, the "plateau of five colors". If you walk the plateau in spring or fall, you will be impressed by the colorful leaves everywhere. The entire 330 m climb occurs over the first 3 km, a quick and hard climb, on paths and steps. It takes about 1.5 hours and includes another Henro-Korogashi site which will challenge our endurance yet again. But if you take it slow and enjoy the views from the climb, you will manage. It is tough but not long.

Finally, we (breathlessly) reach Route 180, turn left, and follow the road for 2 km. We could actually follow it for another 2 km and arrive at T81, but after 1 m you can turn right and reach a parallel route which is the more mystic path through the woods. After passing some military buildings, we pass the okunoin, a very old stone pagoda, and an abandoned cemetery.

We will return along this path later when we will continue from T81 to T82. The stone pagoda was intended as an indicator for upcoming sacred ground, so people arriving on horses or in carriages would have been required to continue on foot to show their respect after this point.

There are no stores, vending machines or restaurants on this stretch, so bring your own food and drinks.

Temple No 81 – Shiromine-ji 白峯寺

Fascination	***
Translation	Temple of the White Peak
Main deity	Senju Kannon Bosatsu
Founded in	815
Location	KM 1029
Distance from last temple	6.7 km
Distance to next temple	5.3 km
Difficulty approaching	Easy, once you are on the plateau
Points of interest	Waterfall, Emperor's Sutoku's grave, Zodiac animals Imperial gate (Chugamon)
Okunoin	Bishamon Kutsu KM 1029

As we move on, the temples become more and more beautiful. The two temples on the Goshikidai plateau are amazing, and so is the landscape. The plateau gets its name "5 colors" from the colors that five of the peaks have in different seasons: white, yellow, blue, red and black. T81 is the temple of the white peak.

The waterfall might have been the earliest sacred spot in this array. To get there and to the emperor's grave - see T79 - follow the unpaved path behind the red and white fence near the temple's parking lot. The sad story of Emperor Sutoku has become popular culture, with rumors he had been killed. The ghost of the emperor even made it into Manga, restlessly seeking justice and vengeance since centuries.

The temple itself is large but spread over several terraces across the forest. The two 13-story stone pagodas, built in 1278 and 1324, are only about 2 m tall but considered national treasures. The main gate (Sanmon), built in 1803, is unusual because of its side-wings. The temple has a number of extra halls and an additional "Imperial" gate. It also represents the twelve animals of the Chinese zodiac.

This temple area is one of the largest along the route, though formerly the temple was formerly much larger and had even more buildings.

T81 – Shiromineji
白峯寺

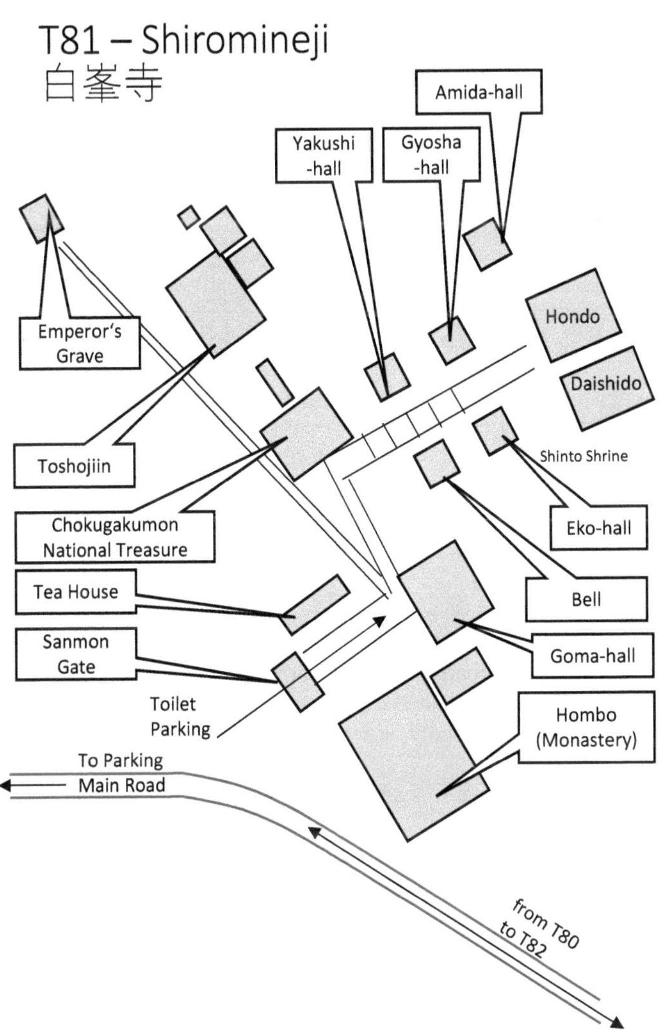

From T81 to T82 – KM 1029 to KM 1034

Fascination	***
Walking Distance	5 km
Elevation gain	175 m (several ups and downs)
Difficulty	Short but hilly walk across the forest
Public transportation	Not available
Points of interest	KM 1030 ⛩O81 Bishamon Kutsu ↗
	KM 1033 ⛩△444 m ↗↗↘↗
	KM 1034 huts 🍽 🚻
Where to stay	🛏 KM 1034 Henro House Kappa

This is a mystic and beautiful walk, basically from the white peak (Shiromine) to the blue peak (Aomine). It will take us about two hours to walk across the forest on the historic Sanuki Henro Trail. The first 2 km take us back the way we came, passing the old stone pagoda and the okunoin O81. The trail offers some beautiful views of the 5-color plateau to our left with plenty of ups and downs.

After another 3 km along the trail and ending in a 10% climb, we reach the road at a Shinto shrine Turning left, where we also find an udon restaurant and a rest hut. The restaurant is modest and run by a friendly, elderly lady.

From the shrine, it is another 1 km with a 10% descent to T82.

Should the forest path be blocked, for instance due to wild boars or heavy rains, it is also possible to walk the entire stretch along Road 180, which is about 2 km longer but offers an easier surface to walk on.

Temple No.82 – Negoro-ji 根香寺

Fascination	***
Translation	Temple of the Fragrant Root
Main deity	Senju Kannon Bosatsu
Founded in	Konin era 810-824
Location	KM 1034
Distance from last temple	5.3 km
Distance to next temple	12.4 km
Difficulty approaching	Easy
Points of interest	33000 Kannon statues Godaimyodo (5 holy kings) 1600-year zelkova tree stump
Okunoin	Jubuji (3 km south of T80)

T82 is located on the blue peak, surrounded by maple trees and cherry-blossoms. Kukai founded a temple in this location named Kazoin or Hanazoin. His nephew Chisho Daishi founded another one nearby called Senjuin or Sendenin, both were unified later as Negoroji, another beautiful temple.

We enter the temple through its Nyomon and walk along a series of stairways for about 100 m until we reach the central part. The main hall is in a central square which is framed by a series of corridors containing 33,000 metal Kannon statues donated by pilgrims. One of the highlights is a wooden carving of 5 holy kings. The temple also displays the stump of a 1600-year-old zelkova tree root that died in 1975 and probably gave the temple its name.

At the parking lot we see a statue of an Ushi-Oni (Bull-Devil) referring to an old legend of an ogre who once lived on the hill and was killed by a famous archer who shot an arrow into its mouth

There are two comfortable free sleeping huts nearby with water and electricity, the hexagonal is open for all and the other one for women only. If you are finished with T82 before 3:30 p.m., you might continue 5 km downhill to B19 and still get your stamp.

From T82 to T83 – KM 1034 to KM 1047

Fascination	**
Distance	12.4 km
Elevation gain	50 m in the beginning, the rest is a descent, later flat
Difficulty	Easy
Public transportation	Not available
Points of interest	KM 1034 beginning of detour to B19 KM 1035-1039 mm KM 1040 Kinashi Station end of detour to B19, bridge over Honzu river KM 1041 Iwata Jinja, hut KM 1043 hut KM 1045 KM 1046 Henro Goya Hut No. 24
Where to stay	Guest House Soraumi near T83

On our next stage, we leave the colorful peaks of Goshikidai and head down to the plain in which Takamatsu is located.

For the regular way directly to T83, we first return the way we came for 300 m, we then continue left, following the road downhill, where we will enjoy amazing views over Seto Inland Sea from our altitude of 300-400 m, reaching the railroad near Kinashi Station after about 5 km.

We need to pay attention zig-zagging our way across the suburban areas, but stickers are posted reliably, and even in case we get off the main pilgrimage route, it is quite easy to find the way if we remember the rough direction.

If we decide to include B19, we need to take a different route to the north-east from T82. The total detour is about 3 km and returns to the main route just south of Kinashi Station (there is a stone pagoda and some graves, take the path LEFT of the stone pagoda).

Temple No. B19 – Kozai-ji 香西寺

Fascination	**
Translation	Western Scent Temple
Main deity	Enmei Jizo Bosatsu
Founded in	739
Detour/Location	5 km downhill from T82 in the western part of Takamatsu. If we include the detour to B19 on the way from T82 to T83, the stage gets only 2.5 km longer
Difficulty approaching	Easy
Points of interest	Jizo Statues

The walk to B19 can be included in the stage from T82 to T83, making the stage about 2.5 km longer to total 15 km instead of 12 km. This is a convenient alternative, as we have done enough walking by now. We can stay in Takamatsu for several nights and visit T83, B19, T84, T85 and T86 in two or three days, which would allow us to include Ritsurin Gardens, or simply to give our tired legs a rest.

For those of us who prefer using public transportation, B19 can be reached by bus from Takamatsu Station to Kozai-Kitamachi.

This charming little temple was founded by Gyoki Bosatsu. It is located on the outskirts of Takamatsu at the foot of the Goshikidai Plateau on the location of the city's former western watchtower.

Temple No.83 – Ichinomiya-ji 一宮寺

Fascination	**
Translation	Temple of the First (Prefectural) Shrine
Main deity	Sho Kanzeon Bosatsu
Founded in	Between 701 and 704
Location	KM 1047
Distance from last temple	12.4 km
Distance to next temple	13.5 km
Difficulty approaching	Easy
Points of interest	Tamura Jinja Shrine O83
Okunoin	Tamura Jinja

There is no public transportation from T82, but T83 is easily reached by train from Takamatsu Station on Koden Kotohira line. We get off at Ichinomiya Station and walking another 500 m.

The temple was founded by Gien and given the name of Daihoin. A few years later, Gyoki restored the temple and gave it its present name. The temple was destroyed by Chosokabe Motochika and the current Hondo rebuilt in 1701.

A temple named after a Shinto shrine? Unlike many other cases, where temples and shrines share the same grounds, this one was NOT divided in the Meiji era, but actually a shrine and a temple were split during the Edo era in the 17th century.

The temple is beautiful, but the shrine part, Tamura Jinja, which also is its okunoin, next to it, is the more interesting place, being the prefecture's prime shrine, and four times larger. It is recommended ti include at least 1 hour to visit the entire premises. People come here for weddings, to get a blessing for their car, and there is an Udon shop on the premises.

The site has numerous smaller shrines, a Sumo ring and a walk with many Torii gates.

From T83 to T 84 – KM 1047 to KM 1060

Fascination	*
Distance	13.5 km
Elevation gain	280 m
Difficulty	Flat, but very steep at the end: 1.5 km/16%
Public transportation	Kotoden Shido line from Ichinomiya to Kawaramachi, transfer to Kotoden Kotohira Line, continue to Kotoden-Yashima.
Points of interest	KM 1048 KM 1050 Sushi, Hut, turn right KM 1051 Sanjo Station KM 1051-1055 Walk along Gobo river KM 1055 turn right, bridge, follow Route 11 KM 1057 Turn left, Katamoto Station KM 1058 ↗ Hut Shikoku-mura KM 1059 ↗↗ Henjoin, hut, Bangai temples
Where to stay	KM 1053 Several options in Takamatsu

Just after the start, we can include a 5 km loop to *Honenji*, a major temple 2.5 km south-east of T83. This one is an unclassified (Bangai) temple. Despite being unnumbered, it is an impressive location with a 5-story pagoda and a sleeping Buddha.

On this stage, we will approach Takamatsu from the south. The stage is split into: 7 km north towards the city, along route 172 and Gobo-river and 6 km leaving the city to the east along Highway 11.

Shikoku-Mura is a nice open-air museum displaying traditional buildings, and I recommend its excellent traditional noodle shop. There is no risk of going hungry on this stage which has plenty of restaurants and convenient stores along the way, but this stage is busy and noisy for 10 km until we pass Katamoto Station and face the Yashima plateau. On the way up, we pass 3 Bangai temples.

Temple No.84 – Yashima-ji 屋島寺

Fascination	**
Translation	Roof Island Temple
Main deity	Juichimen Senju Kanon Bosatsu
Founded in	754 and 815
Location	KM 1060
Distance from last temple	13.5 km
Distance to next temple	5.5 km
Difficulty approaching	Very steep last 2 km, paved
Points of interest	Yashima Plateau Panorama Treasure Museum

On the northeast coast of Takamatsu city there are two landmark hills: Yashima and Mount Goken. Both have temples on top. Yashima actually means "Roof Island", the term "Island" referring to this area being formerly disconnected from the mainland. There used to be a narrow stretch of sea where today we find the railroad. T84 is situated on the southern peak of the Yashima plateau, 286 m above Takamatsu. Apart from the temple, there are several souvenir shops, panoramic points, two premium traditional ryokans, an aquarium and a temple museum on the premises.

For those not willing to walk the steep way up, there is a shuttle bus that operates regularly between Kotoden-Yashima train Station and the temple parking lot on top of the hill on a private road, which is not open to pedestrians. There used to be a cable car connection just 100 m west of Shikoku-Mura. The station has been idle for over 12 years, turning it into a "lost place". The same goes for the station on the other end at the top of the hill.

The temple was originally situated on the more remote northern peak, where a monk named Ganjin built a sanctuary upon his return from China. 61 years later, Kukai moved the temple to its current location. The Kamakura-type main hall and the bell are considered national treasures. A mythical Tanuki racoon-dog also plays an important role here, having once shown Kukai the way through the fog. Tanukis are a symbol of good fortune.

From T84 to T85 – KM 1060 to 1065

Fascination	**
Distance	5.5 km
Elevation gain	223 m
Difficulty	Short, at the end 1.6 km climb at 10%
Public transportation	from T84 parking to Kotoden-Yashima Station, to Yakuri (3 stops), 1.5 km walk, cable car. (It is faster walking downhill and to the cable car, about 4 km = 1 h)
Points of interest	KM 1060 Former cable car station KM 1062 ↘↘ Gempei war memorial KM 1063 Turn left over the bridge KM 1064 Udon, Susakiji KM 1065 Cable car station
Where to stay	KM 1053 Several options in Takamatsu

This is an unusual stage as we will be walking from one peak temple to another one on the next mountain. The distance might not look too long, but it is challenging. A steep downhill path followed by one flat km and a steep uphill stretch. It is not recommendable to try the downhill path during rain, and even in good weather, it is very challenging.

Upon leaving T84 we will pass the former cable car station, a "lost" place, which no one has touched since 30 or 40 years. Once we reach the water after having left T84 at the parking lot, we are on a historical battlefield: In 1185, when the Minamoto and Taira clans were fighting to rule Japan, and the Taira warriors, originating from Shikoku, retreated to the plain near T84, where they felt safe in their home territory. At one point, however, the Minamoto attacked them simultaneously at sea and on land and defeated them. This marked the beginning of the Kamakura era, which lasted for almost 150 years.

There are several traces of the war: graves, graveyards and shrines. We turn left, follow Road 150 for about 1.5 km until we find a historic signpost (the ones with the pointing fingers) telling us to turn left over the bridge. From here, it is another 3 km uphill and we have the option of taking a cable car to T85 for the last 600 m. The fare for a round trip is 930 yen, but if we continue to T86, we only need a one-way ticket.

Temple No.85 – Yakuri-ji 八栗寺

Fascination	***
Translation	Temple of Eight Chestnuts
Main deity	Sho Kannon Bosatsu
Founded in	Tenjo 6 (82)
Location	KM 1065
Distance from last temple	5.5 km
Distance to next temple	6.9 km
Difficulty approaching	1.6 km-climb at 10% at the end
Points of interest	Treasure pagoda, panorama, Nakashobo Tengu Shrine

Although, topographically, both temples look similar, we will notice how different they feel entirely when we visit them. While T84 is exposed on the plateau on top of the mountain, T85 is protected, located in a valley 60 m below the peak.

According to legend, Kukai planted eight chestnut trees in this location before leaving for China.

Today's buildings were built in the 18th century, after the temple had been destroyed several times by armies and earthquakes.

The panorama platform is just 150 m southwest of the main hall. About 50 m north of the main hall, there is a slightly hidden Shinto Shrine where Tengu is worshipped, a slightly funny looking character with a long nose who often appears in connection with Shugendo.

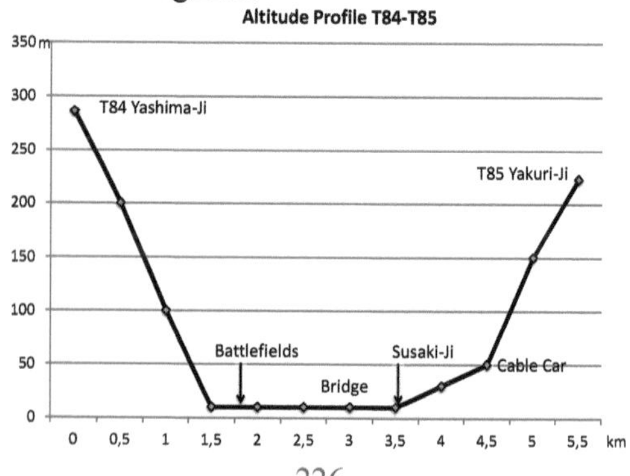

Temple No.86 – Shido-ji 志度寺

Fascination	***
Translation	Temple of Fulfilling Wishes
Main deity	Juichimen Kannon Bosatsu
Founded in	Suiko 33 (625)
Location	KM 1073
Distance from last temple	6.9 km
Distance to next temple	7.1 km
Difficulty approaching	Easy, 3 km downhill and 4 km along the coast
Points of interest	Park, pagoda, ponds, gate, gardens
Okunoin	Jizoji 500 m before the temple

The route to T86 first leads us downhill from T85 on Mount Goken. After 3 km, we will reach the sea and continue along Shido bay until we arrive at Shido Station and Jizoji, an okunoin of T86.

Shidoji is not on a hill but on the coast, surrounded by a park, 4 smaller temples and 2 Shinto shrines. Founded in 625, it is one of Shikoku's oldest temples. Initially, this was the location of the Fujiwara-Clan's mausoleum (there are still 20 tombs from this noble family). Gyoki turned it into a regular temple in 693.

After falling into disuse, the temple was rebuilt in 1670. The main gate, with its two gigantic Waraji sandals, is a national cultural property. The main hall and the Daishido are from the same year, while the 5-story pagoda was completed in 1973. The group of buildings is spread across the huge garden, an exciting walk across several zones. Make sure to visit the entire area, especially the garden behind the stamp office, as some of its gems are hidden.

We have several options for accommodations in Shiso, unless we return to our Takamatsu hostel, by train, if our legs are too tired.

Beyond T86 and Finishing the Pilgrimage

We only have two main temples left to visit, but the pilgrimage is not necessarily over when we reach T88. We can close the loop to complete the circle by returning to T1, and/or maybe include the detour to B20, and maybe do all of this before heading to Koya-San, the sacred city which Kukai founded and where he is buried. Again, there are no rules, but the idea of ending at T1 and not at T88 is most popular. After our long journey it might be surprising that at T88, we are just 18 km away from T10, which we visited on our second day, with just a mountain range in between, which we need to cross.

Here is a summary of the distances to make our planning easier, but let us remember that T87, T88, and B20 are all in the mountains, so walking times should be calculated carefully.

Distances from T86

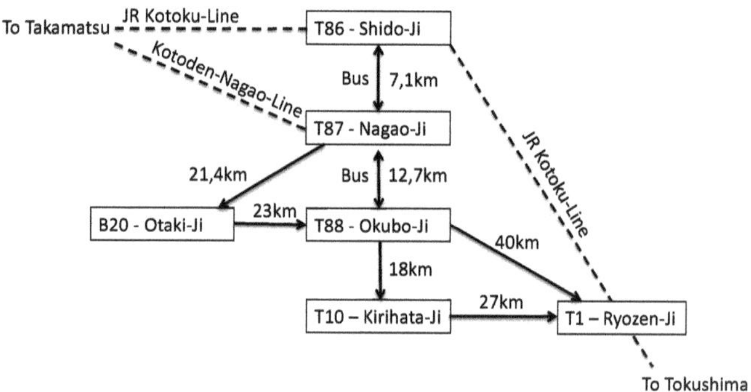

There is a cheap city bus that connects Takamatsu with T87, the Ohenro Koryu Salon (where we can get a certificate of completion), and T88. There is also a simple traditional minshuku near T88.

You will need to create your own plan here, depending on your own focus, schedule and priorities. The most straightforward, "purist" way would be to walk to T88, stay there for the night, and walk from T88 to some location near T10 the next day.

If you want to allow yourself to take the train for some stations but to still mostly walk and to save one night, a nice route to pass the mountain range and return to the low-numbered temples would be to visit T88, returning by bus to Takamatsu and spending the night there.

The next morning, you can take the JR Kotoku to a station named *Sanuki-Aioi* (KM 1122), which is still located on the coast, and take a beautiful 17 km-walk over the mountain range to T3. It is all paved and not too steep. From there, you can walk the 5 kilometers of the first 3 temples backwards to T1. Upon returning to T1, you will get a stamp for your return on a separate page in your stamp book.

From T86 to T 87 – KM 1073 to KM 1080

Fascination	*
Distance	7.1 km
Difficulty	Easy
Public transportation	🚌 from Shido to Asahimachi
Points of interest	KM 1073 🚉 Shido Station 🚌 🛒 KM 1075 🚉 Orange-Town Station KM 1077 O87 Gyokusenji 🛒 🍴 KM 1078 Hut, Henro bridge KM 1080 🚉 Nagao Station 🚌
Where to stay	🛏 KM 1072 Several options in Shido 🛏 KM 1080 Henro House Tek Tek

This is an easy, flat, 2-hour walk southbound along or parallel to Route 3.

Temple No.87 – Nagaoji 長尾寺

Fascination	*
Translation	Temple of the Long Tail
Main deity	Sho Kannon Bosatsu
Founded in	739
Location	KM 1080
Distance from last temple	7.1 km
Distance to next temple	12.6 km
Difficulty approaching	Easy
Points of interest	2 columns
Okunoin	Gyokusenji KM 1079

Not much information is available about this temple. It was founded in 739, probably by Gyoki Bosatsu. Kukai performed a Goma-ritual here before leaving for China.

There are two ancient stone columns from 1283 and 1286 underneath roof constructions, built to commemorate soldiers who lost their lives fighting against Mongol attacks. The columns are national treasures.

Matsudaira Yorishige donated land for the temple in 1681, and shortly thereafter, the hondo was built.

In the Meiji-era the temple was used for other purposes .The okunoin, Gyokusenji, which we passed a few kilometers before reaching T87, was only moved here in 1978 and united with another temple, so probably the temple was only re-installed in 1978.

From T87 to T88 – KM 1080 to KM 1093

Fascination	**
Walking Distance	12.6 km
Elevation gain	690 m
Difficulty	Difficult
Public transportation	🚌 from Asahi-Machi (T87)
Points of interest	KM 1081 🛒 Hosen-ji KM 1082 🛒 Kabe River KM 1083 ↗ Hut 🚻 🛒 (last one!) KM 1085 ↗ 🚌 🍴 🚻 🛒 Maeyama village, Henro Koryu Salon (Museum), certificate, detour to B20, Nagao rest place, hut KM 1086 ↗↗ KM 1087 ↗↗ Kurusu Jinja, hut, climb KM 1090 ↗↗ Henro Korogashi △ 741 m KM 1092 O88 Taizo Mine ↘↘
Where to stay	Yasokubo (minshuku at T88)

The stage to the final temple is not an easy one, and whoever designed the temple route created a spectacular final, a hard stage, a challenge ending at one of the most beautiful sacred places.

During the first half, after 2 km we will walk along the Kabe river gently uphill for 3 km until we reach the village of Maeyama where a dam has been built creating a little lake. The green route in the Route Guide is quieter and a little nicer.

Take your time visit the Henro Salon, it is a little museum with interesting pilgrimage artifacts. If you ever wondered what a stamp books looks like after a pilgrim has completed the route a few hundred times, you will get to see a couple of those. The place is run by volunteers who will issue a completion certificate upon request and keep some statistics.

The next 5 km up Mount Nyotai are extremely tough, unpaved, with a climb of over 10% until we reach the peak at 741 m altitude. From there, the 2-km descent reaches 15% and we pass OkunoinTaizo Mine.

There is a more gentle route with only 300 m of altitude gain, but it is 3 km longer, shown as Route C in the Route Guide. It takes a different direction from the Henro Salon.

If you intend to go up on foot and to return from T88 by bus, be sure to check the schedule for your return, because the last one leaves already at 16:00. It means that you would have to leave the Maeyama village for T88 on foot latest at 12:30.

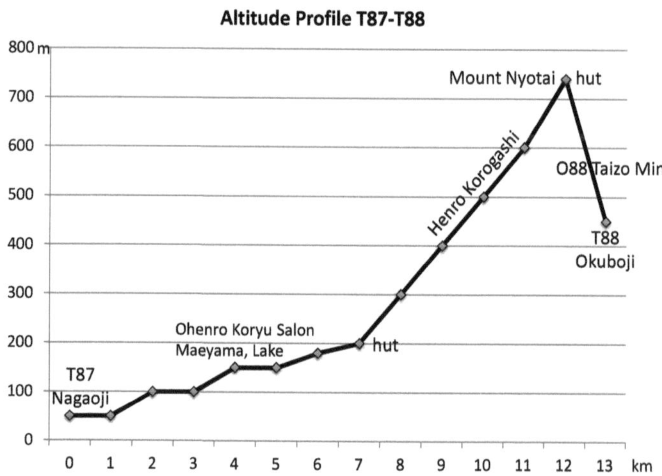

If you intend to visit T87, the Henro Salon and T88 by bus, this would be the schedule as per January 2024:

Time	Activity
12:30	(latest) Visit T87
13:01	Depart Asahi-Machi T87
13:13	Arrive Michinoeki Nagano
	Stay in Maeyama, museum, certificate (2 hours)
15:13	Departure Michinoeki Nagano
15:30	Arrival at T88 Okubo-ji
	Visit T88 (30 minutes)
16:00	Departure from T88

Temple No. T88 – Okuboji 大窪寺

Fascination	***
Translation	Temple of the Big Cave
Main deity	Yakushi Nyorai
Founded in	717
Location	KM 1093
Distance from last temple	12.6 km
Distance to next temple	18 km to T10, 40 km to T3 45 km to T1
Difficulty approaching	Difficult, easy by bus
Points of interest	Eternal flame, staffs for fire ritual, garden, 2-story pagoda
Okunoin	Taizo Mine

The last of the 88 temples is hard to reach on foot, but we are rewarded with a splendid array of buildings in a beautifully colored forest.

The beginnings of this temple go back to a hermitage nearby, possible the okunoin Taizo Mine which has a sacred well. (The availability of water might have made it a perfect place to stay in isolation over a long period) Later on, this temple became the prayer temple of Emperor Gensho (680-748) and must have had over 100 buildings, but then suffered the fate of several destructions, like so many other temples: During the Tensho-era (16th century), once in in a war in 1774 and once in a great fire in 1900.

The Otsuedo holds the staffs of pilgrims left here upon completing the pilgrimage, to be burned in ritual fires twice per year, and an eternal flame commemorates the many victims of Hiroshima and Nagasaki. There are several restaurants and souvenir shops. Do not miss the beautiful garden and views on the east side (downhill). The temple office can issue a certificate of completion in Japanese.

Although there is no rule, today many pilgrims return to T1 and visit Koya-San; after visiting T88.

Temple No. B20 – Otakiji 大瀧寺

Fascination	*
Translation	Temple of the Great Waterfall
Main deity	Senju Kannon Bosatsu
Founded in	unknown
Detour	22 km
Difficulty approaching	Very difficult

B20 is difficult to reach on foot and requires us to spend an additional night somewhere in the mountains. There are no other options, unless we find someone who takes us there by car.

From T88 (alt. 448 m) it is 7.4 km by road to a shrine named Kotohiragu (alt. 287 m) and another 6.6 km on a path with a 620 m climb to B20 (alt. 910 m), so walking it from T88 and back on one day would be 28 km walking with a climb of 800 m. One way to do this would be to stay at Minshuku Yasokubo near T88 for 2 nights and fit in a day hike to B20 and back.

Another option in theory would be to include B20 as a detour from T87 to T88 (the detour starting in Maeyama, KM 1087). So instead of the 8 km from Maeyama to T88 we would have to walk 29.5 km to T88 including B20. However, this would be too much to walk, as there are no accommodations in Maeyama.

There are two accommodations in the mountains that are relatively close to B20: The first, Sanuki Onsen a hot spring hotel on Route 100, from where it is a 10 km-walk with 600 m of elevation gain. The rooms without meal start at 6,800 Yen per night. The second one is Takeyashiki, which is 4 km from T88 on Route 377 between T88 and Kotohiragu, a ryokan offering special rates for Henro.

In any case, the climb to B20 and down is strenuous and difficult to include in the schedule. The temple itself is modest and sharing its space with a Shinto shrine on the peak of Mt. Otaki.

B20 can also be approached from the south coming from Anabuki Station by train from Tokushima. However, the return hike would be a challenging 30 km to be done on one day.

From T88 to T1 – KM 1093 to KM 1137

Fascination	***
Distance	44 km
Elevation gain	330 m to Osaka Toge Pass (3.5 km/10%)
Difficulty	Long, requires one additional night
Public transportation	🚌 to Shiso Station, transfer to Kotoku Line to Itano (for T3), Bando (for T1) or Tokushima
Points of interest	**Part 1: Back to the coast** KM 1093-95 Tunnel alt. 350 m ↘ KM 1099 ↘↘ Hacho Zaka Slope KM 1100-1104 ↘ KM 1104 ↗ Hoshitoge Pass △ 109 m Shortcut to KM 1119 Route 318: 2 km less KM 1105-1110 ↘ KM 1107 🚻 ⛩Mizushi Jinja, KM 1110 Yodai-ji KM 1114 🛒 🍽 KM 1115 🚂 Sanuki Shirotori Station KM 1117 🚌 Hiketa Station, bus to Osaka KM 1119 🚻 🚂 Hiketa Station KM 1120 Coast KM 1121 Bridge 🛒 🚂 Sanuki Aioi Station **Part 2: Over the pass** KM 1123 Turn right, ↗ follow Route 1 KM 1126 ↗ Osaka Toge Pass △ 364 m ， entering Tokushima Prefecture KM 1128 ↘ Road to Awa Omiya Station KM 1130 ↘ 🍽 Onsen KM 1133 T3 Konsenji KM 1136 🛒 T2 Gokurakuji
Where to stay	🛏 KM 1093 Yasokubo at T88 🛏 KM 1115 Business Hotel AZ 🛏 KM 1137 Henro House Ichiban 🛏 Several options in Tokushima

If we wish to close the loop of our pilgrimage, we need to return to T1. Starting from T88, this will be a stage of about 44 km, which takes more than a day on the main route and requires an overnight stay on the way. Due to the lack of accommodations in the mountains, a less purist option would be returning to Takamatsu after visiting T88, celebrating a bit, and then to begin our final stage with a short train ride from Takamatsu along the coast until Sanuki Aioi before heading up to our last mountain range on this pilgrimage. But let us divide the stage into two parts for easier planning: The first part is getting to Sanuki Aioi, which is a town on the coast at KM 1125 we need to pass in any case before going over the mountains.

-   Coming from T88 it is a walking distance of 30 km, but we can stop for the night at some places near KM 1115, which makes it bearable, and walk the rest (2 hours) the next morning.
-   Coming from Takamatsu, it is about 40 km by train (JR Kotoku Line)

500 m from the station, continuing along the coast to the east (the sea on our left) we turn right and follow Route 1 uphill. 400 m later, the road splits into the official Henro Route (to the right) and Route 1 (left). The Henro route is shorter but steeper and not paved, Route 1 is easier but about 3 km longer due to the serpentines. But none of the climbs are tough compared to others that are behind us. From the foot of the hill, we already get a good impression of the serpentines ahead. From the top, we can take a last view of the Seto Inland Sea before leaving the north coast of Shikoku.

At an altitude of 364 m at KM 1129 we will reach Osaka-Toge pass ("Osaka", like the city name, only means "big slope"). On the way up, we re-enter Tokushima prefecture. 6 km later, after heading down the mountain, we are back at T3 (KM 1135), After another 3 km our pilgrimage is completed.

At T1, we will collect our second stamp at the stamp office, maybe register our arrival in the big book next to our departure date, wearing a big smile on our tired face.

Koya-San 高野山

Fascination	****
Translation	Mountain of the High Plain
Founded in	816
Location	2-hour train ride south of Osaka
The approach is usually done by train and cable car, but some Henro prefer the climb up from Gokurakubashi, it is a 4 km walk with an average grade of 7-8%, which will take about 90 minutes	
Points of interest	Everything (See table)

Koya-san is a sacred city in the mountains which is not in Shikoku, but in Wakayama prefecture, about 2 hours by train south of Osaka. It can be conveniently visited after the pilgrimage via Osaka.

This plain, located at an altitude of about 800 m and at the foot of eight peaks, was given to Kukai by Emperor Saga. Kukai founded a retreat where monks could live in peace and isolation. Over the years, Koya-san, which is actually the "mountain name" of the main temple Kongobuji, prospered, became the center of Shingon Buddhism, and expanded to a temple city. In 2004, it became a UNESCO World Heritage Site. Visitors can stay in one of the many temples, take part in the morning rituals, enjoy Buddhist-vegan cooking and the quietude that covers the place after the day tourists are gone and the last cable car of the day has left.

The city is about 5 km long going from west to east, with over 100 active temples situated between the main sacred places. About 50 of them are designated guesthouses, some of them at very high level, serving excellent dinner and breakfast. Koya-san is not a budget place, if your budget is moderate, try staying at the Koyasan Guesthouse, but you will miss the temple magic.

The city can be discovered on foot or by bus. The main attractions can be visited in two half days with one overnight stay, arriving in the morning and leaving the evening of the next day. The following list includes some of the main attractions that can be discovered throughout the day.

Daimon	Built in 1705, the 25 m tall orange gate on the west side marks the entrance to the city. It offers a beautiful view to the Seto Inland Sea.
Danjo Garan	A group of important historical structures: The **Kondo** is a service hall, last rebuilt in 1932. The **Kompon Daito** is the 2-story pagoda with the rounded upper story. We have seen many copies of it at the Shikoku temples, but this one is much bigger in size: 48 m high, built in 1937. The **Fudodo** is the oldest surviving building of Koyasan, built in 1198. The **Miedo** is a replica of Kukai's house, built in 1848
Kongobuji	The main temple and center of religious Shingon affairs for 3,700 Shingon temples. As this is the main temple of Koyasan, its suffix is "-ji". All other temples bear the suffix "-in" which means they are lower in the classification.
Reihokan	A **museum** dedicated to the history of Koyasan.
Okunoin	Here, the term okunoin (inner sanctuary) refers to the huge graveyard east of the city, which we can cross on the Sando, a 2 km walk, starting from **Ichinohashi-guchi** (entrance to the first bridge). There are over 200,000 gravestones, situated under huge cedar trees, many of them belonging to rich families or sponsored by companies. The path ends at the **Kukai Mausoleum**, this is where we collect our Koyasan stamp. One of the buildings is the **Lantern Hall**, where the main lantern has been burning uninterrupted for over 1,000 years.
Nyoindo	The women's temple is in the northwestern part of the city, connected to the okunoin by a shortcut so women could avoid the temples, where they were not allowed until 1872.
Tokugawa Mausoleum	A UNESCO World Heritage Site built in 1643, where several members of the Tokugawa clan are buried.

Ropeway 2,5 km
Koya-San Western Part
Ropeway 2,5 km
Tokugawa-Mausoleum 500 m
Kongobuji Hondo
Saizen-In
Shochi-In
Hojo-In
Myo-O-In
Shinno-In
Seimon Gate
Koukou-Mae
Daito-guchi
Route480
Parking
Danjo Garan
Kondo Main Hall
Kompon Daito Pagoda
Miedo, Sanno-In
Kongobuji-mae
Daimon Gate
Tourist Info
Restaurant Tsukumo
Tofu-shop Park
Shonto Shrine and Park
Tofu Trad. Restaurant
Hairdresser Powerstone Café
Chumon Gate
Hasu Ike Lotus Lake
Daishi Kyokai Hall
Gallery
University
Daimon
Sainan In Café and Hotel
Benten-mae
Kinomi Café
Atago-mae
Family Mart
Rest House Muzuki Parking
Kondo-mae
Bike Rental
Reihokan-mae
Hoon-In Yochi-In
Reihokan Koya Museum
Route. 480
1000 m

Kobo Daishi Mausoleum Torodo
Koya-San Eastern Part
Okunoin Main Cemetary
appr. 900 m
Graveyards
appr.. 2 km
Shojoshin-In
Sekisho-in
Ichinohashi Bridge
Hozen-In
Toukon-In
Koyasan Guest House Kokuu
Tonkatsu-Tei Restaurant
Tofu Laden
Fugen-In
Daien-In
Jyofuku-In
Sanbo-In
Route 371
Souvenir Shop
Restaurant
Okunoin-mae
Ca. 800 m
Route 480
Rengei-dan
Jyochi-In
Eko-In
Kumagai-Ji
Karuka-Yado
Daimyo-In
Tamagawa Ryokan Hotel
Parking
University
Route 371
Saimon-In Guesthouse
Karukayado-mae
appr. 2500 m

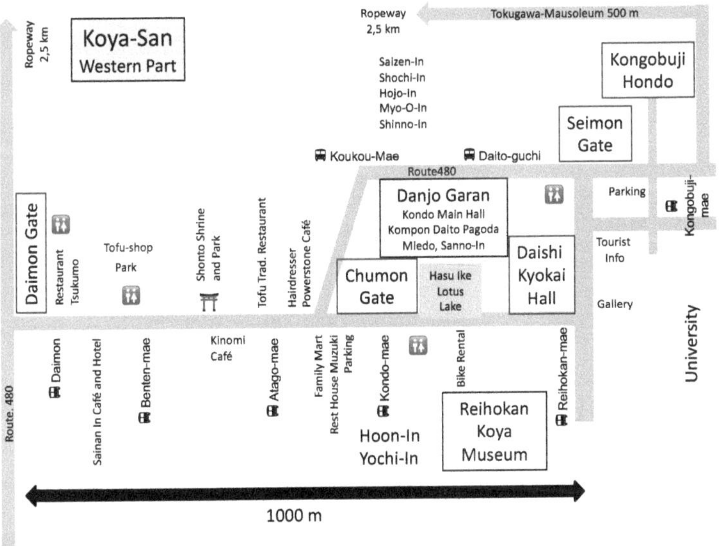

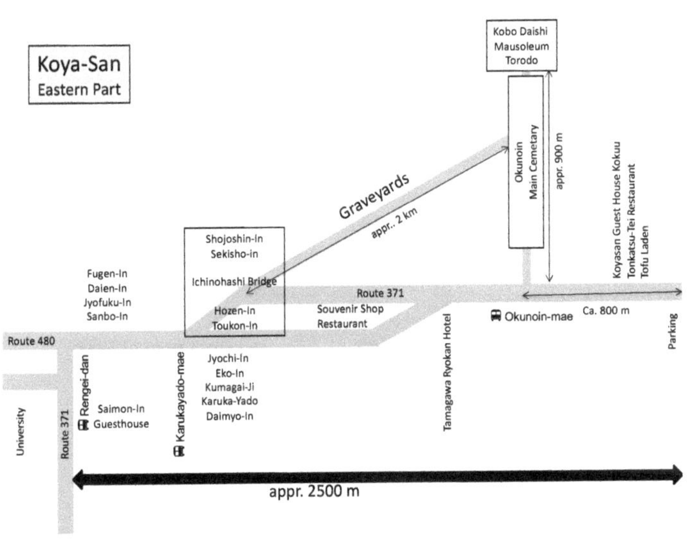

239

Historical Timeline

546-552	Earliest appearance of Buddhism in Japan
668-749	Lifetime of Gyoki Bosatsu
710-794	Nara Period, Nara is capital
774	Birth of Kukai
788	Kukai moves to Kyoto aged 14
794-1184	Heian Period, Kyoto is capital
807	Kukaireturns from China aged 32
835	Kukai passes away aged 61 at Koya-san
1185-1333	Kamakura Period, 1185: Gempei war, Minamoto clan takes over political power, Buddhism is strengthened.
1333	End of the Kamakura period
1336-1573	Muromachi-period, the era of wars
1574-1585	Chosokabe Motochika invades Shikoku and destroys many temples
1573-1603	Azuchi-Momoyama period of unification
1603-1868	Edo period: Japan ruled by Tokugawa clan and remains isolated, Christianity is forbidden, Buddhism supported, c. 100,000 temples are built. Pilgrimage becomes popular.
1827	Nakahama "John" Manjiro born in Kochi Pref.
1851	Manjiro returns to Japan
1852	Emperor Mutsuhito (Meiji) is born
1853-1854	Japan forced to reopen by American threat
1868-1912	Meiji era: Meiji Restauration (Emperor back in political power) Shintoism strengthened, beginning of modern Japan. Shinbutsu-Bunri (1868): Buddhist-oppression, temple splitting, escalated in the destruction of 40.000 temples by 1872; settlement of conflict by splitting shared temple areas into Shinto- and Buddhist areas
1970's	Classification of 20 Bekkaku Temples

Some related Japanese terms

Bangai	unnumbered temple
Bekkaku	Second-class temple
Cho	Distance unit of 109 m
Daishido	Temple hall devoted to Kukai
Fudasho	Major pilgrimage temple
Hakui	Pilgrim's vest
Henro	Pilgrim
Henro Korogashi	Particularly difficult part of the route
Hondo	Main temple hall
Izakaya	Traditional pub
Jinja	Shinto Shrine
Jizo	Boddhisatva guardian of children/travellers
Kannon, Kanon	Boddhisatva, comes in several forms
Kombini	Convenience store (mini supermarket)
Kukai	Founder of Shingon Buddhism, Kobo Daishi
Kobo Daishi	(see Kukai)
Minshuku	Traditional hotel of basic standard
Mon	Gate
Nansho	A place difficult to access
Nokyocho	Stamp book
Nokyosho	Stamp office
Oizuru	White vest without sleeves
Okunoin	Inner sanctuary (Sacred location of a temple)
Osamefuda	Name slip
Osettai	A gift or a favor to the pilgrim
Rakan	The 500 followers of Buddha
Ryokan	Traditional hotel of superior standard
Sando	(Main) road to a temple or shrine
Shugendo	Mountain ascetism
Shukubo	Temple guesthouse
Torii	Shinto-type gate
Yamabushi	Ascetic mountain monk

Reading Suggestions

Shikoku Japan 88 Route Guide by Naoyuki Matsushita
Two on a Pilgrimage by Alfred Bohner
Japanese Pilgrimage by Oliver Statler
Echoes of Incense – A Pilgrimage in Japan by Don Weiss
Visiting the Sacred Sites of Kukai by Tateki Miyazawa
The 88 Temples of Shikoku Island, by Bishop Taisen Miyata
Making Pilgrimages by Ian Reader
Fighting Monks and Burning Dragons by Paul Barach
The Cicada's Summer Song by Lu Barnham

Disclaimer

This guidebook has been written based on latest best information and knowledge, but none of the information provided can be guaranteed, this refers especially to information about public transportation, costs, or conditions of the route.

Thank you!

Angela Dunskus
David Moreton
Don Weiss
Masako Iwamoto
Naoyuki Matsushita

Index